CONSTANTINE VERSUS CHRIST

ALISTAIR KEE

CONSTANTINE
VERSUS
CHRIST

The Triumph of Ideology

SCM PRESS LTD

334 00268 0

First published 1982
by SCM Press Ltd
58 Bloomsbury Street London WC1

Phototypeset by Input Typesetting Ltd
and printed in Great Britain by
Richard Clay Ltd (The Chaucer Press)
Bungay, Suffolk

CONTENTS

Introduction   1

Part One   The Religion of Constantine

I   The Gods at War   7
     1. Divine Patronage   7
     2. Labarum   17

II   Constantine the Friend of God   23
     1. Method and Criteria   23
     2. Model Sovereign   27

III Constantine as Messiah   35
     1. *Remoto Christo*   35
     2. The New Epiphany   37

Part Two   Constantine's Religious Policy

IV   The Life of Constantine   51
     1. Presentation by Eusebius   51
     2. Critical Considerations   58

V   Against Pagan Despisers   70
     1. The Defence of Constantine   70
     2. The Spiritual in the Material   74

VI   The Assembly of Saints   79
     1. A Christian Apology   80
     2. Piety Rewarded   83

VII Legislation on Religion   88
     1. From Persecution to Patronage   88
     2. The Theodosian Code   95

VIII The Unity of the Church   102
      1. The Donatist Schism   103
      2. The Arian Heresy   109

           Part Three The Ideology of Constantine

  IX Constantine's Covenant Religion   117
      1. Pre-Christian   117
      2. Anti-Christian   123

   X The Great Reversal   128
      1. Reflection or Projection   128
      2. In Heaven as on Earth   132

  XI The Labarum or the Cross   141
      1. Locus of Revelation   141
      2. Kenosis   147

 XII The New Imperial Cult   153
      1. In This Sign Conquer   153
      2. The State Religion   159

XIII Constantine and Political Theology   166
      1. Challenging the Tradition   166
      2. Established Religion   170

      Notes   176

      General Index   183

      Index of Biblical References   186

INTRODUCTION

The view that politics and religion should be kept entirely separate from one another is a relatively recent one in world history. The attempt, when it is made, is not undertaken because the two have absolutely nothing in common, but for precisely the opposite reason. Politics and religion not only overlap, but compete in their various functions. They are both human spheres of activity, and through them both mankind has, over the centuries, sought to bring meaning and purpose to life, order and value, restraint over what destroys and encouragement for that which edifies. Whether the attempt to separate them is wise or even possible, our forefathers could not conceive of it, nor if they had would they have considered it a virtue. For better or worse, these two phenomema have shaped our history and culture, and while we can analyse our past we cannot change it. But analyse it we should, especially at those historic moments when the balance of the two changed and the course of history with them. In the history of Europe there is no more dramatic moment than the reign of Constantine, whom men called – the Great.

The subject of this book is politics and religion, the relationship between Constantine and Christianity. It is as complex a relationship as any in European history and for that reason delightfully intriguing, but this book is not written out of delight in such a puzzle. It is a relationship which so often seems full of anomalies, but this book is not simply an attempt to set the record straight. Something happened in the reign of the Emperor Constantine which transformed both politics and religion in Europe, and if we are to understand why we are where we are, for better or for worse, then we must analyse this transformation. Europe as a political entity was changed by it, but so was Christianity. Politics and religion are not the same, and while they work together they also struggle each to overcome the other. The reign of Constantine is remembered as the victory of Christianity over the Roman Empire. Our sub-title indicates a more ominous assessment, 'the triumph of ideology'.

Our subject is an important one, with implications for history, political theory, religious studies, ethics, theology and perhaps even law. Yet we cannot begin where we wish to begin. It is like an ancient site we wish to view from a fresh perspective, but the guide directs us along a well-worn path. It is like trying to update a children's tale: they will have none of it and insist on having it told in the familiar way. Although our subject is relatively unexamined in the history of European thought, yet it will be assumed to be simply a discussion of the conversion of Constantine. To be sure, *this* subject has been repeatedly examined, but it is not our subject. In countless books and articles Constantine and Christianity are reduced to a single question: Was Constantine a Christian? It has been assumed by those who answered Yes and also by those who returned a No, that this is the most important question which can be asked. Assumed also that when this question is answered, then no further questions remain. It is my view in this book, to the contrary, that this question is a relatively unimportant question, for the following reason. Whether the question is answered Yes or No leaves the whole issue of politics and religion untouched. Focussing attention on this question has proved to be a complete distraction from the much more important and underlying issue of the interaction of Constantine and Christianity, and how that interaction determined the future development of European history and culture.

But having said that, we are still jostled by the guides and pressured by the cries of the children. We must address ourselves to this familiar question, which I regard as at best of limited significance and at worst an unfortunate distraction. Apparently I must declare myself on it, else I shall be accused of failing to deal with Constantine and Christianity. Very well, let us make a bargain. I shall not deal with this question as if it were important in isolation from its context. But I shall declare myself on it – in the course of taking up the more fundamental issue, the transformation of both politics and religion in the reign of Constantine.

In dealing with the question of whether Constantine was or was not a Christian, I shall review some contributions to this ongoing debate, this cottage industry of classical scholarship. We shall see, perhaps not surprisingly, that it has generated more heat than light. There are those who are adamant that Constantine was not converted to Christianity, and behind the confidently cynical treatment of the evidence there lies, as often as not, their own rejection of religion. Equally, in the strident tones of many of those who defend

Constantine's conversion, we may detect the rather desperate defence of their own religious position. Few there be who are both sufficiently motivated to pursue the research, yet uncommitted enough to follow the evidence wherever it leads. To those who are fervently for, or fervently against, it must seem that nothing can be achieved until this question is answered, Yes or No. And at the same time, when the question is answered, everything follows: winner takes all. My position is quite different. I do not believe that this is the most important question to ask. Hence I am not anxious to reach a verdict one way or the other. But to adopt this rather smug position is to ensure that I am attacked from both sides. However, although I do not consider this to be the central issue, yet in the course of this enquiry I shall, *en passant*, come to my own answer.

This assurance, if it is no longer smug, may now seem rather coy. The book has already been written, the evidence and sources reviewed. Perhaps it would be as well to declare openly at this point what my answer will be to this supposedly important question. Very well: Constantine was not a Christian. But this tells us nothing about the more profound and perennially important issue of the transformation of politics and religion under Constantine. It is this issue which led me to examine the evidence, and it might be of some interest to the reader to know that, possibly in common with most people who know something of the period, I began with the assumption that Constantine was a Christian. However, this assumption led to too many anomalies and also failed to provide a proper basis for the interpretation of Constantine's actions and motives. I was therefore forced to produce a contrary hypothesis, that Constantine was not a Christian. I expected, as I reviewed the evidence, source after source, that this hypothesis would prove untenable. To the contrary and to my amazement, the hypothesis was not undermined. Further, as a good hypothesis should, it provided an adequate base for handling the questions of intention and motivation. But having said all that, let me reiterate that my view that Constantine was not a Christian does not as yet throw any light on the underlying issue of transformation.

As already indicated, in Part One I begin my analysis of the relationship between politics and religion in the career of Constantine, and at the same time indicate the grounds on which I have come to the conclusion that he was not a Christian. Since this is regarded as an important question, I have spent more time on it than I should otherwise. In Part Two I turn increasingly from the question of Constantine's religion to the matter of the function of religion in Constantine's imperial strategy. During this part it will become clear why I regard the traditional question as of only limited importance. Neither possible answer to the question tells us anything about Constantine's use of religion. However, it is in Part Three that I shall concentrate on the fundamental issue of the transformation of both politics and religion under Constantine. Although on the traditional question I am maintaining that Constantine was not a Christian, I am quite content to have it both ways. That is to say, if any reader remains unconvinced at the end of Part One or even Part Two, this does not invalidate the investigation in Part Three. The fundamental issue is not whether Constantine called himself a Christian or not, but how he actually used Christianity and how, in the course of using it, he transformed it into something completely different. It is for this reason that the traditional question is of only limited importance and why, since it throws no light on the fundamental issue, it is often an unfortunate distraction.

Before we begin, there is one final point which must be made concerning the perspective from which the book is written. Although the subject is historical, the perspective is in turn ideological and theological, the contrasting of the norms of Constantine and Christ. The two sets of norms are not only distinguishable, but are indeed incompatible. Yet in focussing on this dramatic change which took place in the life of the Church and thereafter in society at large, I am not claiming that historically the religion of Christ and the early church continued unchanged, unmodified and undeveloped until the time of Constantine. Some of the characteristic beliefs and attitudes of Constantinian Christianity are to be found in the intervening period. In other words, in claiming that something radically new and fundamentally important came about in the time of Constantine, I am not claiming that he or Eusebius, his biographer and panegyrist, were original in all things. Far from it. Yet, in gathering up lines of thought often already present in the church and developing them in a certain way, they combined to effect something which had never been accomplished hitherto, the replacement of the norms of Christ and the early church by the norms of the imperial ideology. Why it has been previously thought that Constantine was a Christian is not because what he believed was Christian, but because what he believed came to be called Christian. And this represents the 'triumph of ideology'.

PART ONE

THE RELIGION OF CONSTANTINE

I

THE GODS AT WAR

1 Divine Patronage

As a gracious gesture, Constantine allowed his father-in-law, Maximian, to commit suicide.[1] So ended the quite inexplicable coup of
310, the attempted assassination, the life of the retired Emperor of
the West and, it must then have seemed, the career of the young
Augustus, who nevertheless was destined to transform the history
of Europe and with justification assume with the purple the title 'the
Great', which no ruler had thought fit to claim since Alexander of
Macedon. Great things lay ahead of Constantine, but with the death
of Maximian, the odds and indeed the gods were against him.
Between him and supreme control of the Empire lay the structure
of tetrarchy, within which he was but one of four rulers. And apart
from the senior Augusti, Galerius and Licinius, there was Maxentius, ruler of Rome, son of the dead Maximian. But perhaps more
important at this stage was the support of the gods. The Emperor
Diocletian, persecutor of the Christian church, traced his lineage
from Jupiter, supreme head of the Roman pantheon, while Maximian, his lesser colleague in the West, traced his appropriately from
Hercules, the helper of Jupiter. When in 307 Constantine married
Fausta, he had married into the dynasty of Hercules. The execution
of Maximian ended the Herculean legitimation: if Constantine was
to maintain not only his momentum but also the loyalty of his troops
in the aftermath of the death of the widely respected former
Emperor, then he required some new ratifying sign.

Fortunately we need not delve too deeply into the issue of the
extent to which these religious affiliations also reflected the personal
piety of the rulers. But we need not be cynical about their religious
convictions to appreciate that at the time loyalty to a particular god
might coincide with what today would be described as national,
regional or class interests. The line between private and public

dimensions of religion was ill-defined. For his own belief in himself and the credibility of his campaign, Constantine needed a new and dynamic religious legitimation.

The history of the ancient world sometimes appears to be divided between those who were born to rule but did not, and those who came from obscurity to rewrite their destiny. At that moment Constantine looked to belong to the former category, for he had come too far too quickly and now seemed destined to fall back into obscurity. His father was a general, soon to be appointed Caesar in the West by Diocletian. His mother was a Balkan barmaid, capable of supporting her husband in a career until set aside to make way for a political marriage. While a youth, Constantine was sent to the court of Diocletian. He was of course a hostage, but in practice he was able to learn the ways of the Empire. He accompanied Diocletian on his famous Egyptian campaign. He also observed at first hand the persecution of the Christians in the East. The young tribune seemed about to progress naturally to the highest office. But suddenly the two senior members of the tetrarchy, Diocletian and Maximian, retired. Galerius saw Constantine as a threat and the hostage became a virtual prisoner, until he managed to escape and join his father in Gaul. He accompanied Constantius on his last campaign to Britain, and was with him when he died at York in 306. The army hailed Constantine as Augustus, and Galerius had to settle for ratifying him as Caesar in the West. By a series of campaigns in northern Europe Constantine consolidated his position, waiting his moment. In 307 he married Fausta, securing (as we have already noted) his connection with the dynasty of Hercules. But in 310 the crisis arose. For no apparent reason, other than that of the man who mistakenly supposed that he could lay down supreme power and be content without it, Maximian staged a coup against Constantine, plotted his death, and might well have succeeded except for his own daughter. When this pre-television saga of the domestic life of a typical imperial family came to the end of its run, it seemed as if the meteoric career of the young Augustus had reached the peak of its trajectory. At the beginning he never seemed to need reasons why he should succeed, but now he desperately needed reasons why he should not fail.

Perhaps Constantine should never have attempted to legitimize himself by association with the spent force of Maximian and the limited image of Hercules. Now he had no option but to turn back to his roots. In this he had the support of some extravagant panegyrics.[2] First, a dynastic claim was formulated. His family was now to be linked with the emperor Claudius, who had come to power some forty years before. Constantine, it would seem, was born to rule. Secondly, there was a journey which Constantius, his father, was said to have made while in Britain, far to the north, to the place where the gods make feasting, night and day (Aberdeen!). There he was told that the Empire would be inherited by his son. Thirdly, Constantius was by this time deified and presumably in a position to see that this Jovian promise was kept. And fourthly, Constantine was suddenly, if conveniently, re-converted to the sun-worship of his Balkan ancestors. In 310, the panegyrist tells us, Constantine entered a beautiful temple, had a vision of Apollo, accompanied by Victory, and was offered crowns symbolizing not only imperial power to come, but also the legitimation of Sol Invictus in dealing with his enemies, past and present. The chapter which ended with the death of Maximian was closed, and the next chapter in his achievement of power was opening. According to the pane-gyrist, the sun god actually bore the features of Constantine, and certainly Constantine made this close association manifest in his coins and his statues. Heaven agreed with earth: Constantine could again move forward. The war of the gods was ended. Among the old gods, yes, but what of the new?

In the world of men, Constantine made a successful alliance with Licinius. In 310 the Augustus of the East married Constantine's sister Constantia. The following year Maximin seized Asia Minor and Licinius had to turn to Constantine for support. In the world of men Constantine's position was strengthened, and this alliance was to stand him in good stead in the immediate struggles ahead. In 312 he began his campaign from Gaul across the Alps into Italy: the goal was Rome, the enemy Maxentius, the prize undisputed control of the whole of the western Empire. The odds were against him, but what of the gods? The loyalty of his troops, the increasing popular support of those whom his campaign liberated, the non-interference by Licinius, his personal daring, courage and tactical brilliance all combined to hint that he might achieve his aim. Nothing had been left out of his calculations, in the world of men. And yet there was still a doubt in the mind of Constantine.

As already noted, we need not attempt to discern the depth of piety in the issue of religious legitimation, but we must accept that if for no reasons other than politics and morale, it was necessary to choose wisely in the question of the support of the gods. We could even say that in Constantine's case it was an empirical matter. His association with Hercules had not brought results. Now he had turned to Apollo. This association looked more hopeful. But still the doubt remained. There was one other possibility, the God of the

Christians. At first sight this association looked to be out of the question. For almost three centuries the Christians had stood out against the Empire. They had refused to comply with the requirements of the imperial cult, refused to take *sacramentum*, the oath to the Lord Caesar. Not that successive Caesars cared what religious beliefs and practices their subjects favoured, so long as they demonstrated their loyalty to the Empire. Christians had not in fact posed any political threat to the Empire, but unfortunately for them their *religious* scruples had prevented them from taking an oath which was in practice applied as a test of *political* loyalty. Failure to take the test was not heresy, but treason. At first they were not sought out, but denounced on occasion by their neighbours. But whenever Caesar's authority was weak, he would look for scapegoats and initiate a persecution of the Christian minority, *pour encourager les autres*. As the church emerged from the protection afforded it as a Jewish sect, persecution began. At first they were regarded as a suspect minority, misrepresented and charged with all manner of vices and subversions. Yet the barbarity of Nero's persecution in AD 64 went beyond any kind of rationality. By the time of Trajan at the beginning of the next century, simply being an unrepentant Christian was a crime. Towards the end of the century, Marcus Aurelius legislated against new and strange religions and thus laid the foundation for the periodic persecution of Christians which varied from reign to reign, province to province. It was a period of growth in the church, but of decline in the fortunes of the Empire itself. Those who preferred to look outside themselves for the causes of their frustrations and misfortunes found an easy target. 'If the Tiber reaches the walls, if the Nile does not rise to the fields, if the sky doesn't move or the earth does, if there is famine, if there is plague, the cry is at once: "The Christians to the lion!" What, all of them to one lion?'[3] The matter came to a head in 248, during the millennial celebrations of the foundation of Rome. Decius came to power in 249 and shared the popular myth that since the ancient gods had made Rome great, forsaking them, not least for the God of the Christians, was the root of the present reversal. In the following year he instituted the first universal persecution of the church, which continued at various levels of intensity and ferocity for twenty years.

As a 'guest' at the court of Diocletian, the young Constantine observed the next great persecution. It was undertaken as a matter of imperial policy and was to provide a 'final solution' to the problem of church and state. It was initiated in 303 on the festival of the god Terminus, 'to terminate, as it were, the Christian religion'.[4] It was for a strong, reforming ruler such as Diocletian to unify his domains and to eradicate centres of subversion. Constantine had had in Diocletian a good teacher in the art of ruling an empire. But now as he stood poised for the final campaign which would eventually lead to even greater power than that of Diocletian, Constantine came to doubt the wisdom of Diocletian in one most important respect.

Over the centuries of persecution, how many thousands had perished in the most excruciating agony, their devotion to God greater than their fear of Caesar? And how many hundreds of thousands had been tortured, maimed, mutilated or simply terrorized by the threat of such things? But during these centuries, how many died out of devotion to the gods of Rome? Of course the situation did not arise. But the very meaninglessness of the question is unsettling. Would anyone have died out of devotion to Hercules? And would Jupiter have fared better in such a contest? But the blood of the martyrs was the seed of the church. Paradoxically it increased through persecution, it grew strong as Rome grew weak. Diocletian began the persecution in 303. Two years later he abdicated. He was succeeded by Galerius, who renewed the persecution and persisted with it in the East for six years. But in 311 he finally issued an Edict of Toleration. The persecution would come to an end on 'condition' that Christians prayed for the Emperor and the State, a condition already met in practice,[5] a condition which was only to save face. Within days Galerius was dead.

It has been estimated that at the time Christians numbered no more than ten per cent of the population, little represented in the army or aristocracy.[6] But what a ten per cent! In face of persecution they remained firm. Their ultimate loyalties were not in doubt. How could the future Emperor take the side of those who had been outlaws for centuries? It seemed inconceivable. But as we have seen, Constantine had an empirical, even pragmatic, approach to the matter. Should he take the side of those who had opposed his predecessors? Or, to put it in another way, should he take the side of the God who had dismissed Diocletian, a defeated man, and had sent Galerius down to his grave? Now Constantine stood poised to gain political victory, yet about to make exactly their mistake.

We must now consider Constantine's exchange of divine patronage. As we have seen, this was what he needed, and it was an indication of his genius and creative flair that he came to associate himself with the God of the Christians. To those familiar with the material this might seem a very convoluted and secular way to speak of Constantine's conversion. Indeed, we should do well at this point not to use the word 'conversion' at all. Words, which begin by giving us freedom of expression, can at crucial points constrict our under-

standing. They can produce what Marx called 'inverted consciousness',[7] a process described by Wittgenstein as 'the bewitchment of
our intelligence by means of language'[8] and less charmingly by
Alfred Schutz as 'cognitive prestructurization'.[9] The dispute concerning Constantine's religion stems in large part from the use of the
word 'conversion' to describe a transition which took place after the
Edict of Toleration and before the Battle of Milvian Bridge.

The difficulty which arises through the use of the term 'conversion'
is that the issue is falsely reduced to a single question: was Constantine converted to Christianity? On the negative side is the famous
answer given by Burckhardt in 1852.

> Attempts have often been made to penetrate into the religious
> consciousness of Constantine and to construct a hypothetical
> picture of changes in his religious convictions. Such efforts are
> futile. In a genius driven without surcease by ambition and lust
> for power there can be no question of Christianity and paganism,
> of conscious religiosity or irreligiosity; such a man is essentially
> unreligious, even if he pictures himself standing in the midst of a
> churchly community.[10]

On the 'committed' side, the most recent defence of Constantine
comes from Paul Keresztes.

> A study of these documents and reports will show, not that
> Constantine was a perfect Christian in his life, and always well
> informed in matters of doctrine, but that he was a sincere
> Christian, a truly great Christian Emperor and a genuine Apostle
> of the Christian Church.[11]

Burckhardt's rationalist dismissal of religion leads him to misrepresent Constantine. It is unfortunate that Keresztes, in his passionate
need to defend Catholicism, misrepresents Constantine nearly as
much in the other direction.

Clearly we must return to the sources, but we must do so without
such a prejudiced term as 'conversion'. As we have seen, Constantine's approach to religion was not a personal or private one. It was
necessary for him to adopt the most appropriate form of religious
legitimation available. This had in turn led him to associate himself
with and dissociate himself from Hercules. He then turned to
Apollo. But of course he could not simply decide to exchange one
divine patron for another. The decision was his, but it had to have
some element of heavenly confirmation. This is the effect of the
'pagan' vision, as recorded in the *Panegyrici Latini*. The basis of the
decision was not a religious one, in a narrow sense, but a pragmatic

one. Which god was more likely to bring him victory and success? But before we decry such a primitive and unworthy view of religion, let us recall that Elijah, who represented for many Jews in the time of Jesus the epitome of prophetic religion,[12] represented the same 'religious empiricism' when he offered to demonstrate on Mount Carmel that Yahweh was more powerful than Ba'al.[13]

For Constantine, having changed patronage from Hercules to Apollo, the question was whether he had done enough. As ruler of Gaul it was enough, but would it suffice for one whose ambitions extended to Rome and beyond? Apparently not: Constantine decided that he must change or at least extend divine patronage again. In this analysis I am using the phrase 'exchanging divine patronage' to describe Constantine's religious progression. It would be totally misleading to use the term 'conversion'. Constantine underwent no *religious* crisis. The exchanging of divine patronage describes not a religious movement, but the religious dimension of a political crisis. It would be quite false to compare Constantine here with the pilgrimage of Augustine later in that century. Augustine began life with the world-view and morality of his classical education. He proceeded to the religious world-view of Manichaeism and from that to Neo-Platonism, before he at last became a Christian.

> In the midst of that great tumult of my inner dwelling place, the tumult I had stirred up against my own soul in the chamber of my heart, I turned upon Alypius, wild in look and troubled in mind, crying out: 'What is wrong with us?'[14]

This is one of the classical accounts in the history of Christianity of a religious crisis. Its resolution is called conversion. Augustine was convicted of sin and received assurance of salvation through Christ. There is no indication that Constantine underwent an experience even remotely resembling that of Augustine.[15] It is more appropriate to speak of his development in terms of the 'exchange of divine patronage'.

On the basis of his progress to date, how might we expect Constantine to proceed? First, he would make a calculated appraisal of his present divine patronage. Secondly, he would make a rational decision about another divine patron who might be more helpful. Thirdly, he would require a confirming sign or vision that the god ratified this decision. This is in fact the sequence of events reported by his biographer, Eusebius.

> Being convinced, however, that he needed some more powerful

aid than his military forces could afford him, on account of the wicked and magical enchantments which were so diligently practised by the tyrant, he sought Divine assistance, deeming the possession of arms and a numerous soldiery of secondary importance, but believing that co-operating power of Deity invincible and not to be shaken. He considered, therefore, on what God he might rely for protection and assistance. While engaged in this enquiry, the thought occurred to him, that, of the many emperors who had preceded him, those who had rested their hopes in a multitude of gods, and served them with sacrifices and offerings, had in the first place been deceived by flattering predictions, and oracles which promised them all prosperity, and at last had met with an unhappy end, while not one of their gods had stood by to warn them of the impending wrath of heaven; while one alone who had pursued an entirely opposite course, who had condemned their error, and honored the one Supreme God during his whole life, had found him to be the Saviour and Protector of his empire, and the Giver of every good thing. Reflecting on this, and well weighing the fact that they who had trusted in many gods had also fallen by manifold forms of death, without leaving behind them either family or offspring, stock, name, or memorial among men: while the God of his father had given to him, on the other hand, manifestations of his power and very many tokens: and considering farther that those who had already taken arms against the tyrant, and had marched to the battle-field under the protection of a multitude of gods, had met with a dishonourable end (for one of them had shamefully retreated from the contest without a blow, and the other, being slain in the midst of his own troops, became, as it were, the mere sport of death); reviewing, I say, all these considerations, he judged it to be folly indeed to join in the idle worship of those who were no gods, and, after such convincing evidence, to err from the truth; and therefore felt it incumbent on him to honor his father's God alone.[16]

This is not conversion, but an exchange of divine patronage. The basis is not religious experience, but reflection on the failures of other rulers. There is one God who has not yet been adopted as divine patron, the God of the Christians. I must now make a distinction which is fundamental to the course of this present study and crucial to its conclusions. Up till now Constantine had allied himself to pagan gods. Now he exchanged such patronage for that of God. By 'God' I mean the God of Christianity, the God worshipped by Christians. The distinction is this, that Constantine chose

God as his new patron, but he did not choose Christ. This distinction
arises from the sources. It may seem odd to Christians. Yet throughout this book we shall see in source after source, in letters, edicts,
orations and biographies, that Christ plays no part in the religion of
Constantine. It is his distinction, not ours. It is he who chooses God
but omits all reference to Christ. We see this in the conclusion to
which Eusebius comes: 'and therefore felt it encumbent on him to
honor his father's God alone'. Constantius, his father, was not a
Christian. For Eusebius and other Christians, however, it was
possible to see him as a worshipper of God, for two reasons. First,
like other cultured men of his day, he was a monotheist and did not
hold with the ancient Roman pantheon. Secondly, he did not carry
out the edicts of persecution against the church in the West. He was
therefore in some sense a worshipper of the God of the Christians.
Yet he had no faith in Christ. But this is precisely the distinction we
have been making concerning the new religious position of Constantine. He was now a devotee of God, the God of the Christians,
but he did not confess faith in Christ. The exchange of patronage
carried with it no conviction of sin, no blessed assurance, no rest for
the troubled soul. There is no evidence of such a religious crisis in
Constantine, nor of any religious resolution. He had made a decision
about religion, not a religious decision. And the decision brought
him not inner peace, but – so at least he hoped – divine support in his
campaign to become sole ruler of the Empire.

This passage which I have set out in full and examined in detail is
of primary importance in determining Constantine's relationship to
religion, but it must be admitted that the following chapter in
Eusebius is much more colourful and dramatic, and that it is this
chapter which has become associated with the change of patronage.
We have already noted that the rational and calculated decision to
change patronage must be ratified by a sign or vision. After all, the
decision to change must be accepted on both sides.

Accordingly he called on him with earnest prayer and supplica-
tions that he would reveal to him who he was, and stretch forth his
right hand to help him in his present difficulties. And while he was
thus praying with fervent entreaty, a most marvellous sign
appeared to him from heaven, the account of which it might have
been hard to believe had it been related by any other person. But
since the victorious emperor himself long afterwards declared it
to the writer of this history, when he was honoured with his
acquaintance and society, and confirmed his statement by an
oath, who could hesitate to accredit the relation, especially since

the testimony of after-time has established its truth? He said that about noon, when the day was already beginning to decline, he saw with his own eyes the trophy of a cross of light in the heavens, above the sun, and bearing the inscription, CONQUER BY THIS. At this sight he himself was struck with amazement, and his whole army also, which followed him on this expedition, and witnessed the miracle.[17]

The most important question here concerns the meaning or significance of this symbolism. But of course we are not allowed to deal with this question first. Instead we must return to the arena in which the rationalists and the Christians fight it out. Was this a divine revelation, a miracle? On the one side there is Burckhardt dismissing the very idea of such an 'event'. Since such things cannot happen, this narrative is the invention of Eusebius and without historical significance. On the other hand is the tradition most recently exemplified by Keresztes: such miraculous events can and do happen – and therefore this one happened. When we turn to the actual text, we notice that Eusebius assumes that his readers, even those who believe such events can happen, will display some incredulity at this particular vision. But we cannot allow ourselves to be drawn into this traditional battle between rationalism and supernaturalism. As the twentieth century proceeds there is less dogmatism about what can and cannot happen, less dogmatism, too, about how extraordinary phenomena might be interpreted. Instead, we must return to the pattern established earlier. A change in divine patronage should be accomplished by a ratifying sign or vision. If we recall the panegyric concerning the beautiful temple, the question whether Constantine did indeed see the god Apollo, with the face of Constantine himself, is *historically* insignificant compared to the question how Constantine used his status as a devotee of Sol Invictus. So now the question is not whether Constantine had a vision of 'a cross of light in the heavens, above the sun', but how this symbolizes his future career. As Eusebius says, it is a vision in hindsight. The importance of the narrative here is not whether the event happened, but what it symbolizes. When at the end Eusebius claims that the vision was shared by the army, this is clearly an attempt to give the incredible event some objectivity. However, as we shall see, the real objectivity of what is symbolized lies not at that point but in the events which are to come. *They* are to be the real ratification.

Up to this point we have been describing not religion but politics, not conversion but an exchange of divine patronage. It is a matter of rational calculation, not of emotional crisis. But that cannot be the end of the affair. The crunch comes when the new patronage is tested out, and that means tested out in the field of battle. We do not know when Constantine took the rational, strategic decision to ally himself with the God of the Christians, but we do know when the new alliance was tested out.

2   Labarum

In a sense Constantine had inherited the title Caesar and dominion over Gaul. His biggest test was his decision to march on Rome and thus gain supreme control over the West. Yet, it was to be a test not only of his courage, determination and military genius: these he had, but, as we have seen, he decided that they would not be enough. It was to be the first test of his new alliance with the God of the Christians. He was successful in the Rhineland and he gathered support as his campaign progressed through Italy. But nothing would be decided till he faced Maxentius at Rome. And so it was that Constantine came to the Milvian Bridge, like some Old Testament leader whose army was outnumbered by more than two to one, but whose trust was in the Lord. Severus and Galerius had come well prepared but had not taken Rome. Before the battle Constantine had cause to ask himself again whether he was better equipped. In a dramatic and symbolic act he decided to make the new alliance public, so that it might be openly tested.

The sign which had been given in his vision, 'the trophy of a cross of light in the heavens, above the sun', was the sign by which he was to conquer. That seems straightforward enough, but historically it, too, has been the scene of many academic skirmishes.[18] Once again we must avoid the traditional terms of debate. For Burckhardt, since there are no miraculous signs, there is no sign from God. For Keresztes, since there are signs from God, this must be the cross of Christ. Neither position is much concerned with the historical circumstances.

Constantine required a device under which his army must fight. Since, if anything, Maxentius represented the traditions of pagan Rome better than he, Constantine must adapt the imperial device. His new device was publicly to declare his new alliance. If the alliance was to succeed, then it would indeed be under it that he would conquer. But let us take the matter one step at a time. If Constantine had been converted to Christianity, then the device would have been a simple cross. This, the common symbol of Christian faith, would now have been available also to him. The cross belonged to the church, and Constantine as a member of the church would inherit it. But of course that was not the situation. Constantine, as we have seen, was not converted to Christianity. He was not a member of the church. He was not baptized, nor of course did he join in the eucharist. There has been extensive debate about the exact form of Constantine's device, but the evidence which we have reviewed so far – plus the very existence of the debate – indicates that whatever it was, it was not the simple and unmistakable cross of Christ.

The device is normally referred to as the 'labarum', and was an adaptation of the Roman cavalry standard.[19] Constantine therefore did not, like some mediaeval crusader, simply replace the standard with the cross. He chose, for reasons now obscure, to adapt the imperial standard. But he did not adapt it with the cross. Instead, he made his own device. Because he was now allied to the God of the Christians, the adaptation was capable of a Christian interpretation and yet it was not simply Christian.

When we turn to our two historical sources, we must be prepared for two factors. The first is that in the ancient world an action or thought which is attributed to divine inspiration is commonly said to have come in a dream. The second is that it is the intention of both Lactantius and Eusebius to present Constantine as a Christian. Lactantius tells us of the incident on the eve of the Battle of Milvian Bridge.

> Constantine was directed in a dream to cause the heavenly sign to be delineated on the shields of his soldiers, and so to proceed to battle. He did as he had been commanded, and he marked on their shields the letter X, with a perpendicular line drawn through it and turned round at the top, thus ✗, being the cipher of Christ. Having this sign, his troops stood to arms.[20]

Eusebius tends to run together the original account of the 'conversion' (i.e. the exchange of patronage) and the making of the labarum. We return, therefore, to the vision, which Eusebius expects his readers to find incredible. Why should they not, since Constantine himself did?

> He said, moreover, that he doubted within himself what the import of this apparition could be. And while he continued to ponder and reason on its meaning, night suddenly came on; then in his sleep the Christ of God appeared to him with the same sign which he had seen in the heavens, and commanded him to make

a likeness of that sign which he had seen in the heavens, and to use it as a safeguard in all engagements with his enemies.[21]

We must simply recognize that the dream is a mythological mode of expression, affirming the divine inspiration of the making of the labarum. As we shall see, Christ plays no part in the religion of Constantine – certainly not as represented by Eusebius – and therefore the inclusion of Christ, as the source of the inspiration, tells us of Eusebius' interpretation of the labarum rather than of Constantine's intention.

Eusebius then goes on to describe the labarum, which he actually saw at a later date.

> Now it was made in the following manner. A long spear, overlaid with gold, formed the figure of the cross by means of a transverse bar laid over it. On the top of the whole was fixed a wreath of gold and precious stones; and within this, the symbol of the Saviour's name, two letters indicating the name of Christ by means of its initial characters, the letter P being intersected by X at its centre: and these letters the emperor was in the habit of wearing on his helmet at a later period. From the cross-bar of the spear was suspended a cloth, a royal piece, covered with a profuse embroidery of most brilliant precious stones; and which, being also richly interlaced with gold, presented an indescribable degree of beauty to the beholder. This banner was of a square form, and the upright staff, whose lower section was of great length, bore a golden half-length portrait of the pious emperor and his children on its upper part, beneath the trophy of the cross, and immediately above the embroidered banner. The emperor constantly made use of this sign of salvation as a safeguard against every adverse and hostile power, and commanded that others similar to it should be carried at the head of all his armies.[22]

The device which Lactantius describes is simply the Christ monogram, and if this was all there was to the labarum, there would be no mystery or dispute. The monogram, if such it be, is incorporated, according to Eusebius, into something more complex. The monogram is no longer the main symbol. Now it is a cross with a wreath on top. This corresponds to the vision of Constantine, of 'the trophy of a cross of light in the heavens, above the sun'. In this case the wreath would actually represent the sun. And if this is the case, the symbolism is much more complex. We can hardly dissociate from it the fact that Constantine was of the royal house of the sun. Of course the sun was the single most frequently recurring religious symbol at that time, from Persia to Ireland. The Celtic church carved great high crosses, incorporating on the cross the circle of the sun. In this they proclaimed not that Christianity had displaced the ancient religion, but that the religion of the Son gathered up and fulfilled the expectations of the religion of the sun. In the vision, the symbol under which Constantine is to conquer is an eclectic one, representing the alliance between this son of the sun and the God of the Christians.[23]

It will be clear even from this brief discussion why the interpretation of the labarum has been the subject of so much debate. Must we simply plunge in and choose pagan or Christian according to our preconceived views on Constantine or Christianity? No, we must follow the same method as before. Previously, I maintained that whether Constantine was converted to Christianity or not can be answered finally only by following the outcome of his conversion/exchange. Now, I must say that the meaning of the labarum cannot be finally decided by reading Lactantius and Eusebius. The meaning will become clear by the actions of Constantine, or rather by the way in which *he* interprets them.

Against the odds, Constantine defeated Maxentius at the Battle of Milvian Bridge in 312. He had won a great battle, but much more important, his new alliance with God had been tested. He had chosen God, hoping for success. Success had been forthcoming, apparently because Constantine had made a public declaration of his alliance. The labarum was henceforth not only a symbol of his alliance with God, but also the symbol of victory. We shall see that the labarum was not the cross of Christ, which belonged to all Christians. It was the symbol of Constantine's special relationship with God. The labarum belonged to Constantine. For this reason we must conclude that there was more to the labarum – in the intention and interpretation of Constantine – than common Christian symbolism. He worked into the device his own symbol of the sun.

For those who believe that Constantine was a Christian, it is of some concern that the Emperor continued to issue his coins with the symbol of the sun, till at least 323.

> It was during the rule of Constantine the Great that the cult of Deus Sol Invictus reached extraordinary heights, so that his reign was even spoken of as a Sun Emperorship. Constantine was the personification of Deus Sol Invictus on earth, and could consider the statue of the sun in the Forum bearing his name as a statue of himself.[24]

But there is historically no anomaly. The son of the sun had formed a successful alliance with the God of the Christians. He was not required by that alliance to become a Christian. This was a personal relationship, not one mediated by Christ. He had been granted a direct ratification, not simply by a vision in the heavens, whether that happened historically or not, but through the victory at Milvian Bridge. *That* was the miracle. The issuing of such coins would have been inconceivable had Constantine been in fact converted to Christianity.

For those who believe that Constantine had just been converted to Christianity, his actions on entering Rome as victor are also anomalous. According to Eusebius, when the Emperor entered the city to the joyous acclaim of those he 'liberated', he went directly to a statue of himself and had the labarum added to it. The bishop biographer claims this as an action by which 'the pious emperor, glorifying in the confession of the victorious cross, proclaimed the Son of God to the Romans with great boldness of testimony'.[25] But of course it was no such thing. This was not the triumph of Christianity over paganism. It was the victory of the new alliance between Constantine and the God of the Christians. The new factor, which had to be added to the statue, was the labarum. And the labarum was not the cross of Christ, but the personal symbol given to Constantine of his alliance. When we look more closely at the inscription added, we see this confirmed.

> 'By virtue of this salutary sign, which is the true test of valor, I have preserved and liberated your city from the yoke of tyranny. I have also set at liberty the Roman senate and people, and restored them to their ancient distinction and splendor'.[26]

There is no mention here of Christ. The 'salutary sign' is not of salvation from sins, but of liberation from tyranny. Constantine displays the labarum, not as a symbol of victory over sins, but as the symbol of divine support in his political victory over his enemy. This alliance between God and the Emperor is bodied forth in the arch, completed in 315, which commemorates the notable victory. Although it is dedicated by the Senate and people, we may be certain that Constantine agreed to the wording, if indeed he did not himself propose it. They have dedicated the arch,

> decorated with his victories, because, by prompting of the Divinity, by the greatness of his mind, he with his army, at one moment by a just victory avenged the State both on the tyrant and all his party.[27]

As Stevenson notes:

> The arch is an official war memorial. Its sculptures carry no Christian symbols, even on the shields of the soldiers. The gods of Constantine are the sun god and victory.[28]

The important message of the arch is the combination of God and Constantine. They had both contributed to the victory: *instinctu divinitatis, mentis magnitudine*. Constantine had executed his plan for victory, but under divine inspiration.

The labarum was not a sign that Constantine had been converted to Christianity. It is indeed to be the thesis of this book that it symbolized something very different indeed. It was not the cross of Christ but the personal symbol, belonging to Constantine, of an alliance with the God of the Christians. The Emperor's attitude to religion was sincere, but at an empirical and pragmatic level. He had conceived of a new alliance, had symbolized it in the labarum, and had found it confirmed on the field of battle. The alliance would take him to supreme power in the Empire: his religion would therefore bring him the prize which had eluded his pagan colleagues. But what was his religion? For in all this there is no place for Christ.

II

CONSTANTINE THE FRIEND OF GOD

1 Method and Criteria

What was the religion of Constantine? In the modern age it might emerge inadvertently, perhaps in an interview for a Sunday magazine supplement, that a political leader is a religious man, or woman. It is not necessary in the modern Western democracies to be religious to hold office. But, as we have seen, in the age of Constantine religious affiliation could not be simply a private matter. The Emperor must either be divine or at least have divine patronage. Constantine was a devotee of the God of the Christians. But that was not the same as being a Christian. Granted that such a distinction is possible in theory, does it apply to Constantine? This can only be established by reviewing the evidence. And it is of course assumed that the evidence is overwhelmingly in favour of claiming that Constantine was a Christian. Consider his conversion and his adoption of the monogram of Christ. Consider how he transformed the life of the church, restoring property, lavishing it with ever greater gifts. Consider his concern for the unity of the church when schism threatened it and consider his concern for right belief when heresy appeared. We shall indeed consider all these matters, and in some detail. And let us make it clear in advance that we have no new evidence, no manuscripts recently uncovered, no inscriptions newly unearthed. Classical scholars, historians and theologians have made this one of the most over-subscribed areas of research in modern times. What, then, remains to be said? Yet, how seldom in historical disputes do conflicting positions depend on completely different sets of material? And how often in practice is a dispute a matter of arguing over the very same evidence, for it is not new evidence brought to light which proves decisive, but a new perspective on the existing and readily available material. A simple example might suffice. In the synoptic problem it is agreed by biblical scholars that in the case of a narrative common to Matthew and Mark, the Markan form is normally longer. The conclusion is obvious, according to B. H. Streeter. Matthew is a later work, for the author has summarized and condensed Mark. Not so, according to Adolf Von Harnack. The Markan account is longer, but it is the characteristic of a later writer to elaborate with unimportant details, which give an impression of historical authenticity and originality. The evidence is not in dispute: the perspective in each case is different and therefore the interpretation and significance.

The evidence is not in dispute in the case of Constantine. He had a policy towards the church, and this not only included matters of status and property, but extended to the calling of ecumenical councils and the resolution of theological disputes. But how these things are to be interpreted depends on the perspective adopted. The traditional perspective begins with the assumption that the Emperor was a Christian. Yet this is not a matter of historical fact. It would be a circular argument to begin by assuming that since he was converted to Christianity, his actions and his policies show that he was a Christian, therefore it must have been to Christianity that he was converted. No, the assumption that he was a Christian derives in large part from a misunderstanding of his actual involvement in religious affairs. If the evidence is already available, we must pay particular attention to our premises and above all to our method. What was the religion of Constantine? We must not assume that he was a Christian and then find in his every involvement with the church confirmation of this premise. Rather, we must examine his religious involvement and ask what conclusions are to be drawn. If only things were as simple as that! There are three main obstacles. First, there is the difficulty in forming a view which takes all the evidence into account. There are anomalies which argue against his being Christian. We may well find anomalies in the other direction. The second obstacle is the proper evaluation of the historical sources. In his polemical work, *De Mortibus Persecutorum*, Lactantius presents us with a rigorous philosophy of history which goes beyond anything conceived of by the false friends of Job. He presents us with a universe of such a moral fabric that those who persecute the church come to a terrible end. If the facts of history do not confirm this *Weltanschauung,* so much the worse for the facts. In his *Historia Ecclesiastica* Eusebius employs a slightly less bloodthirsty approach, but in his main biographical contribution, *De Vita Constantini,* the framework is the miraculous transformation of the fortunes of the church under the beneficence of Constantine. It tells us a great deal about what Constantine did to religion, but little about Constantine's own religion. Thirdly, although Eusebius is regarded as the first historian of the church in the modern sense, his attributed works must be evaluated critically. Indeed, some of the material may not even come from Eusebius. What are we to make of the orthodox, sermonic and exceedingly boring address, 'To the Assembly of the Saints' (*Oratio ad Sanctum Coetum*)? Even Norman Baynes, who was convinced that Constantine was converted to Christianity, felt unable to give any historical credence to this work.

> The student of Christian apologetic must give the *Oratio* prolonged consideration; the student of Constantine's personal convictions must exercise self-denial.[1]

If we are to allow the answer to our question to arise from the evidence, instead of imposing a preconceived answer upon the sources, where are we to begin? Let us draw up a list of criteria, positive and negative for our starting point.

(i) We cannot begin with the 'conversion' or with the labarum, since they are sufficiently ambiguous that they themselves require to be interpreted in the light of subsequent events.

(ii) Nor can we simply begin with actions, such as ordering the return of property to Christians or the paying of travelling expenses for attendance at an ecumenical council. They too must be understood in a context.

(iii) We cannot begin with edicts of toleration or clerical privilege, since religious policy is not the same thing as religious convictions. It may be based on quite different motives.

(iv) We should do better to begin with a statement, one which deals with precisely the question of Constantine's religion.

(v) And to avoid the possibility that it might be only for the ears of one group, let it be a public oration.

(vi) It should be an extensive and detailed oration, not a few enigmatic phrases capable of various interpretations.

(vii) The oration should be of the Emperor's mature position, as near to the end of his life as possible, not the as yet uncertain sentiments of the new convert.

(viii) As to the occasion, let it be before a mixed audience, some Christian and some not, lest the speaker shape his words to the minds of one group only.

(ix) As a further safeguard, let the occasion be one dependent solely upon Constantine, so that no other party need be taken into account.

(x) To eliminate the possibility even yet that the Emperor might express not his sentiments, but those which his audience might wish to hear, let the oration be spoken not by the Emperor but by one who knows him well.

(xi) And let the orator be sufficiently skilful, that he not only expresses that of which the Emperor is aware, but actually makes explicit what may have been unconsciously held or intuitively performed.

(xii) Finally, let yet another criterion be added, this time to safeguard against any misrepresentation of the religion of the Emperor. Let the orator be himself a Christian, a bishop if you will, who can be expected to make the oration as Christian as it can possibly be – save only that the oration is delivered in the presence of the Emperor, who will not allow himself to be misrepresented.

Twelve criteria; an omen perhaps, but such stringent criteria that they may appear self-defeating. It is most unlikely that such a statement was ever made in Constantine's lifetime, more unlikely still that it should have survived. But those familiar with the literature of the period will already have grown tired of this little charade. The oration which we require was delivered and has been preserved for us. The *Oratio de Laudibus Constantini,* 'In Praise of Constantine', meets all of our twelve stringent criteria.

The oration was delivered at the imperial court in Constantinople in the presence of the Emperor himself.[2] The date, July 336, was less than a year before his death and the occasion was the celebration of his thirtieth jubilee. The oration was composed specially for the occasion by no less a person than Eusebius Pamphili, bishop of Caesarea in Palestine. No doubt Eusebius was qualified to perform this notable function both through his accomplishments as a scholar and also through his close contact with the Emperor in the last years of his life.

It will therefore be clear why this oration fulfils our criteria. Its authenticity has never been doubted. It could hardly have come later in the career of the Emperor. It was composed by a Christian and delivered in the court of the New Rome. Above all, it was given in the presence of the Emperor himself. Although it reflects the views of its author, it must remain within this important constraint, that its subject is actually present and (presumably) listening. This is a much more decisive and historically reliable starting point than the mythology and ambiguity of the vision and the labarum.

We must now examine this important text in some detail, but before we proceed, there is one final critical point to be made. In the course of his *Life of Constantine*, Eusebius tells of festivities in Jerusalem arranged by the Emperor, in connection with the dedication of a new church. Eusebius claims that he has described this

building in a separate treatise, which he will append to the *Life*. He
promises also to add an oration given 'shortly afterwards' on the
occasion of the Emperor's tricennalia.[3] In many of the manuscripts
of the *Life* there indeed follows a long oration by Eusebius, 'The
Oration of Eusebius Pamphili in Praise of the Emperor Constantine,
Pronounced on the Thirtieth Anniversary of His Reign'. The oration
is clearly too long to have been given on one occasion, but on closer
inspection it divides at the end of chapter 10. That chapter draws to
a conclusion an oration which is addressed to the Emperor, is about
the Emperor, and is given in the presence of the Emperor. Chapter
11 is attached to it, with a phrase or two which offers the rest of the
piece to the sovereign, but which was actually given on a different
occasion, not in the presence of the Emperor, but before a Christian
gathering at the dedication of the Church of the Holy Sepulchre, in
Jerusalem.

Drake has argued most convincingly that the content, tone,
perspective, style and motivation for chapters 11-18 are quite
different from the first part, and that the two do not belong together
historically or theologically. He distinguishes them, after the manner
indicated by Eusebius in the *Life,* calling them in turn *De Laudibus
Constantini* and *De Sepulchro Christi*. We need not here repeat the
points made by Drake,[4] but it will be clear that if we proceed on this
assumption, then only the former oration meets the twelve conditions set out above. The oration 'on Christ's Sepulchre' fulfils almost
none. Indeed it is because the first oration has hitherto been read in
the context of the second that Constantine has seemed so obviously
to be a Christian. A quite different, unexpected and at times startling
picture emerges when the first oration is taken by itself. Let us now
examine it in more detail.

2   Model Sovereign

On the Thirtieth Jubilee of the Emperor Constantine, justly called
'The Great', the panegyrists vied with each other in their extravagant
accounts of his character, his deeds, his fame and achievements.
And with good cause; in the history of men even to the present day
there have been few whose real accomplishments have so objectively
outstripped the hyperbole of those employed to flatter. What then
remained for Eusebius to add, new and fresh words of praise, to
express his own admiration for the Emperor and at the same time
the heartfelt gratitude of the church? Certainly not in the further
declamation of such wordly feats. The bishop determined to speak
rather of spiritual things, of the divine virtues of the monarch, above

all of his special relationship with God. Although in the imperial court, he spoke in reverent tones, as if in church or temple, for those who were then in the presence of the Emperor were in the presence of a divine mystery. The Jubilee belongs not solely to Constantine but to the 'Ruler of all' who chose him: it is indeed a religious festival.[5]

What might well strike us today in reading the oration is the unique place claimed for Constantine in the sight of God, and we shall examine this more closely. What would be immediately clear to the hearers of the oration, and no doubt deeply offensive to some pagans, was that the divinity of the Emperor was denied. This tradition has come into the West with the conquests of Alexander the Great in Persia and Egypt. Indeed, it had been the sticking point which had led to the persecution of the church. When Constantine turned away from the ancient gods to the new God of the Christians, he accepted the fact that within this monotheism he could not himself claim divinity nor have it claimed on his behalf. How offensive and degrading it must have seemed to traditionalists. The Emperor a mere mortal! In a real sense the purpose of this oration is to demonstrate that the Emperor was by no means reduced to this lowly state. On earth he had no equal, not because of his armies and his wealth, but because of the unique status accorded him by God and because of his unique place in the divine purpose of salvation. The subject of the oration is the relationship between 'the Highest Sovereign' and 'the model sovereign'.

Thus in the Prologue is the scene set. It is not, after all, a celebration simply of Constantine, but 'a celebration of the Supreme Sovereign'. It is not the religious festival of a divine Emperor, but of the One God. And Eusebius repeats this point throughout Chapter I: 'the One who is Above the Universe', this 'One, the Supreme Sovereign' and 'the One and Only God'. Constantine was truly converted to the monotheism of the God of the Christians, but the oration, having started out in such a bold manner, never attempts to describe the religion itself as Christian. It is certainly the God of the Christians who is referred to: 'this One, the Supreme Sovereign, our triumphant sovereign himself praises to us, having fully per-ceived in Him the cause of his empire . . .' (I,84). This is a clear reference back to his conversion and what we might call the labarum-event, the primitive testing of the covenant in battle. But there is no question of this God being known through Christian revelation. No, varied though the nations within the Empire may be, they are agreed on one thing, 'calling on the One and Only God with an inbred logic, a self-taught and self-learned knowledge'

(I,84). This is a natural theology, and Christ plays no part in it. The cosmos is ruled by God. 'All the heavenly luminaries alike, by His will and word trained to a single strain, covering the long course in aeon-laps, run through the races on heavenly tracks' (I,85). No salvation history, no Christian eschatology: this is the pagan cyclical view of the return of the golden age.

Thus Eusebius asserts the monotheism which Constantine has accepted, and bars the door to any form of deification. But once that is said, he can proceed to speak of the special place of Constantine in the divine scheme of things. It would hardly be fitting to compare the activity of God and of Constantine, and Eusebius turns to another element of pagan religion and classical philosophy, namely the divine Logos. The Logos is second only to God and is that creative force which gave the universe its purposeful form and enlightened it with God's truth.

> He who is above all, before all, and after all, His Pre-Existing and Only-Begotten Logos, yes, the great high priest of the great God, older than all time and all ages, dedicated first and foremost to the glory of His Father, petitions for the salvation of everyone, distinguished with first rank of the universe, but second to rule in the paternal kingdom (I,85).

This is the Logos behind John's Gospel, but not a Logos who was ever incarnate. The Logos directs the cosmos from heaven, but, and now we come to the heart of Eusebius' argument, the Logos has a representative on earth.

> And this selfsame One who would be the Governor of this entire cosmos, the One who is over all, through all, and in all, visible and invisible, the all-pervasive Logos of God, from whom and through whom bearing the image of the higher kingdom, the sovereign dear to God, in imitation of the Higher Power, directs the helm and sets straight all things on earth (I,85).

In this way the pragmatic Constantine was more than justified in his conversion. Had he forfeited his divinity, that illusion, that shadow without substance which had guaranteed his predecessors neither victory or security? But what gain; he was now declared the 'sovereign dear to God', the 'imitation', the agent and counterpart of the divine Logos here on earth.

As the Logos has ruled in heaven from age to age, 'His friend . . . rules on earth for long periods of years' (II,85). Their salvific work is compared.

As the Universal Savior renders the entire heaven and earth and highest kingdom fit for His Father, so His friend, leading his subjects on earth to the Only-Begotten and Saviour Logos, makes them suitable for His Kingdom (II,85).

There is a parallel also in their victories. The Logos, 'our common Universal Savior', defeats the invisible powers of evil that invade the earth, while 'His friend, armed against his enemies with standard from Him above, subdues and chastizes the visible opponents of truth by the law of combat' (II,86). Constantine's wars are apparently not just power struggles, but under the labarum they are crusades, the material dimension of the cosmic struggle for the souls of men. Again, all wisdom and even the faculty of reason come from the Logos, and his friend also proclaims 'for everyone on earth the laws of genuine piety' (II,86). And as the Logos in heaven prepares the kingdom of his Father, so in imitation on earth, his friend cleanses the world of idols and images and welcomes into his court 'holy and pious men'. Constantine does not celebrate the Jubilee as would his predecessors, with the sacrifice of animals, but with the sacrifice of a pure heart and true piety of soul.

In return, God grants him long life and rule, sons to assist him, harmony and peace throughout his realm. This is a return to the pragmatic covenantal basis of his religion, as Drake says: *do ut des,* I give in order that you might give.

Thus outfitted in the likeness of the kingdom of heaven he pilots affairs below with an upward gaze, to steer by the archtypal form (III,87).

The sovereign directs affairs on earth according to a pattern established in heaven. God's will is objectively being realized:

He has modelled the kingdom on earth into a likeness of the one in heaven, toward which He urges all mankind to strive, holding forth to them this fair hope (IV,88)

But surely a mortal could not be so exalted and remain unspotted? Eusebius now proceeds to picture this saintly sovereign as one who wears the purple because it is required of his office, but who understands the value of such outward trappings on some eternal scale. He is surrounded by armies, but he knows himself to be a man like others. In his court he has wealth beyond imagining, but he is not seduced by metals and stones precious to men. He has authority to rule the earth, but he longs already for that heavenly kingdom. (Perhaps a hint that the Emperor's illness is already known to be mortal.) Eusebius pictures him in the midst of revelry as a pious, ascetic figure. Unlike his predecessors, he longs not to be equal with God but to lay down this troublesome life and receive his eternal reward. God 'has brought round the triple cycle of decades', but beyond this life he 'extends it even into far distant eternity' (VI,91). If there was a crisis, it is long since past, at Milvian Bridge. There is but a gentle transition from long rule now, to eternal rule to come.

As if alarmed at his own boldness, the bishop plunges into numerology, ringing the changes on the numbers associated with the sovereign's rule. His prediction, it would seem, is already clearly determined for those who understand such matters. God is pictured as the President of the (pagan) games, and Constantine, because of his skills and virtues, receives the crowns and prizes. Eusebius returns to the theme that what victory the Logos achieves in spiritual matters, the sovereign, his friend, accomplishes in the material world against God's enemies. Those who persecuted the saints and treated them barbarically, the sovereign has in turn defeated. And carrying the victory on has overthrown their idols and stripped them of their honour, and precious possessions. He put an end to the disgraceful and unnatural rites of some of the cults, and by example and gentle persuasion sought to lead the benighted people into the truth of the Logos. No, the pagan gods could neither predict in oracle their fate, nor contrive any defence against it.

And so the new era begins, with Constantine building his new Rome, Byzantium. This heralded the golden age on earth, of peace, harmony, piety. All the achievements of the sovereign were to mirror that golden age promised by the Supreme Sovereign. And so the oration ends as a doxology.

> Choruses of all kinds honor Him with victory odes, and the entire mortal race chimes in with the angelic revellers in heaven. As through musical instruments, rational souls send up to Him through the bodies which enclose them fitting hymns and due praise (X,102).

East and West, South and North, they turn,

> to pursue the pious life under the same customs and laws; to praise one God who is over all; to acknowledge one Only-Begotten Savior, the cause of all good things; and to recognize also one sovereign, rector of the earth, and his sons beloved of God (X,102).

One might be forgiven for thinking that Eusebius considered that all the promises of God had now been fulfilled, that God's will was indeed done now on earth as in heaven, and that with this long awaited consummation world history might just as well end and everyone go home.

We have examined the oration which fulfils our twelve criteria. In it there is no mention of Christ. A Christian bishop addresses a supposedly Christian emperor, giving an account of the latter's religion, but there is no mention of Christ. Those who believe that Constantine was a Christian will press forward with explanations, with reasons, perhaps even excuses. But before we review these interjections, let us pause for a moment and consider the full significance of this situation. Constantine's religion is described in detail by a Christian bishop and yet there is no mention of Christ. In a moment we shall consider pleas for mitigation, but not too quickly. Consider: if circumstances were such that Eusebius could not mention Christ, then surely he could not have even begun to describe Constantine's religion – if Constantine was a Christian. Instead, we are regaled by a bishop-scholar, obviously immensely proud of being permitted to deliver his oration, an oration which has been composed with great care and polished to perfection as a work of art. There is no indication whatsoever that Eusebius felt pressurized by circumstances, or that his treatment of the subject was distorted by some irritating constraints. The work is free-flowing, even self-indulgent, and in it Eusebius says all that he wishes to say to the Emperor and to the world. And Christ is not mentioned, not once. Before we consider any 'explanations', let us ponder this quite extraordinary fact, for fact it is.

Several explanations might be offered. But what is there to explain? Eusebius describes the religion of Constantine in such a way that we should conclude that it has no place for Christ. Why should we suppose there is any need to explain this fact? Of course the need for explanation occurs only for those who before examining this evidence have come to hold the view that Constantine was a Christian. It is that view which needs explanation, not the oration of Eusebius.

As for the explanations, they revolve round one point, that Eusebius could not too openly describe Constantine as a Christian because it would have given offence to the pagans at the imperial court. But as soon as we begin to investigate this argument, it collapses. It is somehow reminiscent of the 'messianic secret' in Mark's Gospel.[6] We can imagine the wider circle of followers of Jesus, after the founding of the church, challenging the inner core of disciples. 'Why did you not tell us he was the Messiah?' The device of the 'messianic secret' means that the disciples claim that they were sworn to silence.[7] The historical explanation is much simpler: they had not known. Similarly, Eusebius is in effect being challenged, 'Why did you not openly declare that he was a Christian?' The device this time might be called the 'Constantine secret', as if Constantine, in order not to offend the pagans, had told Eusebius not to declare openly that he, Constantine, was a Christian. Stated in this way, of course, the device is either absurd or comic. In the days of persecution it had been easy to identify Christians, even when they attempted to disguise the fact. And now, after the end of persecution, are we being asked to believe that Constantine was deeply Christian and yet somehow his closest advisers at the court did not know? There was no Constantine secret. The explanation is much simpler: he was not a Christian. Eusebius did not have to disguise anything. Far from it, he said all that could be said – and that still fell short of declaring Constantine a Christian.

Well, try again. What if the pagan courtiers knew that Constantine was a Christian, but Eusebius, out of deference (and he was never known to run low on that commodity), was constrained not to make a public declaration of this in their presence? Imagine the scene, therefore, in which Eusebius stands in the presence of the Emperor and describes his religion to the pagan courtiers. He (E) knows that they (PCs) know that he (C) knows that they (PCs) know that he (C) is a Christian. But he (E) pretends that he (E) does not know that he (C) is one, so that he (E) will not cause him (C) to offend them (PCs). And this is an explanation!

But as we have seen, Eusebius shows no such concern for the feelings of pagans. He makes his position absolutely clear at the outset, that Constantine is not divine, but human. More important than what the bishop of some obscure hamlet thought, the Emperor obviously accepted this too. It marked a clear break with the pagan traditions, traditions which had deified his own father notwithstanding the fact that Constantius was a monotheist. The only God who required such a rejection of traditions was the God of the Christians. We know that: did it escape the attention of the courtiers?

In the *Life of Constantine* Eusebius sets Constantine in a Christian context. We shall consider this work later, but not surprisingly it tends to christianize the Emperor. But it was one of our criteria that the oration must be in the presence of the Emperor, to avoid misrepresentation. In the oration there is no evidence that Constantine was Christian and that fact was somehow disguised. What we have instead is the introduction into the oration of the Logos, which, according to our eleventh criterion, is an example of the scholar making use of terms which would not be explicitly used by the

Emperor himself. This is in order, but to what use does Eusebius put it? The Logos was a concept common to Greek philosophy and Hellenistic religion. It was the apologetic genius of the writer of John's Gospel to use this concept to describe the person and work of Christ. But as we have seen, the Logos in the oration acts simply in a pagan context. In the oration the Logos is certainly not Christ. When the oration is read in the Christian context of the accompanying oration 'On the Sepulchre of Christ', then reference to the Logos might seem to the casual reader to be a reference to Christ. But in the first oration the Logos is not Christ, neither in person nor in role. We therefore have a very intriguing situation. Eusebius is said to be presenting Constantine as somehow less Christian than he was. But there is no evidence for this. By the introduction of the concept of the Logos it might be said that Eusebius goes as far as he can go to introduce at least a parallel between the religion of Constantine and Christianity. What prevents him from making the comparison more explicit, or indeed openly declaring Constantine a Christian? The answer is not at all complicated or obscure, but lies in our last criterion. What constrains Eusebius from openly declaring Constantine a Christian? Not the presence of pagans, but the presence of Constantine himself. Nothing would have given Eusebius greater pleasure than to be able to declare Constantine a Christian – but it would not have been true. The point can be obscured in documents addressed to other Christians, but it cannot be made in the presence of the Emperor. Those who believe that Eusebius has held back from presenting Constantine as a Christian attribute this to the presence of pagans. But by this time, thirty years after assuming power, twenty-four years after his 'conversion', twelve years after becoming sole ruler of the whole Empire, East and West, and, perhaps as important as any of these, within a year of death, it is difficult to take such a factor seriously. Eusebius held back from declaring Constantine a Christian for the simple reason that everyone knew he was not one.

III

CONSTANTINE AS MESSIAH

1 *Remoto Christo*

In the previous chapter we came to the conclusion that it is possible
to describe the religion of Constantine without reference to Christ.
Although this fact is unexpected and perhaps unsettling, yet there
will be resistance to drawing the conclusion that Constantine was
not a Christian. We have examined and rejected the explanation
that Eusebius was constrained by the presence of pagans in his
audience. Nevertheless, even when admitted, the fact might seem
too negative to bear the weight of such a conclusion. To argue from
the absence of certain terms might seem inconclusive. Indeed, to
speak in this way might recall the method employed in the apologetic
work of Anselm, abbot of Bec. Soon after his appointment as
Archbishop of Canterbury, in 1093 Anselm issued a work on the
doctrine of the atonement, entitled *Cur Deus Homo?* In the Preface
he speaks of its two parts. In the first he deals with the arguments of
unbelievers who claim that Christian faith is contrary to reason. But
he does so by beginning from common premises which all reasonable
people might accept, 'leaving Christ out of view, as if nothing had
ever been known of him'. In the second part, from the same
premises, 'as if nothing were known of Christ', he demonstrates the
necessity of God becomming man.[1] Anselm begins, *remoto Christo,*
from matters of fact and observations, and proceeds to conclusions
which demonstrate (at least to his own satisfaction) the truth of the
Christian faith. Might it not be claimed that Eusebius also argues,
remoto Christo, praying that those who have observed the deeds
and events of which he speaks, will be drawn inescapably to the
conclusion that they point to the truth of Christianity? Would this
explain the absence of reference to Christ, turning a negative
observation into a positive apologetic virtue?

Briefly, the answer is No. Although Anselm begins without

reference to Christ, he is compelled by his own argument at last to bring Christ into the conclusions. There is, speaking without irreverence, a Christ-shaped gap at the end of the argument, which demands to be filled. His verbal picture is incomplete, or to change the metaphor, there is a cruciform piece of the jigsaw missing. Anselm need not put it in place: even his unbelieving hearers are compelled in spite of themselves to acknowledge it. But this is not the situation which faces us in the oration 'In Praise of Constantine'. Its subject is of the Sovereign in heaven and the sovereign on earth, of the election of the Emperor by God to be his servant, of the faithfulness of Constantine, of the division of labour between the Logos and his friend. It is indeed a quite extraordinary narrative, but when it is rounded off at the end it is not incomplete. There is no sense that there is anything or anyone missing. The parallel of heaven and earth is complete: there is no Christ-shaped gap. Eusebius is able to speak of Constantine's relationship to God, unmediated by Christ. He can speak of kingship, without reference to Christ, the King of kings.

In Anselm, Christ is left out of account – for the moment. Never fear, he will appear in the conclusion, by necessity. The oration is delivered *remoto Christo,* but not merely Christ set aside for the moment. Christ is set aside throughout, and there is no move to refer to him in the conclusion. For Anselm, Christ appeared by necessity: for Eusebius, there is no need to mention Christ. The relationship between Constantine and God is direct and unmediated. God has chosen him, without faith in Christ. God has given him a new sign of salvation, the labarum. Through Constantine God has achieved new things: indeed it would appear that through Constantine earth has approximated at last to heaven.

The oration does not present us with an exceedingly subtle apologetic device: Christ is not set aside for the moment, he is excluded from the story. To those who believe that Constantine was a Christian, this situation is quite inexplicable. But if we begin our investigation of the religion of Constantine by listening to the oration of this Christian bishop, then there is no problem to be solved, no difficulty to be explained. How can Constantine be a devotee of the God of the Christians, yet set aside Christ? The answer is as simple as it is offensive to the tradition. Constantine has replaced Christ. In the religion which Eusebius describes, and describes in the presence of the Emperor, Constantine is the new Messiah, and upon him the hopes of the world rest.

2 The New Epiphany

We have already seen that to praise Constantine was no difficult task, but even so, Eusebius begins by placing the sovereign in some isolation beyond men, if not quite on the level of God. He will honour 'the sovereign's own godlike virtues', focus upon 'his more divine qualities' and 'narrate the sovereign's ineffable mysteries'. And even as he denies that the Emperor is divine in the pagan sense, in calling him 'the model sovereign' he is attributing perfection to him. The mystery that he is about to unfold before his hearers is not the mystery of the Sovereign, but the sovereign. Even in the Prologue, we are prepared for the revelation that if this is a mortal man we understand nothing of him approached from the perspective of earth.

The Emperor can only be understood in his relationship to God. It is from this relationship that the Jubilee stems, which is a none too subtle way of stating that the very existence of the Empire owes its existence to that relationship of Sovereign and sovereign. The relationship is as direct and as pragmatic as that. 'This One, the Supreme Sovereign, our triumphant sovereign himself praises to us, having fully perceived in Him the cause of his empire . . .' (I,84). There is no mediation here. The Empire does not exist 'through Jesus Christ our Lord', as the church might sing. No, the Empire and hence the reason for the Jubilee is traced back not to Jesus of Nazareth and the Cross, but to the conversion of Constantine, the labarum and the victory at Milvian Bridge, which was the beginning of the story.

The relationship is personal to the Emperor, and it is through him that God holds the Empire together. But in return the Emperor has made this God known to his subjects. Great soldier, yes, but the mystery of his being extends beyond this role. The teeming multitudes depend on him also for the truth of God: they are 'instructed by the great savior teacher' (I,84). It is through his special relationship to God that their salvation comes: he deserves the title 'savior'. Eusebius is true to his promise: he does not waste time praising the more mundane achievements of his king.

This combination of soldier and teacher has a long history in Greek political thought, at least as far back as Plato. To investigate it further Eusebius turns to another Greek concept, the Logos, the divine principle, eternal and creative, author of the Good, teacher of goodness. This 'Pre-existing and Only-Begotten Logos' (I,85) is now introduced in a thoroughly Platonic mode. The writer of John's Gospel had adapted this tradition, claiming that he 'came to his own',[2] was incarnate in Jesus of Nazareth. But this is not the context of the Logos in the oration. There is no hint that the Logos is to be understood in Christian terms. The model is thoroughly Platonic.

> And this selfsame One would be the Governor of this entire cosmos, the One who is over all, through all, and in all, visible and invisible, the all-pervasive Logos of God, from whom and through whom bearing the image of the higher kingdom, the sovereign dear to God, in imitation of the Higher Power, directs the helm and sets straight all things on earth (I,85).

There is no thought of incarnation here, or rather, in this we are prepared for a much more startling claim which is to follow later: the Logos is incarnate in Constantine. The 'imitation'[3] is not that of a child sitting in daddy's driving seat behind the wheel of the car. No, here we have the duplication on earth of what is present in heaven. Eusebius is explaining to us the mechanism by which God's will is done on earth as it is in heaven. The Logos is co-ruler with God in heaven: 'his friend, supplied from royal streams and confirmed in the name of a divine calling, rules on earth for long periods of years' (II,85). There is a reflection. The Logos is Saviour in heaven while his friend prepares those on earth for the heavenly kingdom.

This is not a Christian model, but a Platonic one. As it continues it is religious, but still not Christian. From earliest times in the church the Cross of Christ was seen as the saving sign, not only over sin but over the demons of the air and over death itself. But as Eusebius describes the new division of labour, the Logos deals with the principalities and powers of evil, 'all those who used to fly through the earth's air and infect men's souls', while his friend 'subdues and chastizes the visible opponents of truth by the law of combat' (II,86). This is not a Christian picture at all, and the decisive point is that the victory is not won by the cross of Christ, but by the labarum of Constantine, since he goes out to combat 'armed against his enemies with standards from Him above' (II,86). The pattern is now clearly emerging. We cannot simply say that Eusebius writes as if Christ were left out of account, as if by some natural theology he were giving expression to the Christian faith without actually naming the Christ or his cross. No, the oration goes far beyond this negative omission. Here we see a positive exclusion. The Logos is not Christ incarnate, because it is in Constantine that the Logos is incarnate. It is not that the servant of Christ inherits victory over the demons in the virtue of the cross. No, in the new divine economy the servant of the Logos is victorious in the material world, and he contends under a sign given specifically to him before his first battle. This is not some subtle apologetic form of Christianity. It is quite a different religion, and from it Christ is not so much absent, for the moment, but permanently excluded.

The Jubilee is the celebration of this divine economy. God has given Constantine the victory on earth. Constantine in return offers not the animal sacrifices of the pagan world, but something much more pleasing to God, 'dedicating to Him his own royal soul and a mind thoroughly worthy of God' (II,86). By the strength and guidance of God, a new world is coming into being, and Constantine selects from it for God something quite unique: 'he has himself rendered a great offering, the first fruit of the world with which he is entrusted, himself' (II,86). He is 'a good shepherd' (II,86), leading his flock by making himself the first sacrifice. The language of this section has resonances with the Letter to the Hebrews, but it is not a Christian passage. To the contrary, what would normally be attributed to Christ is here attributed to Constantine. Not Christ set aside for the moment, but Christ replaced.

In Chapter I we noted the pragmatic, contractual nature of the religion of Constantine. And now, because of his self-effacing devotion to God, Constantine receives his reward, 'additional long periods of rule'. At each tenth anniversary of his rule yet another son is made a Caesar to assist him (so Eusebius, with a certain poetic licence). Once again the situation refers exclusively to Constantine, and yet Eusebius sees in it the fulfilment of an Old Testament prophecy. For the church the transformation was miraculous: persecution stopped and patronage began almost overnight. The Book of Daniel rehearses the history of Israel in which with successive empires, persecution has followed persecution. The writer foretells a time when all this will change and 'the saints of the Most High shall receive the kingdom'.[4] Eusebius quotes this passage, considering it entirely appropriate, but more intriguing is the fact that it is now through Constantine that God has fulfilled his promise. We shall return to this point later, but even if the religion of Constantine is not Christian, yet since he serves the God of the Christians, God's promises in the Bible may be taken to refer to him.

After this biblical aside, Eusebius returns to the pagan context once more. The scene is the imperial games, but now God is the President, and in virtue of Constantine's accomplishments 'He designated him Victor' (II,87), and not just ruler of a plot of land. Now the image is expanded. If the four Caesars, like wild colts, rule segments of the Empire, Constantine rides herd over them, super-

vising from above. But Eusebius uses a more explicit image than
this.

> Holding the reins high above them, he rides along, traversing all
> lands alike that the sun gazes upon, himself present everywhere
> and watching over everything (III,87).

Apollo was often pictured as riding a chariot across the sky, and
here this more than human Emperor, of the royal house of the Sun,
fulfils his more than human responsibilities in the same manner.
Those who would wish to christianize the oration might point out
that by the beginning of the fourth century Christ himself was
pictured as a charioteer in the heavens. But does that make the
oration more Christian – or less? In that case Constantine would
once again be seen to replace Christ, and with some justification
claim ownership of the vehicle. After all, his labarum demonstrated
that he was still licensed to drive it. The image is not Christian, nor
for that matter is it a return to the religion of the past. It is simply an
available image to reinforce the Platonic structure.

> Thus outfitted in the likeness of the kingdom of heaven, he pilots
> affairs below with an upward gaze, to steer by the archetypal form
> (II,87).

Hence the present festivities. The Logos 'has modelled the
kingdom on earth into a likeness of the one in heaven' (IV,88), to
the delight of God the Father, who,

> has rewarded the leader and cause of this excellence with such
> long-lasting honours that not even three ten-year periods suffice
> for his rule, but instead he bestows it for as long as possible, and
> extends it even into far distant eternity (VI,91).

Because Constantine has been so obedient to the will of God, he has
been given long rule on earth. Through him God's plan is brought
to completion and earth approximates to heaven. In these circumstances, Eusebius predicts, the distinction blurs, and *autokrator*
continues his rule even into heaven. At this quite extraordinary
claim Eusebius himself is alarmed and takes refuge in a long
discussion of the nature of time and eternity, the world and its
Creator. God, through 'His Sole-Born Logos, truly the Universal
Common Savior' (VI,92) has prepared a place beyond this world
and 'for those who have lived moderately and piously, a change and
migration from here to a greater place will occur' (VI,93). No
mention of Christ here; no demanding conditions of entry to the

kingdom. All eyes instead are turned towards the Emperor, and the hopes of men lie with him and his special relationship with God.

> In the same way, the honours of our victorious sovereign's world-wide rule, bestowed by the Giver of all benefits, obtain the start of new benefits. For now his reign has fulfilled a tricennial festival, but already it is attaining longer intervals and fosters hopes of benefits yet to come in the heavenly kingdom (VI,94).

And so this particular discussion draws to a close. It began with the prediction that Constantine would be rewarded with eternal rule in heaven. Then after a rambling digression on numerology and other topics, it seems about to close on the same theme. Constantine may hope with assurance, and men may hope through him. He is the mediator of heaven to earth. And even as the section ends, Eusebius casually extends this point into the most startling assertion yet about the peculiar status of the Emperor. Eusebius begins in Pauline vein:

> No human eye has seen this, nor any ear discerned it, for it is not possible for the mind encased in flesh to discern what things are prepared for those graced with piety, such as yourself, most God-fearing sovereign . . .[5]

Constantine indeed is placed here in a select and most distinguished group, those for whom the greatest prize of heaven is prepared. But to be one of any group, even so select, is not the unique place Eusebius has previously claimed for his sovereign, and he goes on to make his most extraordinary statement yet.

> . . . most God-fearing sovereign, to whom alone of those who have yet been here since the start of time has the Universal All-Ruling God Himself given power to purify human life . . . (VI,94).

No reference here to Christ, no indication of the salvific significance of the life and death of Jesus of Nazareth. The history of the world no longer turns on the events which took place three centuries before, in an obscure corner of the Empire. Since the beginning of the world it is to Constantine *alone* that the power of salvation has been given. Christ set aside, Christ excluded and now Christ formally denied. Let us not forget this as we read the last part of the argument.

> . . . to whom He has revealed even His own Saving Sign, by which He prevailed over death and fashioned a triumph over his enemies. Setting this victorious trophy, apotropaic of demons, against the idols of error, he has won victories over all his godless foes and barbarians, and now over the demons themselves, which are but another type of barbarians (VI,94).

The saving sign which was revealed to Constantine was the labarum, not the cross of Christ. And it is through this sign that the barbarians and the demons alike have been defeated; as a result of it Constantine now stands alone as the saviour of the world. The scene is the fourth century, not the first. The world, spiritual and material, was not saved until Constantine.

In this sustained panegyric, which establishes by a new empirical root almost everything that the denial of divinity had apparently given up, there is only one phrase which is in discord, namely, that the saving sign is described as that 'by which He prevailed over death' (VI,94). Is this a reference to the Cross? If so, it is quite out of place in the description of the Labarum, for the Cross did not need to be *revealed* to anyone in the Empire, Christian or pagan. Could it be the Cross? And yet it is not described as the cross of Christ, but the Sign of God himself. But if the saving sign is the labarum, what can it mean to say that by it God has prevailed over death? However, let us not because of this ambiguous phrase set aside the immediate context or the entire oration. We are dealing here with the prediction that Constantine will rule not only on earth but for eternity in heaven. He has been assigned a unique place in the history of the world. Only one enemy stands between him and that prize, death itself. Many years before he faced death, outnumbered at Milvian Bridge, but the sign which was to bring him the title Saviour, first of all saved his life. He has kept faith with the sign and now, as he comes towards the end of his life, the labarum, which has been the sign of everything else for him, will also be the sign that death will not have him. He will indeed rule in all eternity.

Perhaps at this point the audience in the imperial court might exchange glances and wonder what the venerable bishop was about to say next, having surely achieved and far surpassed what might be counted as praise suited to the occasion. But Eusebius after a pause did continue, if in subdued tones, at least carrying forward the concluding thought, of the battle with death and the barbarian hordes. He describes a society completely given over to pagan excesses, sensuous, even bestial, dedicated to the pursuit not of truth but falsehood, devoted not to life but to the god of death. But as Eusebius describes such a society, as if it were uniform throughout the world, it is as if he borrows once more from the New Testament and even from his own records of the confessors and martyrs who kept faith with God through the centuries of persecution. And yet this the greatest historian of the early church presents us with a strangely convoluted account of events. 'In such a situation, what had the Sovereign of the oppressed to do?' (VII,96). As we shall see

in a moment, the secret weapon against his enemies was of course
Constantine. But the great persecution had ended virtually before
Constantine began his career, certainly before his conversion. It
flared up briefly under Maximian and Licinius, but the picture given
by Eusebius is obviously for effect and not for the sake of history.
And who in any case were the persecutors of the saints? They were
the emperors, the imperial court, civil service and provincial governors, not to mention the Roman citizens and even the general
populace of the Empire. Did Constantine attack his own people?
Once again Eusebius adapts history to suit his purpose. The enemy
are the barbarians. Happy solution, for Constantine did in fact
conquer the barbarian threat to the Empire, and at the same time
Eusebius would not offend his audience, since they too would see
themselves on the side of the Emperor against the barbarians, no
matter what their religious positions. God's answer was swift and
terrible.

> These things the Supreme Sovereign enacted from heaven when
> He put forth an invincible warrior as His attendant (yes, this
> sovereign, through his abundance of piety, delights in such a title)
> (VII,97).

Once again, he is 'the image of the One Ruler of All', 'imitating his
Savior' and acting 'as the prefect of the Supreme Sovereign' (VII,97).
We shall return to examine more closely the significance of this
picture of Constantine, but suffice to point out at the moment that
he is heralded here in messianic terms: he comes as the warrior king
to defeat the enemies of God who hold the saints in cruel oppression.
They cry out to God, and he raises up for them a king like David. No
mention here of that other son of David, who 'perceiving then that
they were about to come and take him by force to make him king
. . . withdrew again to the hills by himself'.[6] Constantine is the new
Messiah, equipped to defeat the enemies of God, spiritual and
material, equipped to lead God's people into battle or into
righteousness.

Lost in pagan debauchery, serving gods who were no gods, the
people lived in darkness until 'the manifestation of the Common
Savior to men', 'a certain new epiphany' (IX,99). Epiphany, the
manifestation of God on earth, yet here there is no reference to
Christ. Christ has no place in the entire oration, certainly not in this
context, the advent of Constantine the new messiah. Eusebius says
that no one could have foretold the new epiphany:

> Who foresaw this august and reverent reign, and our gloriously

triumphant sovereign himself, the trophies raised by him over the demons everywhere on earth and the obliteration of the lofty? (IX,99).

There is no doubt about it: the scene described is the new initiative of God in Constantine. There is no reference here to the efficacy of anything done three centuries previously. Constantine acts not simply as a warrior, which he was, but as saviour. The labarum fends off both enemies and evil.

But he, fortified with the armor of piety, arrayed against the multitude of his foes the Saving and Life-Giving Sign like some safeguard and shield against evils, and gained a victory over his enemies and the spirits alike (IX,99).

Eusebius then refers to the statue in Rome commemorating Constantine's defeat of Maxentius. It incorporated 'the Victory-Bringing Sign',

this great trophy against all enemies, this explicit and indestructible salutary Sign of the Roman Empire and safeguard of the Universal Kingdom (IX,99).

In all this Eusebius is speaking of the labarum and not the cross. Once again, the security and the salvation of the Empire depend on Constantine, and both are symbolized in his personal standard, the labarum. He instructed the people in battle: he instructs them now in prayer and sets aside Sunday as a day of prayer. He restored religious buildings and raised up new ones.

And suddenly, as the oration draws to a close, Eusebius again surprises us with yet further claims on behalf of Constantine. Restoring the buildings for the worship of the true God reminds Eusebius of two sites in the Eastern Empire, of special importance. One was at Antioch, begun in 327, of which Krautheimer writes:

The location of the Golden Octagon in or adjoining the palace precinct; the person of its Imperial founder; and its dedication to the divine force uniting Church and Empire, combine to suggest that it was designed as the palace church where the Emperor, God's counterpart on earth, would attend services.[7]

But it is the other one which is much more crucial to our enquiry. The historical background to it involves a discovery made by his mother Helena as she visited various traditional sites in Palestine.[8] Apparently while on pilgrimage in Jerusalem, she was guided by a dream to uncover a buried vault in which were then found three crosses. Not surprisingly, they were taken to be the crosses of Calvary and one of them was confidently identified as the true cross of Christ. Constantine built upon that site the Church of the Holy Sepulchre. It is this foundation which Eusebius describes, and in it he comes closer than anywhere else in the oration to speaking of Christian origins and by association implying that Constantine acknowledged Christ. But what does he actually say?

> In the Palestinian nation, in the heart of the Hebrew kingdom, on the very site of the evidence for salvation, he outfitted with many and abundant distinctions an enormous house of prayer and temple sacred to the Saving Sign, and he honoured a memorial full of eternal significance and the Great Savior's own trophies over death with ornaments beyond all description (IX,101).

It is possible that Eusebius, in view of the discovery by Helena, is referring to the cross of Christ in the phrase 'the Great Savior's own trophies over death'. The reference is not explicit, but this may well be the intention. What is clear, however, is that these trophies are distinguished from the saving sign, which must still refer to the labarum. Eusebius can refer to this place as 'the very site of the evidence for salvation', but as we have seen, this is not the religion of Constantine. Salvation comes to him by the labarum, some three centuries later. And insofar as he is the saviour of the world, this site in Palestine is but a witness to what is achieved through him.

> In this same region, he recovered three sites revered for three mystical caves, and enhanced them with opulent structures. On the cave of the first theophany he conferred appropriate marks of honor; at the one where the ultimate ascension occurred he consecrated a memorial on the mountain ridge; between these, at the scene of the great struggle, signs of salvation and victory. To be sure, all these the sovereign adorned in order to herald the Saving Sign to all; the Sign that, in turn, gives him compensation for his piety, augments his entire house and line, and strengthens the throne of his kingdom for long cycles of years, dispensing the fruits of virtue to his good sons, his family, and their descendants (IX,101).

Here Eusebius is clearly referring to three traditional sites associated with Christ. But just as clearly, they are honoured not because of their now decisive significance, but because of their witness to the saving sign. Once again it is made clear that this saving sign is not the cross of Christ, but the labarum, which in Constantine's pragmatic, covenantal religion, has already brought him its own reward, is responsible for the very Jubilee now being celebrated, and is the foundation of this kingdom from generation to generation. It is in this ninth chapter of the oration that we have the most explicit recognition of the existence of Christ. Does this weaken the presentation of Constantine as the new Messiah, the new epiphany of God? No, since no conclusions are drawn from the passage. Indeed it hardly belongs within the oration at all, since it is not describing the religion of Constantine. It belongs more appropriately in subsequent chapters, in which we shall deal with Constantine's religious policy. And policy is quite a different matter from personal conviction. It was not Constantine who went seeking out these Christian sites. But once they were drawn to his attention by Helena, perhaps it was expedient that the Emperor should respond positively. Does it weaken the case? If anything, it strengthens it, for having introduced these references to Christ, Eusebius draws no conclusions about the efficacy of Christ's death, resurrection and ascension. The persecutions and idolatries, the debaucheries and madness that he has just been speaking about are historically still to take place. The new epiphany, the one which is to be decisive, lies yet in the future, though 'heralded' here. The saints have still to cry out to God to rescue them. God has still to send his 'friend', the invincible Constantine, previously friend of Sol Invictus. The chapter concludes not with a reference to Christ, but with the now familiar confirmation of Constantine the new messiah. 'Thus have the deeds of God become clear through the divine efficacy of the Saving Sign' (IX,101).

This rather surprising interruption to the panegyric came about not through any intention of retracting what had already been claimed, but rather through association of ideas. Eusebius was speaking about Constantine's religious policy, which included restoration and building of new churches. His thoughts moved to a foundation of special importance to him, namely the Church of the Holy Sepulchre. Indeed we now draw towards the end of the oration, which is followed by a separate piece originally delivered on the occasion of the dedication of that church. After this digression, Eusebius returns to his earlier line of thought.

The oration is ending: he has spoken at length about the sign, but claims that much more could yet be said. Previously we noted that Constantine *alone* has been given the power to bring salvation to men. Now Eusebius makes such an exclusive claim for the Emperor's labarum.

It alone has everywhere eclipsed the age-old lies about the gods and consigned the error to darkness and oblivion. It has cast the light of understanding upon the souls of men and revealed to all the One True God (X,101–2).

Eusebius is not writing of events three centuries before or of the cross of Christ. He speaks of the transformations which he has himself seen and experienced during the period since Constantine came to rule.

Of such benefits to mankind the cause plainly is this great and wonderful Sign, through which all that was evil no longer exists, whereas what was not before now shines forth to all in rays of peity (X,102).

The watershed of history is now, not three centuries ago. What is *now* revealed, was *not before*. Once again, it is clear that the life and death of Christ have no efficacy in this scheme of things. It is not that in accordance with events long ago, or in continuity with them, or inspired by them, Constantine saves the world. No, the salvation of the world is now wrought by the events of the life of Constantine, symbolized by *his* saving sign.

And so the oration finally comes to an end. The sovereign is hailed as 'rector of the earth'. He is the pilot who steers 'by a favorable Sign'. He is the victor to whom God has already given the earth, but in addition God (according to Eusebius' best information) 'intends to declare him a partner of greater goods' (X,102). But considering what the bishop has already claimed on behalf of his sovereign, perhaps it is as well that modesty finally breaks through and the oration 'In Praise of Constantine' is at last brought to an end, if not to its conclusion.

How was it received? Perhaps there would be a few stifled yawns, a good deal of shuffling of sandals and anxious looking at sundials to see if it were time for dinner. Or perhaps it was received with wild acclaim: nothing like it had ever been heard in that or any other imperial court; or perhaps with stunned silence, in view of the quite extraordinary claims made. We do not know. Do not know! Eusebius has just painted a picture of the Emperor which makes Flash Gordon look like a part-time social worker, and we do not know! This distinguished scholar and Christian bishop has just spelt out with the utmost clarity how Constantine has displaced Christ, and the labarum has taken the place of the cross, and we do not know how the oration was received. Perhaps it was regarded as a draw: the pagans were glad it was not openly Christian, the Christians content with its biblical images. Perhaps neither side took it at face value, that Eusebius, confidant and friend of the Emperor, was actually describing the religion of the sovereign. Within a few years, as the church grew stronger, the second oration, delivered earlier at the dedication of the Church of the Holy Sepulchre, was deliberately attached to the first. It was not delivered in the presence of the Emperor but to a Christian audience. When the two orations are run together, the latter, the Christian oration, provides a context in which the religion of Constantine is now read as explicitly Christian.

PART TWO

CONSTANTINE'S RELIGIOUS POLICY

At the outset of this study I recognized that the famous vision and labarum of Constantine were not self-explanatory, and adopted the method of establishing Constantine's religion from a quite different source. The source was the oration 'In Praise of Constantine', which fulfilled twelve very stringent criteria. What emerged was a quite different picture of Constantine's religion, but one which provided a basis not only for the correct understanding of the vision and the labarum, but also for dealing with apparent anomalies. These anomalies derive for the most part from the assumption that the Emperor was Christian. Without that assumption his own religion, his attitude towards religion and his religious policy were perfectly consistent.

The oration has provided us with an unexpected and even alarming view of Constantine's religion. To this position and its implications we shall return in Part Three. There is more to be said on that account, much more and much worse. However, in Part Two we must examine the main sources of our knowledge of Constantine to determine whether this new view of Constantine's religion is confirmed in these other writings and whether it provides a more coherent and comprehensive view of his religion.

This may at first seem unlikely. These other sources, which do not fulfil our twelve criteria, will be 'compromised' in various ways. For example, some come from Eusebius when he is writing to other Christians. None is a sustained presentation of the religion of the Emperor addressed to him personally. In some the Emperor himself writes, but is he writing *ad hominem*, adopting the terminology of his hearers. As we shall see, it is all too easy to begin with the assumption that Constantine was a Christian and to read into these sources evidence to confirm the assumption. But if we have in mind this new position which emerges from the oration, we shall see to our surprise that the texts themselves do not support the assumption about Constantine's Christianity.

In dealing with the oration I noted that those who begin with this assumption are claiming that Eusebius, in order to cause no offence to pagans, avoided making explicit Constantine's Christian faith. And yet in Chapter III we observed Eusebius present a religion in which Constantine actually replaced Christ. To veil explicit recognition is one thing, but positively to exclude Christ is an entirely different matter. After reviewing the sources of Constantine's attitude towards religion and his religious policy, in Part Three we shall return to continue our examination of the implications of the religion which Eusebius attributes to Constantine. Then it will be clear that this religion is not simply non-Christian but positively anti-Christian.

IV

THE LIFE OF CONSTANTINE

1 Presentation by Eusebius

Although Eusebius is regarded as the first historian of the church, his *Historia Ecclesiastica* is not a history in the modern sense. It preserves most valuable material, but it is actually written to illustrate and confirm a philosophy (or theology) of history. Similarly, *De Vita Constantini* is not simply a biography of the Emperor. It deals with the transformation in the life of the church which was brought about by Constantine. It is in fact a doxology, a work of faith offered to the glory of God. In contrast to the oration 'In Praise of Constantine', the story is not told from the perspective of the Emperor but from that of the church. We must therefore be prepared for a Christian context and therefore inevitably a tendency to christianize the religion of Constantine himself. For this we should be prepared, yet more surprising is how little christianizing takes place.

It would require a multi-volume work to encompass the character, the life and the achievements of Constantine the Great. Eusebius, saddened by the death of his king, is speechless, 'unable to utter a single phrase' on the subject.[1] Not for long, however, and soon he is off, launched into perhaps his favourite subject, Constantine the 'friend of God the Sovereign'. It is hardly surprising that the *Life* should echo many of the points made in the Oration, since the Emperor died the year following the Jubilee. Indeed, as I have just indicated, many of the same phrases are used. However, the subject is subtly changed. It is no longer Constantine in himself, but Constantine as an example to strengthen the evidence for Christianity. The work will therefore be selective. Eusebius is not going to treat of all battles, legislation, policies or the general character of his rule: 'the design of my present undertaking being to speak and write of those circumstances only which have reference to his religious character.' (I.11) So Eusebius begins with the familiar themes of the faithful Constantine and his divine rewards, the invincible conqueror under the trophy given him from God.

We need not go through the treatise in detail. It is, as Eusebius has indicated, a highly selective document which gathers together incidents in the life of Constantine of particular religious significance, including edicts affecting the life of Christians and the status of the church. In the oration we have been examining we are presented not with history, *wie es eigentlich gewesen ist*, but history interpreted to bring out its 'real' meaning. The real meaning in this case concerns Constantine's unique relationship to God. Now in the *Life* we are presented not with history, but with history interpreted. The subject is not Constantine, but rather what God has achieved through Constantine. The change in subject may seem unimportant, but it means that in the *Life* we have less of Constantine and his religion and more of Eusebius and *his* religion. It is for this reason that we should be prepared for a christianizing of Constantine, for here he is presented not in his own terms but in a setting provided by the philosophy of history developed by Eusebius. Of particular interest, therefore, for our purposes is the specifically Christian dimension of the *Life*, which, as we have seen, was entirely absent, actually excluded from the oration.

Some of the material Eusebius claims to have obtained from the Emperor himself, but most of it must already have been at least in note form at the time of Constantine's death. But since the final redaction took place after the restraining presence of the Emperor was removed, we must brace ourselves for a quite new picture of Constantine, as a ruler fully and consciously Christian in all his actions and motives. And yet when we read the *Life* no such picture confronts us. As already noted, under the circumstances the presentation of Constantine as fully Christian could hardly count against our emerging view, since the picture would be influenced by Eusebius' apologetic motivation. But contrary to expectation we do not find such a picture of the Emperor, and therefore our view receives unexpected support even from this unlikely direction.

That is not to say that the *Life* is as a-Christian or anti-Christian as the oration. It contains many references to Christ and Christian faith. However, when these are examined more closely, most of these references relate to Eusebius and not to Constantine.

To the casual reader, the *Life* appears to be a fully Christian work and Constantine appears within it as a Christian monarch. However, when we look more closely, dividing material into several categories, then we must conclude that the evidence is surprisingly thin.

(i) *Ambiguous terminology*. There is a close relationship between
the oration which we have been considering and the *Life*. Many of
the themes are common to both: Constantine as the witness of God,
the example of piety as well as faithfulness; the sovereign rewarded
for his service to God; his prosperity, victory, longevity derive from
God; he is the friend of God. There is also continuity in the
terminology used in speaking about God. This becomes important,
since to the casual reader some of these terms might seem to refer to
Christ. To a Christian, 'Saviour' would normally be used of Christ,
yet as we might expect from our examination of the oration, it is
normally used in the *Life* to refer to God. 'But God, that God, I say,
who is the common Saviour of all . . .' (I.3). It may be that the term
actually comes from Constantine and would be a further indication
that although ambiguously close to Christianity, he was not a
Christian. Thus in his letter addressed to Alexander and Arius,
Constantine writes of 'Our great God and common Saviour of us all
. . .' (II.71). Eusebius claims that Constantine considered God to
be 'the Saviour and Protector of his empire' (I.27). His success was
due to 'the powerful aid of God his Saviour . . .' (II.23). But
Constantine also used this title in writing or speaking of God. In his
address to the Council of Nicaea he speaks of 'God our Saviour'
(III.12). The same phrase is used in a letter which Constantine sent
to Eusebius, 'through the favoring providence of God our Saviour
. . .' (IV.36). The title 'Saviour', therefore, must normally be taken
to refer to God and not Christ in the *Life*, so far as its reference to
the religion of Constantine is concerned. The same is true of the title
'Lord', which Christians might assume to refer to Christ. Thus
Eusebius, writing of Constantine's arrangements for his tricennial
thanksgiving, speaks of the 'Sovereign Lord' (IV.40). But Constantine himself uses the title in a letter to Eusebius, 'the almighty God,
and our Saviour, and Lord of all' (III.53). In a letter to Sator, King
of Persia, Constantine speaks of God as 'he who is Lord of all . . .'
(IV.10) and later of 'that God who is the Lord and Father of all'
(IV.13).

These references form a selection of the uses of terms which at
first sight might suggest that Constantine was a Christian, but in
context it is always clear that the Emperor is speaking of God.
Eusebius also uses them faithfully in this sense.

(ii) *Religion of Eusebius*. There are many other examples where
'Christ', 'Saviour', 'Son' or 'Lord' are used, but which on closer
inspection express the religious faith of Eusebius and not of Constantine. To begin with, there are examples which simply reflect
Eusebius' view of events. He speaks of those who persecuted the

church, having 'driven from house and home the servants of Christ
. . .' (III.1). Describing the persecution by Licinius: 'he threatened
with death those who professed the Saviour's name' (I.52). Many
pagans became Christian as a result of Constantine's policies, 'some
applied themselves to the saving doctrine of Christ . . .' (III.57).
These phrases simply indicate how Eusebius as a Christian understands events. Their use gives the *Life* a Christian dimension, but it
does not come from Constantine.

There is, however, a second series of examples in which Eusebius
speaks in such a way as to suggest that Constantine shared his
position. In examination of the oration, we touched on the motivation for the building of the Church of the Holy Sepulchre. We shall
examine this again in a moment, for it is dealt with also in the *Life*,
but I have already suggested that it cannot be assumed that Constantine's motivation was Christian. Yet Eusebius makes this assumption, or at least chooses to interpret the action in this way.
Thus the site is described as 'the blessed locality of our Saviour's
resurrection . . .' (III.25). The church is to be 'erected near the
Saviour's tomb . . .' (III.29). It is the place of 'the Saviour's
sufferings' following 'the murder of the Lord . . .' (III.33). There
are many such examples, which convey the impression that Constantine thought of the place and the project in Christian terms.
This is a fairly mild example of Eusebius christianizing his material,
but it reinforces the feeling that this is a Christian work and that
Constantine's position is naturally Christian. Once that assumption
is made, then other passages read naturally. 'All these things the
emperor diligently performed to the praise of the saving power of
Christ, and thus made it his constant aim to glorify his Saviour God'
(III.54). Everything we have heard of Constantine in the the oration
and so far in the *Life* would suggest that this statement is perfectly
accurate, except for the reference to Christ. Eusebius is attributing
Christian motivation to Constantine, but this is simply a reflection
of Eusebius' own motivation. A similarly gratuitous addition is to
be found in the account of Constantine's preparation for the battle
against Maxentius. 'Assuming therefore the Supreme God as his
patron, and invoking His Christ to be his preserver and aid, and
setting the victorious trophy, the salutary symbol, in front of his
soldiers . . .' (I.37). The connection of Constantine, God his patron
and the labarum as his trophy is familiar. The addition of Christ is
quite out of place in the light of the oration, but also, as we shall
increasingly see, within the *Life* itself.

(iii) *Explicit Christianity*. When these and other similar examples
are taken into account, there still remain some in which Constantine

appears to be explicitly Christian. Three points might be made in this connection. The first is that such examples are very few indeed. They do not provide the basis for claiming that Constantine was Christian: they are anomalous as they stand. The second point is that we can quite easily understand how they arose, given, as I noted at the outset, that this is a Christian work and that Eusebius will tend to christianize the presentation of Constantine. In other words, what is surprising is not that such examples occur, but how very few there are. Third and more curious still, while Eusebius on these rare occasions claims that Constantine is a Christian, it is the overwhelming evidence of Eusebius himself that this is not the case. Let us examine these examples to see how they could have arisen.

Let us display at least a little critical discrimination and perhaps some awareness of human nature as we consider an intriguing example of this claim.

> For truly he maintained a continual testimony to the Christ of God with all boldness, and before all men; and so far from shrinking from an open profession of the Christian name, that he rather desired to make it manifest to all that he regarded this as his highest honor, now impressing on his face the salutary sign, and now glorying in it as the trophy which led him on to victory (III.2).

What lies behind this rather strident assertion? Eusebius here protests too much. 'So far from shrinking from an open profession of the Christian name . . .' That indeed must have been the most disappointing – perhaps the only disappointing – feature about Constantine as far as the church was concerned. Eusebius has hit the nail on the thumb here. Everything about his attitude towards the church and his essentially profound devotion to the God of the Christians must have led them to expect that as a matter of course he would take that final step. The final step seemed such a short one to them and such a logical one. They could not understand his position otherwise: it was anomalous. But he would not take the step, and Eusebius has instead to settle for the fact that Constantine makes a public display of the *labarum* while he will not identify himself as a devotee of the Crucified One.

When Eusebius says that Constantine testified to his Christian faith, he is not describing a fact but giving expression to the heartfelt desire of the church. But the oration and the *Life* simply do not bear out Eusebius' claim. Among modern scholars Eusebius has no lack of critics of his objectivity, but let this at least be said on his behalf, that if his interest was in disguising the facts about Constantine, misrepresenting his actual position, then Eusebius has made a very poor job of it. He had the opportunity of completely obscuring the historical position, but he has not done so. He could have rewritten the facts so that they upheld his claim that Constantine was a Christian, 'who alone of all sovereigns had openly professed the Christian faith . . .' (IV.74), but at least in this respect Eusebius was a greater historian than many of his contemporary critics.

Our emerging view of Constantine's religion still stands, not in spite of Eusebius, nor by ignoring him or explaining him away. It stands because he provides the evidence which continues to support it. But after all that has been said, there still remain a number, a surprisingly small number, of explicitly Christian statements attributed to Constantine. The largest number fall within the category of being *ad hominem*: they tell us about his audience rather than about himself. They occur in letters written by Constantine to Christian churches or church leaders. For example, there is the letter to Bishop Macarius, concerning the building of the Church of the Holy Sepulchre in Jerusalem. 'Such is our Saviour's grace, that no power of language seems adequate . . .' (III.30). Or again, the letter to the church in Antioch recommending that they not appoint Eusebius as their bishop: 'O holy faith, who givest us in our own Saviour's words and precepts a model, as it were, of what our life should be . . .' (III.60). There is the letter to Eusebius praising the bishop's lecture on Easter: 'It is indeed an arduous task, and beyond the power of language itself, worthily to treat of the mysteries of Christ . . .' (IV.35). What are we to make of such apparently Christian references? Are they, so few in number, to count against the weight of evidence in the contrary direction? Or rather, should we not say that their very paucity of number indicates that they do not reflect the historical position of Constantine, but rather one of two things? Either they are included for the benefit of the recipients, in order to enlist their support for what is included in the letters, or they indicate some of the slight christianizing which Eusebius occasionally undertakes.

And finally, apart from such *ad hominem* references, there are several events which are presented by Eusebius as Christian. The first, of course, is the vision which accompanies Constantine's conversion, not in the original, but in a repetition later during the night. '. . . then in his sleep the Christ of God appeared to him with the same sign . . .' (I.29). If we exhibit some scepticism here, it is not about a vision: there is no call for such positivism. No, once again the doubts arise from Eusebius himself. Everything he tells us in the oration, and most of what is set out in the *Life*, indicates that

Christ played no mediating role between Constantine and his Saviour God. Eusebius would like to think it a Christian vision and Christian conversion, but elsewhere he is honest enough to present the religion of Constantine as a-Christian.

Then there was the decree on Sunday observance. 'He ordained, too, that one day should be regarded as a special occasion for prayer: I mean that which is truly the first and chief of all, the day of our Lord and Saviour' (IV.18). Of course this tells us nothing about Constantine's own religious position, but something about his religious *policy*. And when we recall his continuing association with Sol Invictus, it is not entirely irrelevant that this decree should refer to the *Dies Solis*.

Eusebius tells us that Constantine was careful to observe Easter. 'The emperor himself, as a sharer in the holy mysteries of our religion . . .' (IV.22). By the way, do you find that encouraging? Eusebius has an unhappy way of assuring us of doubtful things. In this particular example he manages to make it clear that the Emperor stood over against the Christians. But the main point he makes is that at Easter 'his religious diligence was redoubled . . .'

> As soon as day itself returned, in imitation of our Saviour's gracious acts, he opened a liberal hand to his subjects of every nation, province and people, and lavished abundant bounties on all (IV.22).

But what does this tell us about Constantine's religion? He had not been baptized, and therefore clearly did not participate in the Easter eucharist. Did he by example encourage all Christians to join in the Easter celebration? No doubt, and the reason is not far to seek. One of the reasons for his calling of the Council of Nicaea was that the church was divided over the date of Easter. The date and even the celebration were not nearly so important to Constantine as the threat to the unity of the Empire. Small wonder he rewarded those who celebrated the feast at the official time. To this we shall return in Chapter VIII, 'The Unity of the Church'.

And finally there is, of course, the baptism of Constantine. 'Being at length convinced that his life was drawing to a close . . .' (IV.61), he sought baptism. It certainly does not sound like a conversion experience: more a calculation of some kind. Clearly Eusebius understood the baptism as the (long, long overdue) final seal on Constantine's commitment to Christianity. But once again we must ask whether this was in fact Constantine's view.

The time is arrived which I have long hoped for, with an earnest

> desire and prayer that I might obtain the salvation of God. The
> hour is come in which I too may have the blessing of that seal
> which confers immortality (IV.62).

We recall that in the oration Eusebius speaks of Constantine passing
directly into an eternity of rule in heaven. Does this explain the
Emperor's view of baptism? He did not see it as being washed in the
blood of the Lamb. Christ was no mediator for him. The significance
of the event lies rather in its timing. He wanted to be baptized, but
postponed it till the end of his life. This has normally been taken to
mean that he wished at this late stage to have, through baptism, his
sins forgiven. But this is not what Constantine has in mind. Rather,
he sees baptism as the conferring of immortality, and that comes
appropriately at the end of his earthly rule. An unusual view, but
one which is spelt out by Eusebius in the oration and now by
Constantine in the *Life*. And to underline it, let us read the words of
the Emperor after his baptism.

> Now I know that I am truly blessed: now I feel assured that I am
> accounted worthy of immortality, and am made a partaker of
> Divine light (IV.63).

Right to the end of his life, Constantine stands over against the
church because of his unmediated relationship with God. And as if
to emphasize this, Constantine notes that if his timing is wrong and
by any chance he happens to live for some time after baptism, then
he will be able 'to associate with the people of God, and unite with
them in prayer as a member of his Church . . .' (IV.63).

Eusebius has done it again. In what appears to be a passage
demonstrating that Constantine was a Christian, he manages to
convey to us that before his baptism Constantine never did unite
with the church in worship, and that the baptism itself was to
accomplish something within Constantine's religion and not to
incorporate him within the Christian church. Precisely at the point
where our position might seem to be challenged, it is suddenly
confirmed and shown to be entirely justified.

2   Critical Considerations

(iv) *Comparative material*. We have not been able to deal with all
the material in the *Life*, but we have dealt with examples of all types.
That is to say, nothing has been overlooked because it would have
caused problems for our position. We have chosen the most challenging examples. Nor have we taken the easy way out of denying

the historicity of the material when it became difficult to handle. If truth be told, the material has proved surprisingly easy to deal with. It would have been unsatisfactory, for example, simply to dismiss the conversion material or the baptism passage as 'unhistorical'. Perhaps because of this we have seemed rather uncritical, as if we were naively ready to accept anything Eusebius said. Not so, but for the sake of the discussion, much better to take the worst that Eusebius can set before us and still maintain our position.

But now that we have emerged from this examination without having to take the easy way out, let us note that there is evidence that Eusebius has christianized his material at times. By definition we cannot always be sure of this, because the original form is now overlaid by the christianized form. The only way in which we would be absolutely sure is if we knew the original form, and had also before us the christianized form. Fortunately, we have in fact examples of such comparative material and we can now take time to examine two examples.

The first of these two incidents concerns the building of the Church of the Holy Sepulchre in Jerusalem. Eusebius gives an account of the matter in III 25–40. It begins with the motivation that it is to honour this holy site: 'and this he did, not on the mere natural impulse of his own mind, but being moved in spirit by the Saviour himself' (III.25). Eusebius therefore makes the decision a specifically Christian one. He tells us that the site had been deliberately covered and obscured: the sacred cave and the immediate surroundings had been filled with earth. Upon the site there had been erected a temple to Venus. Eusebius implies that the site was known to be that of the burial of Christ, but successive emperors and administrators of the area had (of course) done nothing to prevent the idolatrous and pagan practices. Not surprisingly, therefore, we hear that Constantine ordered the dismantling of the temple. And if that were not enough, he ordered that the site should be excavated. Quite unexpectedly, when the cave was cleared of polluting earth, 'the venerable and hallowed monument of our Saviour's resurrection was discovered' (III.28). Having first of all set out merely to restore the site, Constantine then authorized the building of a church. The Emperor therefore writes to Bishop Macarius telling him of the miraculous finding of 'that monument of his most holy Passion' (III.30) and of the plans now to build there 'since it has brought to light a clear assurance of our Saviour's passion' (III.30). He continues with the instructions for the church. Eusebius adds a detailed account of the architecture and the fittings. 'This temple, then, the emperor erected as a conspicuous monument to the Saviour's resurrection, and embellished it throughout on an imperial scale of magnificence' (III.40). Eusebius also mentions churches built on the sites of the birth of Jesus and the ascension. These are all Christian establishments, and according to Eusebius they were built because of the Christian faith of the Emperor. If we had no further material on these buildings, we should have to conclude that the Emperor was motivated by Christian faith. However, we do have alternative material which gives a different account, one consistent with Constantine's position up till now, and consistent with our view of his religion.

Eusebius himself goes on to tell us about the admirable actions of Helena Augusta, the Emperor's mother, who very late in her life made a pilgrimage of various sites in Palestine, to 'survey this venerable land' (III.42). She dedicated two churches on the sites of the birth and ascension of Christ. So that at Bethlehem one was built, and 'the emperor himself soon after testified his reverence for the spot by princely offerings, and added to his mother's magnificence by costly presents of silver and gold, and embroidered hangings' (III.43). It would therefore appear that it was the Christian Helena who took the initiative in seeking out the traditional sites and also dedicating churches upon them. It would be perfectly consistent with our view if Helena had requested that the Emperor build churches or at least meet part of the expense of the fittings. And by the same token, this would be compatible with Constantine's policy of helping Christians, without implying that he took a Christian initiative in the matter.

If this were true of the two sites mentioned, we should expect it also to hold for the Church of the Holy Sepulchre. It would seem unlikely that Constantine would take the initiative in having the traditional site of the burial of Christ excavated. As Eusebius recounts the matter, it is quite unexpected and altogether fortuitous that the cross of Christ is discovered there during the excavations. We should expect the reverse to be the case: that by chance a cave was uncovered, within which were three crosses, and, the conclusion being drawn that one was the cross of Christ, a church be erected on the spot. That is what we should expect, and that in fact corresponds to another incident in Helena's pilgrimage. It is not included by Eusebius, but his summary reference to the cross indicates that he was not only well aware of it, but thought it necessary only to mention it in passing, so well would it be known to his contemporaries.

The incident is recounted by Theodoret in his *Historia Ecclesiastica*, in which he tells how Helena, just before her death in her eightieth year, visited the site of the Passion. Discovering that it was used for pagan worship, she ordered the site cleared. At that time three crosses were discovered. 'All were of opinion that one of these crosses was that of our Lord Jesus Christ, and that the other two were those of the thieves who were crucified with him.'[2] Bishop Macarius was able to identify the cross of Christ by arranging for a woman who was sick to touch each in turn: the one which effected her cure was the authentic cross of Christ.

Historians will cringe at such gullibility, and we may see behind the main characters in the drama that little band of hand-rubbing residents who are the ancient counterparts of those who are only too willing to rip off religious pilgrims, who in turn are only too willing to be parted from their money for the sake of finding their hearts' desire. Fortunately we need not comment on the historical value of such a 'find', nor on the apparent confusion of the site of the execution and the site of the burial. Our concern here is to show that it was Helena who took the initiative in both finding the site and persuading her son to pay for the erection of a church there. The incident of the building of the Church of the Holy Sepulchre does not demonstrate Constantine to be a Christian, but we are fortunate that Eusebius himself has provided us with comparative material by which to see the christianizing process at work.

Eusebius goes on to tell us of another foundation, at the traditional site of Mamre. (Following the Septuagint, Eusebius spells it Mambre.) The early church believed in the pre-existence of Christ and found references to his presence and activity in the Old Testament. Some of the passages were typological, for example, the Suffering Servant of the exilic Isaiah: 'He was despised and rejected by men; a man of sorrows, and acquainted with grief . . .'[3]. More mystically Paul sees Christ prefigured in the incident of the water-giving rock which Moses struck at Horeb. 'For they drank from the supernatural Rock which followed them, and the Rock was Christ.'[4] But there are other occasions which seem to have no typological or even symbolic significance, and yet the church came to associate them with Christ. Thus does Eusebius interpret one of the three divine figures who greet Abraham at the oaks of Mamre.

> But having heard that the self-same Saviour who erstwhile had appeared on earth had in ages long since past afforded a manifestation of his Divine presence to holy men of Palestine near the oak of Mambre, he ordered that a house of prayer should be built there also in honor of the God who had thus appeared. (III.61)

In this case also it would appear that Constantine, as a Christian, takes the initiative in honouring what was by that time regarded as a Christian site.[5] It is followed by a very sharp, even threatening, letter from the Emperor to Macarius.

However, there would seem to be a parallel here with the case of the Church of the Holy Sepulchre. In this case the pleading is not by the Emperor's mother, but by his mother-in-law. Let us not be so uncharitable as even to suppose that the sharpness of the letter to Macarius reflected the sharpness of the tongue of Eutropia, mother of Fausta. The point is that the initiative again comes from a Christian, but once the matter is raised it falls within Constantine's policy of aiding the Christian cause.

We need say no more on the matter: it is clear that Eusebius has christianized the motivation. But in view of what is to be said later in Chapter X about the 'covenantal' character of Constantine's religion, we should note that Constantine's interest in the site, once brought to his attention, might well be in Abraham himself. Constantine's religion was a religion of theophany, and he might well have had a special reverence for this site, not in its christianized form, but as a place where God manifested himself to the great father of covenantal religion: '. . . there God first appeared to men; there he gave the promise to Abraham . . .' (III.53). However, this additional point is not integral to our present discussion of the christianizing work of Eusebius. If he could so easily christianize the two events we have examined, he could certainly, by the odd word or phrase, have christianized the *Life* throughout.

(v) *Christ omitted.* In concentrating attention on the references to Christ in the *Life* I may well have given a completely distorted impression of their place within the work over all. Statistically, Christ is referred to, in some manner, in Book I in only six out of fifty-nine chapters and in Book II in only three out of seventy-three chapters. This is the more extraordinary when we consider that Eusebius has already restricted his subject to the religious activity of the Emperor. But in maintaining that the *Life* does not present Constantine as a Christian, we must now move on to the negative evidence, which proves to be even more extraordinary, that is to say the absence of any reference to Christ in passages where reference would seem altogether unavoidable for a Christian.

First, there is the fact that although the church and churches are mentioned frequently through each of the four books, Christ is never associated with the terms. It is always the 'church of God' and never the church of Christ (I.12,13,23,44,49; II.1,20,45,51; III.3,24,58,59,63; IV.1,17,18,28,32,34,45). Even statistically, this is a quite extraordinary characteristic for a work which is taken to be

explicitly Christian. And in keeping with Constantine's reluctance
to use the phrase 'church of Christ', Eusebius himself refrains from
using the phrase even in his general narrative. The entire work,
therefore, has a consistently a-Christian tone about it.

But secondly, it is not simply the absence of reference to Christ,
but rather the contexts in which Christ is absent which prove to be
almost incredible. There was, for example, the Arian controversy,
which threatened the unity of the church. Eusebius describes it in
II.61–72. The theological dispute was over the relationship of the
Father to the Son, yet Christ is not once mentioned. Constantine
was primarily concerned with damage to the unity of the church,
and wrote a letter to the two leading protagonists in Alexandria,
Bishop Alexander and Arius the presbyter. The context will be
discussed more fully in Chapter VIII. What might we expect to be
the main argument used by the Emperor to encourage the two to
end their division? He could have looked back to Paul, who wrote
letters to a divided church in Corinth. 'For just as the body is one
and has many members, and all the members of the body, though
many, are one body, so it is with Christ.'[6] But Constantine does not
appeal to Paul, nor does he recall this image of unity in Christ.
According to Paul, unity is not something that men devise, but a gift
of Christ which they recognize. 'For by one Spirit we were all
baptized into one body – Jews and Greeks, slaves or free – and all
were made to drink of one Spirit.'[7] This christocentric argument for
unity follows a chapter setting out Paul's teaching on the eucharist.
The sacramental Christ binds the church together. But Constantine
makes mention of neither the social nor the sacramental unity in
Christ. It is hardly conceivable that a Christian could write concerning division within the church without recalling these images from
Paul. But if that is difficult to conceive of, it is beyond comprehension
that there is no reference to the farewell discourse of Jesus to his
disciples, in John's Gospel. Was there antagonism and ill-feeling in
Alexandria? Then the call for unity might be to echo the new
commandment: 'Love one another; even as I have loved you . . . By
this all men will know that you are my disciples, if you have love for
one another.'[8] But Constantine makes no mention of Christ or the
new commandment. Were the antagonists developing new positions
on which to base the truth of the faith? What could have been more
salutary than the words of Christ: 'I am the true vine.' 'Abide in me,
and I in you.'[9] But Constantine does not turn their minds to this
powerful metaphor. When it comes to assessing whether the *Life*
presents Constantine as a Christian or not, then we must say that the
occasional use of the name 'Christ' is completely offset by the

deafening silence in such crucial passages as the letter to Alexandria. It is as if Constantine will not even use Christ-language *ad hominem*. Instead, the arguments used are those now familiar to us from the oration 'In Praise of Constantine'. Constantine argues that such theological division is against his design for religious and political unity in the empire. His work is to defeat the Devil, and division is victory to the Devil. As a political leader he argues that there is nothing substantial between them: they should resume fellowship (unity). At last Constantine turns to a model on which unity might be restored. Yet it is neither Paul nor Christ, but philosophical schools. He argues, cajoles and pleads with them. He speaks of God, Divine Providence and the Common Saviour, but at no time does he speak of Christ. When that performance is set on the balance, the odd Christian reference, which may in any case come from Eusebius, does nothing to tip the scale.

It is not, therefore, the absence of reference to Christ which is decisive but rather the contexts in which that absence occurs. We have just examined Constantine's attempt to deal with the emerging split between Alexander and Arius. It was not successful, and the Emperor took the initiative in calling a general council of the church. This has been taken as an indication of his Christian commitment, but if we are to pay more attention to Constantine himself, then we see that it is a matter of religious unity, which undergirds the political unity of the empire. But surely here Constantine will argue, at least *ad hominem*, that they must agree in Christ. But Christ is not mentioned.

The account is found in III.5–14. It begins and ends with reference to Easter, the festival which is not only most central to the Christian religion but also most distinctively Christian. Yet Constantine makes no reference to Christ, and nor does Eusebius. We are told of the arrangements for the Ecumenical Council, the areas represented, the virtuous character of the participants and even their relative ages. There is a dramatic description of the entrance of the Emperor and his reception by the council. And yet there is no reference to Christ. Most significant of all is the address by Constantine in which he speaks to the council of his wishes for the church and of the 'blasphemy' of division. But he does not appeal to them in the name of Christ. Instead, and in keeping with what we already know of him, he refers to his divine calling and to the victories which God has given him. Having put down every enemy, how distressed he is to find a new enemy and threat to the empire, namely division within the church. He appeals to them in God's name to end their disunity.

And throughout he neither mentions Christ, nor does he make any appeal to them as a Christian or indeed to them as Christians.

According to Eusebius this address won them over. Historically this is not so, but at least we must acknowledge that there is nothing Christian in the whole section. It ends with a glorious celebration of Easter, still without any mention of Christ. This, then, is the second example of a context in which one might think that reference to Christ would be unavoidable. Were these the very words of the Emperor? If the passages were fully Christian, replete with many references which could only have come from deep Christian conviction, then perhaps we should have been forced to argue that they had surely been christianized. The reverse is the case. No reference to Christ is to be found. Who knows whether they are the *ipsissima verba* of the Emperor, but what conceivable reason would Eusebius have for censoring *out* any references to Christ, to de-christianize? The position itself, however, is perfectly clear. As it stands the *Life* does not present Constantine as a Christian.

Let us take a third example, if further evidence is required. It is a long edict by Constantine and the heading is 'Law of Constantine respecting Piety towards God and the Christian Religion'. It is found in II.24–42. And in these nineteen chapters dealing with piety and the Christian religion there is not a single reference to Christ, not even an ambiguous one. But perhaps by this time we need not go through the passage theme by theme. From what we already know of Constantine it is not really surprising. Indeed, we should now anticipate that he will speak of piety to God without referring to Christ. The two subjects are quite different for him. And similarly, he is quite prepared to advocate the Christian religion without practising it himself. Nevertheless, for completeness we must draw attention to the fact that he is able to deal with the persecution of Christians, both martyrs and confessors, without mentioning Christ for whom they suffered. He proclaims his decisions concerning restoration of property and civil rights to the church without reference to Christ and he ends with an 'earnest exhortation to worship God' without reference to Christ. If Constantine had been a Christian, would he not have linked himself in some way to those whom he now addressed? But although using the royal plural, 'we boast and believe ourselves to be the servants of God' (II.31), at no time does he declare himself to be the servant of Christ. It would not have been difficult for Eusebius to christianize this boast, yet he does not do so.

We must conclude that the *Life* does not present Constantine as a Christian. He is said to have been converted to Christianity at the beginning and baptized a Christian at the end. We have already examined these two events in detail and found that even if the events took place, their interpretation does not confirm the claim that the Emperor was a Christian. There are references to Christ in the *Life*, most of them by Eusebius. Only a few are by Constantine, and these for the most part are *ad hominem* or examples of christianization. But the few examples do not in themselves counter the overwhelmingly a-Christian treatment of major themes which for a Christian would include unavoidable references to Christ.

(vi) *English translation.* So far we have been discussing Eusebius' presentation of Constantine. This work was originally composed in Greek and, as we have seen, has hardly any Christian element within it. There is one final group of examples which we might mention briefly: they do not come from Eusebius, but rather from the translation. The original English translation was done anonymously for Samuel Bagster & Sons and published in London in 1845. It was revised, but not substantially, by Ernest Cushing Richardson at Hartford, Connecticut, in 1890 for the first volume of the Second Series of the *Nicene and Post-Nicene Library of Christian Fathers*. The Bagster translator obviously believed that Constantine was a Christian, and this has affected his presentation. In passing, we might note that Richardson also shared his belief. Indeed, in his Prolegomena to the *Life* he goes out of his way to provide us with five conclusive examples intended to end all debate on the matter. 'Was Constantine a Christian? Let each one apply his own test.' It is a rhetorical question, yet on closer inspection *not one* of these five examples, presumably the best that can be found, includes reference to Christ! The point, however, is that the Bagster translator actually christianizes the work quite independently of Eusebius. The examples are of two kinds.

The first series of examples concerns the chapter headings to the English translation. There are no headings in the Greek text, and while it is useful to have an indication on the contents of each chapter, inevitably there is a certain amount of interpretation written into the summaries. In I.16 there is an account of an action which Constantine took to determine for himself who were 'worthy servants of God'. The heading, however, replaces this phrase by 'willing to confess Christ'. The people concerned would be the same, but the heading introduces reference to Christ where, for whatever reason, Eusebius did not wish to do so. In the next chapter, Eusebius describes the virtuous character and behaviour of his Emperor. As usual, Christ is not mentioned, nor the word Christian. However, the translator takes it upon himself to add the heading 'Of his

Christian Manner of Life'. A further example concerns a statement by Licinius concerning the question of divine assistance. The heading is, 'What Licinius, while sacrificing in a Grove, said concerning Idols, and concerning Christ'. There is no mention of Christ in the text, nor even an ambiguous phrase we might refer to him. Or again, there is the typical reference to the cross. As we have seen from the oration 'In Praise of Constantine', and to some extent from the *Life*, Constantine used the labarum in an almost superstitious manner, as if like the blood on the doors of the ancient Hebrews in Egypt: those who sheltered behind it would escape evil and receive victory. In II.7 we have such a picture of Constantine in the battlefield with the labarum, 'the salutary trophy', 'like some triumphant charm'. But the chapter heading is 'That Victory everywhere followed the Presence of the Standard of the Cross in Battle'. Yet Eusebius (in our view quite correctly) does not make this identification *simpliciter*. Such examples have the effect of creating a Christian context in which it is simply assumed that the Emperor was a Christian.

The reference to the cross brings us to our second series of examples. In IV.21 we have a good example of a christianizing heading: 'He orders the Sign of the Saviour's Cross to be engraven on his Soldiers' Shields'. We might well wonder where this summary comes from, since the phrase 'Saviour's Cross' does not appear in the Greek text at all. The answer is that it comes via the English translation of the chapter. There we find the phrase 'the standard of the cross'. It is a short step, given the translator's assumptions about Constantine and the labarum, to refer to this as the 'Saviour's Cross'. Yet the phrase which is translated here as 'the standard of the cross' is τὸ σωτήριον τρόπαιον.[10] For Eusebius this Greek phrase is actually a technical term, referring to the labarum. It is normally translated 'the salutary trophy'. It is not the cross of salvation, as it would be for Christians, but rather the symbol of the protection and victory which God has given to Constantine. To translate it as 'the standard of the cross' is therefore completely to alter the meaning of the phrase and to defeat Eusebius' intention in using it consistently in the way he does. In the next chapter we find a rather different example. This concerns the Easter celebrations, a passage to which we referred in an earlier discussion. At that time we argued that Constantine did not himself take part in the Easter eucharist, but given his religious policy and the Easter controversy he encouraged the church to unite in its celebration. 'As soon as day itself returned, in imitation of our Saviour's gracious acts, he opened a liberal hand to his subjects . . .' (IV.22). The title 'Saviour', as I have already argued, comes from Eusebius and not from Constantine. The actions are Constantine's, but the interpretation is that of Eusebius. But to the casual reader, the phrase 'our Saviour' blurs this distinction, for it might well suggest not only that Eusebius speaks as a Christian to Christian readers, but includes the Emperor within this Christian grouping. The word 'our' does not appear in the Greek text. Eusebius is not claiming that Constantine acted liberally because of 'our' Saviour, i.e. the Saviour of Constantine, Eusebius and the readers. The translator has chosen to insert 'our' to christianize the passage. The importance of the point is not, however, simply in this crude christianizing, but rather, once again, that it thwarts a careful position which Eusebius has developed. The position is elaborated more extensively in the oration, as we have already seen. No one who has the oration in mind could lightly pass over the claim that Constantine here acts in 'imitation' of the heavenly sphere ($\mu\iota\mu o\acute{\upsilon}\mu\epsilon\nu o\varsigma$, $\mu\acute{\iota}\mu\eta\sigma\iota\varsigma$).

There are many examples of the addition of 'our' to Saviour through the work, but a final instance might indicate how confusing the end result becomes. In IV.5 we read of Constantine that 'with full confidence in his Saviour's aid, he raised his conquering standard . . .' By this time it is clear that 'Saviour' here refers to God and not to Christ, just as the 'conquering standard' refers to Constantine's labarum and not to the Cross of Christ. Yet the heading for the chapter is 'Conquest of the Scythians defeated through the Sign of our Saviour'. This is another example of the christianizing of Constantine by the translator because of the heading which he adds. But as in the previous examples, the importance of the issue is not that the christianizing goes beyond the Greek text, but rather that it actually distorts the picture which Eusebius has carefully drawn, more carefully drawn in the oration. Eusebius could easily have included such Christian references himself. He must have had very good reasons, historical, cultural, or theological, for deciding against them. It is unfortunate that the reader of the English translation has this position obscured: it would be even more unfortunate if scholars were then to read the Greek text with assumptions already formed, which come from the Bagster translator rather than from Eusebius.

In my examination of the *Life* I began by expecting Eusebius as apologist to present Constantine as a Christian. This, I claimed, would not necessarily damage my position, since Constantine's position historically would almost by definition have been less Christian. However, on closer examination we have found that there is very little material indeed which represents Constantine as a Christian and most of that can be accounted for as serving the apologetic purpose. The overall impression is that Eusebius has, for whatever reason, deliberately refrained from presenting the Emperor as a Christian in explicit terms. The *Life* in its final form was of course published after the oration, yet most if it would already exist, at least in rough form, before the oration was composed. The *Life* reads like a first draft of a position which is coherently and consistently worked out only in the oration. It is for this reason that I noted the continuity in themes between the two works. But the *Life*, as an earlier project, would include material which was loosely tied together as a biography: the oration is a much more carefully composed piece. There are passages and incidents in the *Life* which are historically quite incredible and some which are naive and quaint. When we turn to the oration, however, we are dealing with a more tightly argued work: not mythology but ideology. But contrary to our expectations, the *Life* presents us with a picture of Constantine who, even when deeply involved with the church, remained completely un-Christian. There seems to be no possible reason for this, apart from the obvious one, that in this respect Eusebius was an able and honest historian.

V

AGAINST PAGAN DESPISERS

1 In Defence of Constantine

In the *Life of Constantine* IV.45, Eusebius tells us that he took part in the festivities on the occasion of the dedication of the Church of the Holy Sepulchre and, not surprisingly, delivered himself of an oration on the subject. The ceremony took place in September 335, and although the Emperor was not present, Eusebius dedicated the treatise to him. In IV.46 he promises to append the text to the *Life*. At the same time he says that he will be adding the oration delivered at the tricennial celebrations. In fact only the Jubilee Oration is to be found in the manuscripts of the *Life*. However, it is probable that the oration 'In Praise of Constantine' consists of only ten chapters and that the remainder of the appendage is in fact the lost oration 'On Christ's Sepulchre'. Chapter X draws the first oration to a suitable conclusion, while the opening words of Chapter XI would indicate not only a new beginning but a rather different subject. Drake makes a very interesting observation.

> It is possible, therefore, that a comparison of the two orations may indicate ways in which the Emperor's presence caused Eusebius to treat similar topics differently; these in turn could prove useful in separating Constantine's policy from Eusebius' interpretation.[1]

While there is something to be said for this argument it has to be qualified for three reasons. The first is that the final form of this second oration may have been delivered before the Emperor. Eusebius tells us that he 'had begged permission to pronounce a discourse on the subject of our Saviour's sepulchre in his hearing'.[2] Eusebius was sufficiently vain about his associations with the Emperor that it is likely that it is the oration in the form delivered in the presence of the Emperor which is appended to the *Life*. Chapter XI begins with an address to Constantine. A second reservation about Drake's argument is that Eusebius does not seem to be sufficiently devious substantially to misrepresent the position of the emperor. If such an act was important, then the Emperor would surely find out. Eusebius does not seem to wish to go behind the Emperor's back, whether through fear or through dedication to his sovereign. And thirdly, the *Life* in its final form was issued after the death of the Emperor, yet, as we have seen, Eusebius did not take the opportunity even then substantially to christianize his work.

The whole argument is yet another example of a very questionable assumption, namely that Eusebius did not wish to describe Constantine's actual religious position. From the evidence we have reviewed so far Eusebius describes it very accurately, so to discuss circumstances in which he would be less inhibited or constrained is fundamentally misguided.

There is today a phenomenon which might be called 'television for the blind': an irritating breed of sports commentators insist on keeping up a non-stop verbal description of exactly what viewers can in any case see taking place on their screens. Eusebius tells us that at the dedication of the Church of the Holy Sepulchre he delivered an address describing the architecture of the building and its fittings (IV,46). Since he was presumably describing it to people who were capable of looking at it themselves, Eusebius might at first seem the forerunner of our contemporary compulsive commentators. Eusebius does in fact give some details of the building (III,34–40).

There might well therefore be some confusion about the treatise to which we now turn, 'On Christ's Sepulchre'. Originally it was delivered in Jerusalem to other Christians, but in the absence of the Emperor. Originally it would contain some detailed description of the building. However, the form that we have now is somewhat different. The description of the building is omitted. Indeed it is only in the last chapter that there is a residual reference to the new church. Whatever its original purpose, the treatise is now addressed to the Emperor, and is offered not in praise of the new building but in praise of the sovereign himself. It is now an *apologia* to the Emperor and not a tourist brochure for a church in Jersualem. And for this reason it is brought closely into line with the oration 'In Praise of Constantine' and also with the *Life*.

When examining the *Life*, we looked in some detail at the two accounts of the motivation for founding the Church of the Holy Sepulchre. The reconstruction which we favoured was that Helena reported the 'find' which she had made in Palestine and requested the Emperor to authorize a suitable church to be raised on the site. The fact that the Emperor was not even present at the dedication would be consonant with this approach. Our purpose in examining the passages was to consider the extent to which Constantine was presented in the *Life* as a Christian. However, we did suggest that the actual events behind the whole episode would indicate that Helena was very gullible indeed. Whether Constantine shared her view or not, we can scarcely imagine now the damage that it caused to his attempt to promote the Christian religion throughout the Empire. At a time when Constantine was attempting to turn his people from pagan practices and beliefs, from rites regarded as crass and unworthy of the spiritually enlightened, we can scarcely imagine the ridicule with which this whole episode of Helena's 'find' must have been greeted by cultured pagans.

> But those who in the blindness of their souls are ignorant of matters divine hold the deed a joke and frankly ridiculous, believing that for so great a sovereign to bother himself with memorials to human corpses and tombs is unfitting and demeaning.[3]

We must admire Eusebius' courage in saying this to the Emperor's face. He was repeating the kind of thing said behind Constantine's back, and although Constantine would wish to know what was being said, it is a brave man who will tell such a monarch the truth. All credit to Eusebius. But it also shows us his real devotion to Constantine. It was not possible for the Emperor to defend himself against such attacks. His opponents were using the whole affair as grounds for arguing for a return to the traditional religion of Rome, which for all its faults did not go in for *this* kind of naive nonsense. The treatise is therefore now offered to the Emperor not as a description of the Church of the Holy Sepulchre, but as a theological justification of the Emperor and his religious policy in general. It is to be 'revelations about solemn mysteries', mysteries in which the Emperor needs no instruction, but which when expounded will silence his critics. All know of his virtuous life, but some do not know how to interpret his religious policy.

Perhaps it was with some relief that Constantine heard that Eusebius had come to his aid. On the other hand, when we are in trouble, assurance of help from some quarters might alarm us even more than the problems with which we are beset. It may be that Constantine would have preferred not to be defended by this bishop whom apparently he regarded as of rather limited ability.[4] But more central to our investigation is the fact that Eusebius in the treatise seeks to defend two things at the same time, Constantine's religious policy and the truth of the Christian religion. He addresses the Emperor: 'I pray that I may be a kind interpreter of your intentions and become the reporter of your devout soul . . . (XI,104). If the treatise is more Christian than the oration 'In Praise of Constantine', it is because of its dual prupose. Our interest will be in whether Constantine is presented as a Christian in the course of a treatise in which Eusebius is seeking to establish the truth of Christianity to its cultured pagan despisers.

Eusebius makes this dual purpose clear at the beginning of the treatise. He continues to speak of the Logos, as in the oration, but since he is now defending Christianity, he allows himself a more explicit identification of the Logos with Christ. But he does not claim that this is Constantine's position. The second of his two themes, the defence of the Emperor, comes in his claim that 'his zeal for the memorial of the saving immortality did not develop without God's aid . . . (XI,104). And it is here that we must be clear about the twin motivations. In order to defend Constantine against the scorn of pagans, he has to demonstrate that the sepulchre and indeed the cross are to be understood in a spiritual context and not in a crass superstitious way. Our point is that this leads Eusebius to a defence of Christianity, but it does not entail that Constantine believed what Eusebius believed. It is the confusion of these two issues which has led to the reading of the treatise as if it presented Constantine as a Christian. As we have seen, in the *Life*, Constantine appreciated that it was a sophisticated theological treatise, but there is no evidence that it described his own religious position.

Having said all this, we come to the end of a brief introduction to the treatise. 'At this point, then, discussion of these matters may begin' (XI,104). As already indicated, if Eusebius ever composed a work describing the Church of the Holy Sepulchre, that work has been almost entirely set aside. If he not only described its architecture but offered a religious commentary upon it, that work has been for the most part set aside. If the present treatise is to be entitled 'On Christ's Sepulchre', it is no longer to describe the church, but rather to demonstrate that the building of the church was a spiritual and not a superstitious act. And in order to achieve this, Eusebius must set the act of building in a much wider context. Eusebius had no doubt about how to proceed. As in the oration, 'In Praise of Constantine', the key is *'mimesis'*. He begins the final form of the treatise as if he were presenting a teleological argument for the existence of God. Once again it is the Logos who has given the world its rational, planned and purposive form. If we are impressed by the

world around us, how much more then should we be impressed by
the Maker of such a world! If we have reverence for such material
phenomena, how much more should we revere the invisible Creator!

2   The Spiritual in the Material

At this stage Eusebius is intent on opposing paganism and establishing the existence of the one Supreme God. 'Like fools at heart, the
followers of polytheism have drifted into horrible error . . .'
(XII,109). Anyone who understands the complexity of the universe
must not stop with the material world but go on to believe in the
existence of God and the creative activity of his Logos. The Logos
is described very much in the same terms as in the oration, though
on occasion Eusebius, almost by association of thought, crosses over
from the neutral position of the oration to a more explicitly Christian
identification. For example, having spoken of 'the God-Generated
Logos' he goes on to quote from the Prologue to John's Gospel
(XII,108). But even more so than in the *Life,* what is more obvious
is the restraint. The Logos for the most part is still described in a
non-Christian way. This is essential for the conclusion to which
Eusebius hopes to bring the argument.

   From the opening discourse on natural theology, Eusebius returns
to a more detailed denunciation of pagan society. In turn he
condemns the gods of Rome, Greece, Egypt and Phoenicia. As in
the oration, he repeats the charges of sexual perversion and debauchery, of immorality and even human sacrifice. From natural
theology and the necessity of the recognition of God and his Logos,
Eusebius turns to the necessity of God's intervention in human
history in order to save mankind through the Logos. And at this
point he is specifically Christian. The Logos in this case does not
simply permeate the universe, but 'He condescended to commune
and converse with mortals through the instrument of a mortal body,
with the intention of saving humanity through the resemblance'
(XIV,115). The theology is closer to Athanasius' *De Incarnatione*
than Paul, but the position is unquestionably Christian. This,
however, corresponds to the first of Eusebius' twin motives. If he is
to demonstrate that the honouring of the site of the Holy Sepulchre
is a spiritual action, he has to demonstrate the connection between
the Logos and the site.

   And here we move to the heart of the problem. God determined
that he must save mankind by sending the Logos to men in human
form.

For how otherwise could the divine and intangible, the immaterial
and invisible Being manifest Himself to those who sought God in
creatures and below on the earth, who were unable or unwilling
to contemplate the Creator and Maker of all things, than through
a human shape and appearance? (XIV,115).

The problem was that men sought the divine in human and material
form: this was the very source of their errors. But the divine solution
was to enter the human and material in order to be found. Not in
some general, pantheistic or animistic way, but by incarnation in
one particular man. Hence the paradox, that it is in this human and
material form that the errors of idolatry are to be overcome. But to
those who do not understand the mystery, Christianity will appear
to be yet another example of the worship of the human and material.

Eusebius makes it quite clear that the Logos is not to be identified
with a man. While the Logos was incarnate, the power and presence
of the Logos were still operating everywhere within the universe.
And the body in which the Logos was incarnate could ultimately
suffer no harm: to the contrary, that life was surrounded by miracles
and proofs of the indwelling of the Logos.

At last Eusebius comes to his main point of interest, the death
and resurrection. From what he has already said the Logos could
not simply discard the body which had been used in the incarnation.
The Logos must be seen to overcome evil, the demons, the Devil
and death itself, and this could not be demonstrated if the body had
somehow been made subject to death. The promise of immortality
to his followers must be based on the immortality of the incarnating
body. To give assurance of immortality, therefore, it was necessary
both to die and rise from the dead, and to do both not secretly but
publicly. The resurrected body is the 'trophy over death' (XV,118),
the 'trophy of immortality' (XV,119).

Eusebius has therefore moved from natural theology to a historical
theology. In both cases he refers to evidence upon which his beliefs
are founded, and the implication is that anyone of goodwill might
draw the same conclusions. But that is not enough. He wishes to
make his conclusions not probable, but undeniable. There is a final
'proof', as he calls it, that what he has been describing is true.

Together, at the same critical moment, as if from a single divine
will, two beneficial shoots were produced for mankind: the empire
of the Romans and the teachings of true worship (XVI,120).

Eusebius identifies polytheism and paganism as the root causes of
human emnity and conflict. He believes it is no mere coincidence

that as the idols are cast down and the demons defeated by that 'victory trophy', that 'salutary instrument', that is, the risen body of Christ, so mankind is at last united under one Empire and eventually under one Emperor. The *pax christi* is manifest in the *pax romana*.

Our concern here is with the argument of Eusebius, not with its validity. He makes no mention of the fact that it was because Jesus was a potential threat to the existing peace of Rome that he was executed. There is no mention of the persecutions which took place precisely because Christianity was an obstacle to the unity of the Empire. Yet our knowledge of these events comes to us in the main from Eusebius himself, the writer of the first great *Historia Ecclesiastica*. Clearly he is telescoping history to make his point. His twin motives are to bring together Christ and Constantine and to demonstrate their empirical relationship. Or rather, judging by the oration, he wishes to show that the Logos which was active in Palestine is the same Logos who has now unified the known world under his friend.

Eusebius goes on to speak of the changes which are now on record by which the new religion spread throughout the world and brought to an end the old pagan practices. In fact there is a curious assimilation of the Saviour and the sovereign, when the former is described in phrases which in the oration have been used to praise the latter: it is the Saviour who 'constantly had to do battle to defend himself, and yet displayed superhuman virtue, so as to flourish day after day, and stay young throughout his whole life' (XVI,122), a picture which in another context would have described the young Constantine. Eusebius then refers back to the beginning of the treatise to those who then doubted: 'this most of all shut every scoffing mouth' (XVI,122). By assimilating Constantine and Christ, he makes the vindication of Christianity at the same time a vindication of the Emperor's religious policy in general and his founding of the Church of the Holy Sepulchre in particular.

The proof continues now with reference to the confessors and martyrs of the church, who were maintained by the life of the Risen Saviour to suffer all hardship and indignities until at last the persecutors themselves were drained of strength and life itself. Eusebius refers to the transformation of the situation since that time. Elsewhere he would immediately have spoken of the work of the Emperor, but now the assimilation continues, and what would normally be said of Constantine is said of the Saviour.

In contrast he at once erected victory trophies everywhere on earth, adorning the entire inhabited world once again with holy temples and the solemn dedication of oratories (XVII,124).

So confident is Eusebius of this line of argument that it would seem that it is not even necessary to defend Constantine with regard to the dedication of the church: that is attributed to the Logos.

With such arguments he expects to overcome 'the detractor's hardened intellect' (XVII,124): the spread of the church, the humble beginnings among unlettered people, the fulfilment of prophecy, courage in adversity. The points go on and on.

> The whole length of the day would fail me, my Emperor, if I should try to collect and combine into one account the manifest examples of our Saviour's divine power . . . (XVII,126).

Increasingly the treatise has nothing to do with Constantine, but is simply an *apologia* for Christianity. As the Emperor is addressed at the outset, so as the work comes to a close the author respectfully returns to involve the sovereign directly. He has, as he promised, expounded the mysteries of revelation, but certainly not for the sake of Constantine. Indeed Eusebius insists that the Emperor stands in a quite unique position in this respect, 'for you have frequently received perception of the Saviour's divinity through actual experience, and have become not by words but by events themselves a herald of the truth to all' (XVIII,126). This is the much more familiar theme that the career of Constantine is in itself the demonstration of the power of God. Or again, Eusebius requests that the Emperor might instruct his audience and the public at large by recounting 'the manifest support by your Champion and Guardian God' (XVIII,127), in affairs both military and civil.

The treatise then ends with the only reference to the Church of the Holy Sepulchre, which was the occasion of the defence of Christianity and the Emperor.

> For all these reasons, then, it is reasonable that you have heeded these manifest proofs of the Savior's power and have displayed to all men, believers and non-believers alike, a house of prayer as a trophy of His victory over death, a holy temple of a holy God, and splended and great offerings to the immortal life and the divine kingdom – memorials of the All-Ruling Savior entirely fitting and suitable for a victorious sovereign. This you have put round the Sepulchre that bears witness to the immortal life, impressing on the Heavenly Logos of God the imperial seal as victor and triumphator, and in clear-cut and unambiguous terms making unto all people, by deed as well as by word, a pious and devout confession (XVIII,127).

At the outset Eusebius had undertaken both to describe Constantine's action and to interpret it. We have seen that there is a tendency to blur the distinction, so that it is Eusebius' own religious position which provides the interpretation of an objective act. The deed is not in doubt, but is it, as Eusebius adds, a 'devout confession?' We have already noted that in this treatise Eusebius is inclined to historical licence. His primary goal is to demonstrate the truth of Christianity. The vindication of the Emperor will follow from that. Inevitably, therefore, once he has provided the demonstration, to his own satisfaction, he is led on to the conclusion that the Emperor is vindicated. But is he vindicated because of his own Christian faith, or because the essentially spiritual nature of the action has been brought out? We must reaffirm our earlier position, that Constantine agreed to build the Church of the Holy Sepulchre, but did not do so as a Christian. Indeed, once again we must be impressed by the fact that even in his full-flowing *apologia* for Christianity Eusebius deliberately avoids an explicit claim that Constantine was a Christian. The treatise is much more Christian than the oration, but that is because Eusebius is responsible for the argument: it is about his religion, and Constantine is almost forgotten in the main part. But the historical Jesus is not mentioned. The Incarnation is entirely taken up with the activity of the Logos, who is then responsible for Constantine, the counterpart of the Logos in the governing of the world. And at the end Eusebius goes out of his way to dissociate Constantine from the received revelation and to focus attention, rather, on the new revelation granted to him. Once again there is no suggestion that the historical figure in Palestine is in any sense the Mediator for Constantine. It is proper that the Emperor should honour the historic site, because it was there that the Logos manifested one side of the saving event: the other side, according to Eusebius, is the Logos manifested in Constantine.

It is for this reason that the solution to the problem Eusebius faced at the outset might well be the same *mimesis* as we found in the oration. At the outset he uses a teleological argument. The invisible Logos expresses and affirms spiritual values by his creation of material things. As we saw, it would be idolatry to identify the material as the divine. But this is precisely the error made by those who scorned the building of the Church of the Holy Sepulchre. As the Logos in Heaven, so his friend on earth. The Emperor expresses and affirms spiritual values in the creation of material forms. The object of the treatise is to interpret this action, to show why the cave of death should be honoured as the fount of life. The action belongs to Constantine, but the Christian interpretation belongs to Eusebius.

VI

THE ASSEMBLY OF SAINTS

As we continue the examination of sources which might clarify for us the nature of the religion of Constantine, we come to an oration which is attributed to the Emperor himself. In the *Life of Constantine* Eusebius tells us that Constantine delivered many orations, which were then translated into Greek.

> One of the discourses thus translated I intend to annex, by way of specimen, to this present work, that one, I mean, which he inscribed 'To the Assembly of the Saints', and dedicated to the Church of God . . .[1]

Such an oration would be very useful, though of course it would not fulfil our criteria, since Constantine might adapt his message to the religious beliefs of his audience. However, we must point out that there has been considerable discussion about the authenticity of the work.[2] Since there are many Christian passages in the oration, it is tempting to take the easy way out and declare it inauthentic! In this way it would not count against our view that Constantine was not a Christian. But no one enjoys a walk-over in tennis, when the opponent has to withdraw before the contest begins. If truth be told, we should prefer to face the challenge of this oration, rather than simply set it aside. Even so, according to Norman Baynes we may not be allowed this luxury. We have already noted his judgment of the oration.

> The student of Christian apologetic must give the *Oratio* prolonged consideration; the student of Constantine's personal convictions must exercise self-denial.[3]

It would appear therefore that, justified by the authority of Baynes, we need not examine this document.

Yet there remains a nagging doubt. Eusebius apparently considered this to be an oration by Constantine. Given his credulity in such matters, perhaps that counts for very little, but it would be more satisfactory if we could explain this belief. Let us consider the internal structure, form and content of the work.

There are twenty-six chapters in the oration 'To the Assembly of the Saints', without any formal division. Baynes is quite right to say that it reads as Christian apologetics. But on closer inspection, this is true only of Chapters I–XXI. We might therefore consider the possibility that what we have is a composite work, consisting of an original document, Chapters XXII–XXVI, which might indeed come from Constantine, though it would hardly constitute a full-length oration, plus another document, Chapters I–XXI now preceding it. It is this first part which forms a traditional Christian *apologia*. The second reads quite differently. We shall examine the evidence for this proposal in a moment, but it would deal with the problem which Baynes ignores, namely that Eusebius believed the oration to be by the Emperor. It would be easier to account for this if the document, or at least part of it, had indeed associations with Constantine. And as we shall also discover, while the first section is Christian, the second section is quite consistent with our view of Constantine's own religion. It is for this reason that we have not taken the easy way out, simply setting the oration aside entirely. Far from undermining our view, it actually confirms it.

1   A Christian Apology

On the view which we are now presenting of the *Assembly*, the first part has been added to the original by a Christian writer who, understandably, wished to christianize the religion of Constantine, or more probably – in the pseudepigraphical tradition – sought to add the authority of the Emperor to his own views of religion and philosophy. Not surprisingly, while that part of the *Assembly* which may well come from the Emperor is lively and direct, the first part is heavy and convoluted. It makes very heavy reading and, if we are correct, was never delivered as an oration. Its effect would have been comparable to the spell of the wicked witch in 'The Sleeping Beauty'! It is a rambling, disorganized piece which may itself have been added to more than once: although it is Christian, it is not consistently Christian. Although the setting is Easter, the first part of the *Assembly*, after the opening paragraphs, has nothing to do with this feast. It is supposed to be by the Emperor, yet there is nothing, apart from one phrase in Chapter II, to suggest that it is written by anyone of special standing.

Following a brief reference to Easter in the introductory Chapter, the *apologia* is not linked to any specific time or place. The author contrasts the realms of grace and nature. Although God created nature, men have taken it to be self-sufficient and have turned their backs on the Creator. Thus good was turned into evil, and so the generations of men lived blindly until 'the radiance of the Saviour's presence appeared'.[4] In this case 'Saviour' refers to Christ, who brings justice into the world and provides the example of purity, until the time of his ascension, leaving his church to maintain the pure worship of God. But soon evil broke out again, specifically in the form of persecution.

It is not crucial to our argument, but as in the case of Luke's Gospel, it may be that this introduction is not the first part of the *Assembly* to be composed, but the last. It may have been added to bring out the association with Easter, which is missing from the rest of this part. The chapter does not go well with the main sections. Chapter II may well be a previous beginning, in which the work is associated with the Emperor and also with the 'assembly of the saints', i.e. an audience of Christians. Christians are already familiar with the mysteries and must forgive the way in which the matters are dealt with. In view of the style and scholarship lying behind the subsequent chapters, this is of course a self-effacing little plea. They are to attend 'not to him who speaks, but rather to the pious zeal which hallows his discourse'.[5] This is the only indirect reference to the Emperor as author, and is an attempt to link the additional material to the second part, which we are suggesting may well have been by the Emperor.

With these two introductory chapters out of the way the oration now begins. The first section is Chapters III–V, though it is not always clear what is the subject, since even the author acknowledges that he allows himself constantly to digress. The author is not only an apologist, but a theologian conversant with the contemporary christological controversies. He is careful to make clear the 'generation' of the Son from the Father, of the Father's 'substance'. Then follows a teleological argument, that the Son has control over the world. The order and harmony of its parts is witness to the unity of God. Discord among men comes from the pagan belief in many gods. The author associates such beliefs also with cults in which immorality abounds. In Chapters VI–VIII the author directs his argument towards those who refuse to acknowledge the divine order. Order they acknowledge, but they call it fate, sometimes the law of fate. But (*pace* Hume) a law of fate implies a legislator. And behind law lie principles. Those who speak of fate also distinguish good and evil, and these judgments do not come from fate but depend upon God. While men may be to some extent responsible for the circumstances of day-to-day living, the motion of the sun and moon, the cycle of the seasons, the eternal stars in the heavens are witness to an order more than human in origin. The author goes into many details, the usefulness of the olive tree, the distribution of precious metals, the utility of others such as copper and iron. Whatever the origin of the piece, it has nothing at all to do with Easter; it is not necessarily even Christian, and its author is unlikely to be the Emperor, but a rather pedantic scholar (probably a lower second-class degree in Philosophy of Religion). The third section examines the works of pagan writers. In Chapter IX he specifically comments on the shortcomings of philosophers. Pythagoras was too much influenced by pagan cults, while Socrates was too clever by half, more concerned by his skill in argument than seeking the truth. Plato receives two cheers but he also wanders from the truth. In Chapter X pagan poets are, perhaps surprisingly, praised for their grasp of fundamental truths about death and judgment, but much of their work is wide off the mark.

Now follows Chapter XI, which is specifically Christian. As we have noted, the first three sections are on philosophy of religion, with no fundamentally Christian dimension. They may have been composed on another occasion or even by another author. We now turn to a Christian *apologia* which could have been an independent piece. Like the previous section it has reference neither to Easter nor to the Emperor. If the earlier sections dealt with traditional arguments for monotheism, this fourth section deals with attacks on Christianity. The author calls upon Christ to inspire him in his defence of true religion. For example, some people have said, apparently, that Christ was quite justly executed. This would not be an unnatural view among Roman citizens, but the author brings forward a theological defence, that is, the death of Christ took place to show forth the love of God. There is of course no common ground between such a historical/legal view and a theological view. But the writer goes on to condemn the pagan religion which lies behind the detraction. Indeed he becomes heated and abusive about it, and to that extent is quite different from the rather cool intellectual author of the first three sections. Having silenced this criticism, at least by the violence of his counter-attack, the author proceeds to deal with other questions, such as Christ's unique claim to be the Son of God, and what is meant by the incarnation. This leads into a rehearsal of the main points in the life of Christ, and finally ends in a rather fulsome doxology to the Saviour of mankind.

After this brief but very committed defence of Christianity, we have a fifth section, Chapters XII–XIV, which though not perhaps by the first author, takes up further issues of a philosophical nature. There are the questions of free will and the knowledge of God, and why God did not create all men with the same moral character. Thereafter we come to another Christian section, Chapters XV–XXI, in the form of an account of the life and works of Christ, confirming faith and destroying the unjust. But all this had been foretold in the scriptures. The section continues with the praise of Moses and, perhaps surprisingly, of Daniel. However, the author has singled out prophets who worked among pagans and converted them by their steadfastness. The section ends with the author seeking to show that Christ was not only foretold in the scriptures, but also in pagan sources. He includes an acrostic of the Erythraean Sibyl, 'Jesus Christ, Son of God, Saviour, Cross', and also some lines from Virgil. Whether because of this classical context, this first part of the *Assembly* comes to an end in a doxology, not this time to Christ, but to 'Piety' and 'Clemency'.

This has been a brief outline of the first part of the oration. It connects at no point with Constantine and has no essential connection with Easter. It is quite incoherent, and is probably composite, being gradually added to by two or possibly three different authors, each seeking to gain imperial standing for his own approach to those issues which most concerned him. There is no division in the text, but the first part comes to a suitable ending here, and from this point a new part begins, new in content and in style. Style is always to some extent subjective, but let us concentrate on the difference in content.

2   Piety Rewarded

This second part does not read as one argument, and may also be composite, but the content is quite different from the first and corresponds to what we already know of the religion and the concerns of Constantine. Chapter XXII is an invocation of Piety; indeed, the reference to Piety in the previous chapter may be to form a bridge between the original and the added chapters. But the address is direct, in the first person singular. 'To thee, Piety, I ascribe the cause of my own prosperity, and of all that I now possess.' Logic-chopping, metaphysics and classical allusions are left behind. This is the first characteristic of the religion of Constantine: what he has comes from God and is a reward for his faith and obedience. 'This truth the great city itself allows with joy and praise.' Not speculation but history. The writer, and we shall refer to him as

Constantine, brings forward the empirical proof of the connection between his religion and his prosperity. It all began with the defeat of Maxentius at Milvian Bridge and the triumphal entry into Rome. The rest of the chapter is a rather gory description of the torture of those who had faith in God. Constantine turns to address the persecutors. How could they call such atrocities obedience to gods, and even if it were, is that not the very reason why such gods should be rejected?

Chapter XXIII continues the debate, but from another direction: 'Compare our religion with your own.' Not for Constantine the religion which tortures and mutilates. Yes, he on occasion gives direction to correct error, but it is in love and not by fear. Instead of taking advantage of the poor, he provides for their needs – and, he adds with due modesty, it is done without hypocrisy. This is true religion, and those who follow it do not die but are received into their eternal reward. This is a theme which we have already met in the oration 'In Praise of Constantine', that Constantine will not die but inherit eternal life through a continuous process uninterrupted by death. Constantine is not unaware of his virtues (perhaps he had read about them in Eusebius!), but he sees a parallel between heaven and earth. As obedience has its reward in human custom, so God will also reward those who are obedient to him. So ends this first section. It has no reference to Christ, and it covers some of the familiar points we have already encountered in other works.

The second section, Chapters XXIV and XXV, turns abruptly to a different theme, but one also connected with the Emperor. The chapters are concerned with the example and fate of Decius, Valerian, Aurelian and Diocletian. In each case they persecuted God's faithful but were punished for it. After rehearsing the well-know incidents associated with their deaths, Constantine comes to the conclusion: 'do not these things every way afford convincing proofs of the providence of God, and his affectionate regard for the interests of mankind?' This philosophy of history, which is at the same time a form of religious legitimation, is fundamental to the religion of Constantine as presented by Eusebius.

The third section follows on from this, though its subject is not a specific rehearsal of the history of the emperors. Chapter XXVI begins with the familiar theme: 'When men commend my services, which owe their origin to the inspiration of Heaven, do they not clearly establish the truth that God is the cause of the exploits I have performed?' He outlines once again his practice, that spiritual preparation must precede military campaigns if there is to be any assurance of victory. Whatever has been done for the common good has been achieved also through a combination of work and prayer. 'For righteous prayer is a thing invincible; and no one fails to attain his object who addresses holy supplication to God . . .' This is the religion of Constantine: he who prays wins. This chapter may well be addressed to a Christian audience, to an 'assembly of the saints'. Indeed, in this second part of the piece it is the only chapter which is addressed to the church. And yet here, as elsewhere in the second part, Constantine does not speak of Christ. As in the other writings we have examined, 'Saviour' refers to God. The oration draws to a close.

> Hence it becomes all pious persons to render thanks to the Saviour of all, first for our own individual security, and then for the happy posture of public affairs . . . For he is the invincible ally and protector of the righteous: he is the supreme judge of all things, the prince of immortality, the Giver of everlasting life.

This is entirely consonant with the religion of Constantine. However, I do not wish to disguise from the reader who does not happen to have the text available at this moment that I have omitted an important phrase:

> at the same time entreating the favor of Christ, with holy prayers and constant supplications, that he would continue to us our present blessings.

Does this one reference at the end, tucked away in a subordinate clause, tip the whole balance in favour of a Christian Emperor? Does this phrase, which interrupts the flow of Constantine's argument and is quite incompatible with his general position, mean that only now is his true religion appearing? Or is this phrase inserted by a pious hand when the scribe sees the title 'Saviour', assumes that the reference must be to Christ, and takes it upon himself to add his own sentiments to those of the Emperor? Norman Baynes is prepared to set aside the entire oration: are we not permitted to question a phrase as we attempt to salvage at least part of the work for Constantine?

What are we, therefore, to make of this strange work? First, we must say it is not by Eusebius, at least judging by the writings which we know to be by him. Secondly, it is an incoherent composite work from beginning to end. Of the many divisions within it, the one which we have indicated at the end of Chapter XXI is the most significant, and represents a change both in author and religious position. We may apply Baynes' observation to the first part, that it tells us something about Christian apologetics (at its worst) but nothing at all about the religion of Constantine. Attention therefore must be focussed on the second part, Chapters XXII–XXVI. This could be by Constantine: we shall never know. But if it is our intention to expose my view of Constantine's religion to as severe a test as possible, then let us take it that it is by Constantine, or at least, as in the case of the writings of Eusebius, that it reflects the position of Constantine. We should therefore note, thirdly, that the themes of this part are mutually compatible, stand in contrast to those of the first part of the work, and express the position of Constantine with which we are already familiar. Only one subordinate clause mentions Christ, and this reference, which we have disputed, can hardly alter the balance of the chapters. After all, if the writer were a Christian addressing Christians there are other places at which the name of Christ would have been appropriate, for example instead of an invocation to 'Piety'.

Although I approached this piece with some misgivings, it does not in fact undermine my position, but actually confirms it. That is my sole purpose in dealing with the oration. However, we might note in passing that there are several difficult problems which are still outstanding, though quite irrelevant to our interests. For example, why did Eusebius include this literary chop suey as a *prime* example of the Emperor's orations? He includes it 'by way of a specimen'. It would be like offering to praise the poetry of Milton by producing a piece by Pam Ayres. Eusebius mentions this oration in the *Life* just before two chapters containing references to Easter. The *Assembly*, as we have it, purports to be delivered at that feast. We have already noted that in Chapter III the author is conversant with christological problems which came to a head at the Council of Nicaea. And in the *Life* we noted that Constantine could, in the *Assembly*, be addressing Christians on the feast day without referring to that one issue which he held more important than any other, namely the unity of the church. We have already discussed this in Chapter IV, and also Eusebius' account of how Constantine himself behaved during the feast.[6] The second part of the *Assembly* has no reference to Easter, and it is inconceivable that Easter could have been the original occasion, from which the theme of unity has been omitted.

As we have seen, there is nothing apart from the first chapter to suggest the piece is given to an 'assembly of saints'. And if the Easter reference is suspect, so also is this setting. The fact that Eusebius characterizes it as being 'To the Assembly of the Saints' must mean that it was already in circulation under that name and in its final form. If there is any historical basis to the work, then, as suggested, it may be in the second part. But all these problems, fortunately, are quite irrelevant to our main interest. Either the work as a whole is to be set aside, as Baynes suggests, in assessing the religion of Constantine, or only the last few chapters are to be considered historically authentic, as I have suggested.

I have taken seriously the possibility that at least part of the *Assembly* is historically authentic, dating back to Constantine, to forestall criticism that I have avoided testing my position against this particular oration. In doing this I may have seemed rather gullible. In his critical edition of the text of the *Assembly*, published at the turn of this century, Ivan Heikel reviewed literature from the nineteenth century which disputed the authenticity of the whole document, beginning with Rossignol, *Virgile et Constantin le Grand*, published in 1845. After dealing with the main contributions, Heikel considers the internal evidence and external historical references to the work and concludes that it must be from at least the fifth century and that it was still later before it was joined to the *Life*. 'Hopefully the "Oration to the Assembly of the Saints" will no longer be used as a source for the history of Constantine or his time.'[7] Complex though this continuing debate is, we need pursue it no further. We cannot be accused of taking the easy way out. If Heikel is correct, then the whole oration is irrelevant to our position. If Baynes is correct, the *Assembly* is equally irrelevant to us. But if, by my own more discriminating approach, part of the work can be used to test my view, I must conclude that my position is not undermined in any way. The *Assembly* tells us nothing about the religion of Constantine which was not already known and certainly does not provide grounds for believing that the Emperor was a Christian.

VII

LEGISLATION ON RELIGION

In Part One it became clear that Constantine was a religious man. He was not Christian, and indeed his religion might well be regarded as very shallow and superficial. Yet he had religious convictions and they were strongly held. However, in Part Two we have found difficulty in extending our knowledge of his religion. Instead, our sources have made it clear that religion was important to Constantine in his political life. In this chapter we shall illustrate this from the legislation which he enacted concerning religion, and in the next chapter we shall see how important religion was in his attempt to unify the Empire.

1   From Persecution to Patronage

We can scarcely begin to imagine the response of the Christian church to the enlightened policy of Constantine. From torture, degradation, and arbitrary attack they were rescued at a stroke. And if that were not enough, the policy went further than simply leaving them in peace: it positively discriminated in their favour. It must indeed have seemed to them a miracle wrought by the hand of God. This provides the perspective for Eusebius when he wrote his *Historica Ecclesiastica*, paraphrased by G.A. Williamson in the Penguin translation as *The History of the Church from Christ to Constantine*.[1] It is indeed the story of the fortunes of the church from the beginning, but also of the ill-fortunes of those who persecuted it, from the Jews to Licinius. This philosophy of history was not unique to Eusebius. A more strident and bitter example, already noted, is to be found in the work of Lactantius, a slightly older contemporary, *De Mortibus Persecutorum*. Lactantius dwells with relish on the manner of the deaths of those who persecuted the church. The Emperors are presented as gross and bestial almost beyond belief. Of the cruelty and arbitrariness of Galerius he claims, 'it seemed as a favour, on account of old services, when one was permitted to die in the easiest manner'.[2] The unrestrained immorality of Maximin Daia was such as to suggest that 'under the reign of this adulterer, chastity had been treason'.[3] Such polemical philosophies of history were intended as *apologiae* for the vindication of Christianity over its enemies, both individuals and pagan cults. Eight centuries previously, Isaiah proclaimed hope to Israel when the people suffered captivity in Babylon. God had chosen the king of the Persians to rescue them: 'He is my shepherd, and he shall fulfil all my purpose.'[4] But if Cyrus was unconscious that his imperial policy also served the will of God, Constantine, the new shepherd, acted consciously in the full knowledge of what he must do.

Stated thus, of course it seems clear that Constantine was a Christian. He was the conscious agent of God, and his policy was only the outworking of his new Christian faith. But as we have seen, such sentiments, though they express the faith of Christians, cannot be attributed to the Emperor himself. It might seem strange that Constantine's first action when he gained control of the West was to end persecution and reverse the discrimination against the church. Yet it was not at all strange. Shrewd, yes, but not at all incredible. As N. H. Baynes has pointed out, the persecution itself was imperial policy: 'the martyrs and confessors after the middle of the third century had suffered primarily from the intransigence of the Roman State, and not from the animosity of their pagan fellow-citizens.'[5] We might say that the persecution itself was not a religious matter. As from the beginning, the persecution by the state was to deal with the threat to the unity of the Empire. If by all objective standards this policy had failed, why should Constantine not change the policy? And if indeed it had been counter-productive, why not positively reverse the policy? We can all be wise with hindsight, but at least we can say that the policy of acting as the patron rather than the persecutor of the church was a wise political decision. Whether and how it was also a religious policy requires careful evaluation.

If Constantine did not act as a patron of the church simply because he too was a Christian, it is tempting to conclude that nevertheless he acted thus because of his new devotion to the God of the Christians, that fine but real and important distinction with which I began. Yet we have not discovered any evidence to support this conclusion. The covenant was a personal one between God and Constantine. If he trusted in God then he would be victorious. Well, he did so trust and he gained his reward, Rome. Of course we should not expect him to continue the persecution of the Christians, but there seems no obvious reason why he should adopt such a positive policy towards the church. And it certainly was not a religious consideration that led him to adopt the policy. The policy, like the prior policy of persecution, was a political one. It certainly provides no grounds for judging that Constantine was a Christian.

The first document which we must examine is the *Edict of Milan*, promulgated in 313. As presented by Eusebius, this is a historic document issued jointly by Constantine and Licinius. Scholars today are somewhat sceptical of such an agreed text deriving from the meeting of the two. As recorded by Lactantius, it is a letter addressed by Licinius to the eastern provinces now under his control, but one which reflects the agreement which he had made to implement in the East the policy which Constantine was already pursuing with regard to religion in the West.[6] Such questions about the origins of the document are not of first importance, since according to Baynes,

> The facts for which the 'Edict of Milan' once stood are still facts, though the Edict itself has gone the way of many another symbolic representation of historical truth.[7]

In order to test my hypothesis I shall assume the document reflects the position of Constantine. If it does not, then of course it cannot count for or against.

In the Edict persecution was brought to an end: 'no one whatever was to be denied the right to follow and choose the Christian observance or form of worship . . .'[8] By this time we are not at all surprised by the fact that there is nothing in the Edict to indicate that Constantine was himself a Christian. Indeed the assumption that he was, and that this was his motivation in promulgating this policy, runs into difficulties with an apparent anomaly, namely that toleration is extended not simply to Christianity but to all forms of monotheism. The quotation continues; 'and everyone was to have permission to give his mind to that form of worship which he feels to be adapted to his needs, so that the Deity might be enabled to show us in all things His customary care and generosity.' But in our view there is no anomaly. We have discovered that Constantine was a monotheist, but not a Christian. It is therefore not at all surprising that his toleration operates within a certain religious band of options. He disapproves of pantheism, since he himself is a monotheist, but he can hardly prescribe only Christianity, since he himself is not a Christian. If this is the negative aspect of the policy, the ending of persecution, there is, in the second place, the positive policy of restoring to Christians the property which had previously belonged to them. Some of that property might have been sold since its confiscation or given away in the form of a gift. If there is any dispute, then the dispute is to be taken up with the local authority or judiciary, but whether compensation is to take place or not: 'All this property is to be handed over to the Christian body immediately, by energetic action on your part without any delay' (X.5).

The Emperor's motives in both aspects of the policy are quite clear. On the first, as indicated at the end of the quotation, it is 'so that the Deity might be enabled to show us in all things His customary care and generosity'. On the second, it is 'so that in this also our liberality may further the common and public tranquility'. The religious policy then is quite explicitly taken for the following motives. It represents an extension of the causal relationship of obedience and reward which Constantine has already experienced. And it is to repair the social fabric of the Empire that he requires all confiscated property to be returned. In neither case can we conclude that the policy indicates that Constantine was a Christian.

Eusebius includes three further documents indicating Constantine's policy on religion, as it concerned the church. These arose from the Donatist schism and will be discussed in that context in the next chapter. The first is a statute issued as a letter to Anulinus, Proconsul of Africa. Christian property is to be restored in its entirety, and this order has to be carried out both energetically and meticulously. The only indication which the Emperor gives of motivation is that the policy 'is in keeping with our benevolence that when things belong by right to another man we wish them not only to suffer no damage, but also to be restored' (X.5).

The second letter is addressed to Caecilian, Bishop of Carthage. Constantine declares his intention to give substantial grants to the church in North Africa. His chief religious adviser, Hosius, Bishop of Cordoba, was to oversee the actual payments and is authorized to make more money available if necessary. The only relevant detail on the question of the religion of Constantine is the final greeting: 'May the divine power of the great God keep you safe for many years' (X.6). Must we simply note that it is not a Christian greeting? Surely it is more significant than that? If Constantine were a Christian, would he not in these circumstances add some reference to Christ?

The third letter is also addressed to Anulinus, and this time concerns the status of Christian clergy. The effect of the instruction was to exempt full-time clergy from public duties which might have distracted them from their religious duties. But it is the reason which the Emperor gives for this exemption which is of interest to us at this point.

Many facts combine to prove that the sad neglect of religious observances, by which the highest reverence for the most holy, heavenly Power is preserved, has brought great dangers upon the community, and that the lawful restoration and preservation of the same has conferred the greatest good fortune on the Roman name, and wonderful prosperity on all mankind – blessings conferred by divine benevolence (X.7).

This is a most revealing statement. From what we have already seen of Constantine and his religious policy, it is quite clear that he has two things in mind. The first is his discovery of the connection between obedience to God and material success and prosperity. The second is that his encouragement of Christian worship assists this process. And yet the passage quoted contains no reference to Christianity. It can hardly be said that his policy is 'restoration and preservation' of religion. His policy is actually the replacing of the old religion(s) with the new. The language and the sentiments expressed in the passage, however, are entirely at one with a very old tradition dating back to the earliest period of the Empire. As A. D. Nock has pointed out, 'It is clear that down to the fourth century A.D. it was widely held that the prosperity and even the safety of Rome depended on the accurate performance of traditional ceremonies.'[9] Constantine did not, of course, believe this, but it is interesting that he uses this traditional argument to justify the clergy of the new religion as if they had been clergy of the old. The shrewd politician often finds that in order to go forward he must pretend to go back. But at least we can conclude of this material that it provides no grounds for claiming that Constantine was a Christian, or that his policy was motivated by Christian commitments.

We examined the *Life of Constantine* in some detail when discussing the religion of Constantine. Eusebius includes examples of Constantine's actions with regard to religion, which, while they do not add to our knowledge of his own religion, further exemplify his religious policy.

First of all there is the letter to 'the inhabitants of the province of Palestine', advocating Christianity. The Emperor brings forward but one argument. There is a difference between those who follow the Christian religion and those who oppose it. Those who follow the Christian religion 'are rewarded with abundant blessings'.[10] Those who oppose it 'have experienced results corresponding to their evil choice'. This view was rejected by the writer of the Book of Job in a very convoluted work. It was rejected by Jesus in the most straightforward way,[11] even though it has been accepted by

Christians at various times. It was quite central to the religion of Constantine, and in this letter he assumes that it is an argument which should also appeal to Christians. He goes on to say that this is the lesson of history: that those who have sought justice, obedience to God and the service of their fellow men have been successful in what they attempted. By contrast, those who have acted in the opposite way 'have received a recompense proportioned to their crimes'.[12] The faithful have, of course, suffered at times, but what character it has wrought in them! The persecutors have in the end been defeated and put to flight (II.26). Those who have opposed the divine will have invariably ended their lives in ignominy and suffering, a suffering intensified by the prospect of their eternal fate. How is it, then, that the situation has been so transformed, that from 'the remote Britannic ocean' throughout the Empire evil has been overcome and virtue rewarded? Constantine is forced to overcome his natural modesty and acknowledge that it has all been brought about through him, 'the instrument' of God (II.28). Indeed, after the opening sentences Constantine has been speaking of his own religion, and certainly he does not mention Christ. It was he who carried his campaign eventually into the East and brought to an end the sufferings of those persecuted for their faith (II.29). It is tempting to think that Constantine is here advocating his religion because it is true, but truth he does not discuss. The only argument is reward, and we must conclude that he wishes his subjects to practise monotheism because individually they will suffer if they do not, but more generally the Empire will lose the rewards which it now enjoys.

The second letter (II.30–34) is an edict calling on those who went into exile rather than give up their religion, now to return and receive back their good names and their property. Those who have been compulsorily exiled are to return, and those politically disgraced by reason of their religion are to return to home and honour. Soldiers who had been downgraded are to be reinstated or to be given an honourable discharge. Constantine orders the release of those of noble birth who have been forced to undertake menial work and also the ending of the enslavement of free men who have been taken because of their religion. We have already met this aspect of Constantine's policy, to restore the unity of society and end the divisions and bitterness caused by persecution. One of the most divisive questions concerned property, and to that he now turns.

The third letter deals with the return of confiscated property (II.35–42). Many Christians lost property, as martyrs, confessors, or as exiles. Their property is to be restored, or if they are dead, at least to their families. In some cases it may not be possible to find close relations who might receive the property. When this happens, then the local church is to be given the property instead. The logic, presumably, is that this is the nearest community because of the common faith. During the intervening time some will have profited from the use of this property, such as land, a house or garden. The property is to be restored, but realism indicates that the profits cannot be handed over in their entirety. The law is to apply to individuals, but since the state also benefited from confiscation, the treasury is liable to observe the same law. Constantine concludes by pointing again to the fact that he has brought evil to an end: his legislation is to remove its lasting effects.

Eusebius also reports that discrimination was brought to an end in the imperial government and Christians were again permitted to hold high office. Constantine also issued edicts against polytheism, as might be expected.

A fourth letter is to Eusebius, with copies sent both to bishops and to provincial governors. In it the Emperor orders that more churches be built, that ruined churches be restored, and that others still be enlarged. This is to be done at imperial expense, presumably in anticipation of the great increase in numbers becoming Christian (II.46).

Finally there is a fifth letter, rambling over a variety of subjects (II.48–60). Indeed, we have referred to these chapters as 'letters' only for convenience. It is not clear that the individual items ever belonged together. This letter is addressed 'to the people of the Eastern provinces'. He speaks in prayer of his policy. 'My own desire is, for the common good of the world and the advantage of all mankind, that thy people should enjoy a life of peace and undisturbed concord' (II.56). Although some have not turned from their errors, he will not compel them as they did others. 'For it may be that this restoration of equal privileges to all will prevail to lead them into the straight path' (II.56). He is willing to allow them to continue in pagan worship. This would appear to be an anomaly, but not if Constantine's primary concern is with the unification of the Empire. He does not absolutize Christianity.

These letters, edicts, laws, tell us little specifically of the motivation of Constantine's religious policy, but they illustrate and support our earlier view that his primary concern is a political one, the unification of the empire and the extension of the benefits enjoyed under his régime. They do not provide any evidence to suggest that he was a Christian. Indeed the premise of this policy is, as we have seen, deeply un-Christian.

2   The Theodosian Code

In our customary manner we have marched towards the sounds of
gunfire. In examining the legislation of Constantine we have looked
to those edicts and letters preserved in Eusebius. This Christian
context would make the legislation appear as clearly motivated by
Christian faith as possible. And yet no such motivation appears. We
must now turn to another source, one which is more historically
reliable and one in which the legislation is placed in a very different
context.

In 429 the Emperor Theodosius appointed a commission of
experts to make a collection of the imperial edicts, beginning with
those of Constantine and continuing to the present. In 438 the *Codex
Theodosianus* was at last issued in sixteen books. Its historical value
is not simply that it gathers together the legislation of the Empire
during the period, and through the *Novels* the further legislation
down to 468 and thus virtually the end of the Western Empire, but
that the original forms of edicts are preserved and additions are
clearly set out in succession. Thus we have the edicts attributed to
particular emperors, along with the subsequent additions by which
later rulers developed or modified the laws. Fortunately we need
only concern ourselves with the legislation attributed to
Constantine.

The first and most striking fact is that in the first fifteen books
there are only three edicts of Constantine concerning religion. Most
of the edicts on religion are to be found in the final book. In
Euscbius' accounts of Constantine, his life, work and thought, we
are given a picture of a ruler whose primary motivation is religious
and whose main concern is to transform the position of the Christian
church. The *Codex* is an imposing volume, and as we struggle
through section after section, title after title, and book after book,
we cannot fail to be impressed by the burden of administration with
which Constantine coped so admirably. In the *Life of Constantine*
religion is the central preoccupation of the Emperor. In the *Codex*
he legislates on civil servants and brothels; freedmen and slaves;
betrothals and divorces; aqueducts and river patrols; grain, fish and
oil; chariots and gladiators; magicians and astrologers; rape and
incest; ragmen, miners, physicians and lawyers; tax collectors and
swine collectors. And in the midst of this plethora of executive
decisions, religion neither appears nor requires to be mentioned.
This is the first point that must strike us in dealing with the *Codex*.
It is salutary but true that religion did not dominate the life and
work of Constantine. Rather, religion took its place within the

constraints of imperial allocations. In the sixteen books the experts determine that it should not come first but last. Constantine's policies are not determined by religion: his religion is determined by his imperial policies. Indeed, as we have seen, religion is part of his strategy.

The second point that emerges is that there is not a single example in the whole collection of any Christian commitment on the part of Constantine. Nor will it do to say that this would be inappropriate: subsequent legislation by his successors is often openly and specifically Christian. Indeed, one of the three examples from Books 1–15 is of particular interest since it provides us with an independent account of the legislation concerning the *Dies Solis* and thus an opportunity of contrasting it with Eusebius' interpretation of Constantine's ruling on Sunday. In the *Life* (IV.18), as we have seen, Eusebius attempts to impose a Christian interpretation on the legislation concerning Sunday, 'in memory, I suppose, of what the Saviour of mankind is recorded to have achieved on that day'. Yet when Constantine issues an edict clarifying what may and may not be done on the day, he uses the pagan phrase 'dies solis' to describe it.

> Just as it appears to Us most unseemly that the Day of the Sun, which is celebrated on account of its own veneration, should be occupied with legal altercations . . .[13]

Here is apparently another anomaly, that the Emperor should revert to the pagan justification of observing this day. Yet it is an anomaly only for those who assume that he was a Christian. Indeed it confirms our view very well. The Emperor, who is a devotee of the God of the Christians but not of Christ, is able to honour the day of the Christians, but not as a Christian. Is he dissembling, disguising his true colours? Far from it, he states quite clearly, this sovereign of the house of *Sol Invictus*, that it is as the Day of the Sun that this day is to be observed throughout the Empire.

The other two references in Books 1–15 and most of the references in Book 16 are concerned with the legal status of the church and its clergy. The more radical concerns the decisions and testimony of bishops. It comes in Book 1, which is mainly taken up with defining the rights and duties of imperial officers. This would imply that bishops were here considered not simply in their ecclesiastical office but as imperial dignitaries. Indeed, so extraordinary is the edict that its historical authenticity has been called in question. Fortunately this question need not concern us, but only the extent to which it might count as evidence of Christian commitment on the part of the

Emperor. Even if it were not authentic, it is clearly an early document, since it appears as the first of the *Constitutiones Sirmondianae*. (These documents, which predate the *Codex*, were first published by Jacobus Sirmondus in Paris in 1631 and are held to preserve earlier forms of sixteen edicts.) But neither in the *Codex* nor in the *Constitutions* does the edict present Constantine as a Christian.

It must be concluded, therefore, that in the first fifteen books of the *Codex* religion was not of primary importance for the Emperor. There is no positive evidence of any Christian commitment. But before moving on, perhaps some counter-evidence might be noted. Perhaps it may seem a small point, but Constantine makes no objection to the greeting given him by former soldiers. 'Augustus Constantine! The gods preserve you for us! Your salvation is our salvation' (7.20.2). They obviously do not see him as a threat to their religion, rather as the upholder of the traditions on which their future depends. And there is no lack of examples which would seem to confirm *their* view of Constantine, over against those who think that behind the facade there stands a Christian Constantine secretly loathing such customs and values.

> If any man by an infamous conspiracy should give to barbarians an opportunity to plunder Romans, or if any man should share the spoils acquired in any other way, he shall be burned alive (7.1.1).

No weakening of the old reign of terror here, nor in the treatment of informers.

> The accursed ruin caused by informers, the one greatest evil to human life, shall be suppressed; at the beginning of an attempt it shall be strangled in the very throat, and the tongue of envy shall be cut off from its roots and plucked out . . . (10.10.2).

A man of his time, perhaps, yet clearly not converted to Christian values in public life. But a final example must surely raise doubts about Constantine's own commitment to Christianity. In legislating for punishment in the case of high treason, Constantine rules that in the case of a slave accusing his master or a freedman his patron, 'a hearing shall be denied such a slave or freedman, and he shall be affixed to the cross' (9.5.1). To continue the practices of burning alive and strangulation is one thing, but to continue the crucifixion surely must count *against* Christian commitment.

In Book 16 we find collected edicts referring specifically to religion. Or rather, referring to institutions of religion rather than religion itself. This is an important point because the edicts together well illustrate Constantine's religious policy, but in the course of delivering them there is not a single comment which would indicate a religious commitment. Several deal with the status of the clergy.

> Those persons who devote the services of religion to divine worship, that is, those who are called clerics, shall be exempt from all compulsory public services whatever, lest, through the sacrilegious malice of certain persons, they should be called away from divine services (16.2.2).

At many points 'Interpretations' are added to the *Codex* which derive not from the work of the original commission, but from its application by jurists in the period up to the Breviarium of Alaric II in 506. In this case the Interpretation suggests that the clergy are not to be distracted from their religious duties by having to act in capacities such as tax collectors. At the same time Constantine was aware that some people actually became clerics in order to avoid such public service (16.2.3). On occasion rich families arranged for one of their members to become a cleric in order to gain exemption from public service. The Emperor ruled that in such cases 'he shall be removed from the clergy and shall be delivered to the municipality' (16.2.6). Although such legislation forms part of Constantine's religious policy and is enacted without reference to any Christian commitment, he does distinguish here, as elsewhere, between religion which is to be supported and pagan cults. There were cases of Christian clergy being forced to perform functions for such cults. The Emperor legislated against this, saying that 'if any person should suppose that those who devote their services to the most sacred law may be forced to the ritual of an alien superstition, he shall be beaten publicly with clubs . . .' (16.2.5).

There was also legislation concerning property. 'Every person shall have the liberty to leave at his death any property that he wishes to the most holy and venerable council of the Catholic Church' (16.2.1). (There are several references to the Catholic Church in Book 16, titles 2 and 5. These will be discussed in the next chapter.) However, we may doubt if Constantine had in mind simply the increase in the wealth of the church. If rich families had to assume their municipal duties, the church with its new wealth also had obligations. 'For the wealthy must assume secular obligations, and the poor must be supported by the wealth of the churches' (16.2.6). Once again, legislation on the church served the end of social cohesion.

There are two further topics which are dealt with in Book 16, of particular interest to our enquiry about the religion of Constantine. Christianity was originally just another messianic group within sectarian Judaism. It might therefore seem strange that from an early stage it has been anti-Semitic. It was the challenge of that other sectarian leader, John the Baptist, that being Jewish was not enough: 'and do not presume to say to yourselves, "We have Abraham as our father". . .'[14] But by the time of Paul being Jewish will not do at all. 'Paul's position was unquestionably that of anti-Judaism.'[15] By the turn of the century the writer of John's Gospel identifies the Jews with the forces which killed Jesus and rejected God. 'There is no way to rid Christianity of its anti-Judaism, which constantly takes social expression in anti-Semitism, without grappling finally with its christological hermeneutic itself.'[16]

Are there any indications that Constantine was a Christian? It is perhaps a rather uncomfortable observation to make, but if being anti-Semitic is inherent in Christianity, it may be important to note that Constantine displays some very anti-Semitic attitudes. In his letter to the Council of Nicaea he appeals to the church leaders, 'Let us then have nothing in common with the detestable Jewish crowd . . .'[17] Yet such a remark would be slim grounds for maintaining that he was a Christian. The issue was the unity of the church, the occasion the division over the celebration of Easter. Some followed the traditions of the Passover. Hence Constantine in dismissing the Jews is actually attempting to unite the church. Once again we can be sure that it is consistent with his religious policy, but it hardly constitutes evidence for Christian faith.

There are several references to the Jews in the *Theodosian Code*, Book 16, Title 8. They run the gamut from being anti-Semitic to being pro-Jewish. There have been reports of converts from Judaism being stoned, and the Emperor, in highly pejorative terms, warns of the penalties if the Jews attack 'any such person who has fled their feral sect and has restored to the worship of God, such assailant shall be immediately delivered to the flames and burned, with all his accomplices'.[18] It was a minimum objective of the Emperor's religious policy that religion should not be a divisive issue in society. Although he was not prepared to persecute Jews, he did not countenance their interference with the church. Thus in the *Constitutions* he takes the side of Christianity. 'We command that if any Jew should unlock for himself the door of eternal life, should deliver himself to our holy worship, and should choose to be a Christian, he shall not suffer any disquietude or molestation from the Jews.'[19] In this quotation the Emperor clearly identifies himself with Christians, at least over against the common enemy. If that were the only saying of Constantine which remained extant, then it might suggest he himself was a Christian. However, it can hardly neutralize the accumulated evidence in favour of our view so far. Roman Emperors had trouble with the Jews before Christianity emerged from sectarian Judaism. Although numerically they were not a threat to the Empire and were therefore given special status, nevertheless Constantine sees in Judaism a threat to the capacity of the church to unify the Empire. Other cults he can dismiss as unworthy, but in this case he must, in common with Christians, attack Judaism as false. The irony, of course, is that, as we shall see in detail in Chapter IX, 'Constantine's Covenant Religion', the Emperor's own religion was in many respects closer to Judaism than to Christianity. In this *Constitution* he is defending his policy, not his religion, from the threat of the Jews.

A more neutral and less anti-Semitic tone is found in the edict declaring that, 'If any Jew should purchase and circumcise a Christian slave or a slave of any other sect whatever, he shall not retain in slavery such circumcised person.'[20] Although in the setting of an imperial edict the Emperor purports to be concerned about Christians and those of 'any other sect', he has a special concern for Christianity because of its vulnerability to Judaism. However, there are other laws concerning Jews which, far from being anti-Semitic, actually confer rights on Jews or specifically extend rights to Jews which might otherwise in local situations have been denied. 'By a general law We permit all municipal senates to nominate Jews to the municipal council' (16.8.3). Or again, 'We command that priests, rulers of the synagogues, fathers of the synagogues, and all others who serve the synagogues, shall be free from every compulsory public service of a corporal nature' (16.8.4). It would seem that Constantine was willing to treat Judaism in exactly the same way as any other monotheistic religion, in accordance with his liberal policy on religion. But since his religious policy was to use the church to unify the Empire, he would not allow any actions by Jews which threatened or weakened the church.

In these matters we see that Constantine had views on religion, but that his policy on religion was perfectly consistent. It served his political aims. His edicts on religion cannot be derived from Christian commitment. Indeed here as elsewhere anomalies arise only when the assumption is made that he was a Christian. For example, there is the edict concerning soothsayers. 'If it should appear that any part of Our palace or any other public work has been struck by lightning, the observance of the ancient custom shall be retained, and inquiry shall be made of the soothsayers as to the portent thereof' (16.10.1).

The problem is still with us. Recently a cathedral organist reported that during an electrical storm the roof of the church had been struck by lightning, rain had found its way in and ruined the organ. Attempting to be helpful, it was pointed out that insurance companies refer to such accidents as 'acts of God', and he was invited to draw the appropriate conclusion about his playing. If Constantine assumed that his obedience to the God of the Christians brought prosperity, he could not explain a lightning attack as coming from God. What more natural than that this son of the house of the Sun should turn to soothsayers? Of course the Old Testament prophets knew how to interpret such chastisement, but as we shall see, Constantine's religion was not as subtle as that. Constantine's religion was personal, eclectic but not Christian, and his legislation on religion was primarily designed to serve his imperial objectives.

VIII

THE UNITY OF THE CHURCH

At the end of the previous chapter we were able to conclude that Constantine's legislation on religion was not enacted for religious motives, but as part of a religious policy. It did not demonstrate the Emperor's Christian commitment; it showed that he used religion as a means to a political end, namely the unification of the Empire. It was therefore intended to strengthen monotheism in general and Christianity in particular, in view of the importance of religion in Constantine's overall strategy. However, on occasion Constantine took a much closer interest in religion: he actually intervened in the affairs of the church. We then have the Emperor sitting among the bishops and theologians, concerning himself with matters of orthodoxy. As in the general case of legislation on religion, it is often assumed that Constantine could only have concerned himself with such matters because of his own Christian faith. His interventions in church affairs are therefore taken to be motivated by Christian commitments. His interventions are then taken to be further demonstrations of his religious convictions. But this argument is no more valid here than in the previous chapter. Constantine's interventions spring not from religious convictions, but because certain developments threatened the unity of the church. If the church was to be a means to an end, an instrument in the unification of the Empire, then any threat to the unity of the church was a threat to his religious policy and ultimately to the unity of the Empire itself. The unity of the church could be broken in two different ways, through disputes concerning practice and disputes concerning doctrine. Schism and heresy were not matters of theological importance to the Emperor, but of political importance. We shall illustrate this from the two most famous interventions, the schism of the Donatist Church and the controversy over Arianism.

1   The Donatist Schism

The year 312 was a momentous one in the history of Europe. Constantine defeated Maxentius to enter Rome and exercise sovereignty over the entire Western empire. Religion, he believed, had played its part, and it was central to his strategy as he turned towards the larger goal, the unification of the whole of the Empire, East and West. A united church was essential to this plan, but in that year Mensurius, bishop of Carthage, died and the appointment of Caecilian to succeed him was to divide the church and thereby threaten Constantine's ambition (or vocation, as he more coyly described it). The Emperor immediately intervened in the dispute. The theological issues are complex and fascinating, but there is no evidence to suggest that these played any part in Constantine's calculated moves.

Only the previous year Maxentius had been forced to put down a revolt in North Africa, not least because it threatened to interrupt grain supplies to Rome. In this new ecclesiastical dispute Constantine rightly detected nationalist sentiments and sought to achieve by peaceful means what his predecessor had tried to bring about by force of arms. But the main reason for his intervention was political, to maintain the unity of the church as an instrument in his imperial policy. Four years later, when the dispute still continued, he recognized the need to investigate the causes of the division, but in 312 he assumed that decisive action would heal the schism. He did not act as a Christian, concerned for the truth of the matter, but as a commander who assumed that the issue could be settled by throwing his weight on the side of the incumbent.

The schism is associated with the name of Donatus of Casae Nigrae. The Primate of Numidia had the right to consecrate the bishop of Carthage and in this case his choice was Majorinus, and upon his death in 313, Donatus. Donatus had therefore the support of the Numidians, but also of the populace of Carthage. Caecilian had the support only of the clergy of Carthage. Not surprisingly, Caecilian was regarded as schismatic by the majority, who referred to themselves as the Catholics.[1] However, all this altered with the intervention of the Emperor. He took the side of Caecilian and the 'Catholics', by which he meant the supporters of Caecilian. And since there was sympathy for Caecilian in Italy, the dispute has been recorded not as the Caecilian schism, but as the Donatist schism. This may seem a relatively unimportant matter of nomenclature, but its significance was far-reaching. The Emperor did not intervene for religious reasons, yet his action had important consequences for religion.

In 249 Decius became Emperor, and in the following year initiated the first universal and systematic persecution of the church. There were many martyrs and confessors, clergy and lay people throughout the Empire, and many 'lapsed', that is, those who in face of threats of terrible torture fulfilled the required sacrifice to the gods of Rome. The persecution continued intermittently till 259, and the church was deeply divided on the treatment of the lapsed. For over forty years there was toleration, in name if not in law, and during that time the church became increasingly integrated into the life and institutions of the Empire. Although, therefore, there are many parallels between the persecution by Decius and that which was suddenly unleashed by Diocletian between 303–305, the situation of the church was significantly changed and with it the response to the persecution. Few of the new converts, especially in the Romanized cities and provinces, were willing openly to confront the authorities. Their lives were lived within the Empire, and they did not have the former alienated view of the church of the martyrs.

> Christianity was no longer confined to unprivileged and non-romanized groups. Its leaders were being drawn from all classes. The numbers of bishoprics had increased greatly. In the towns it was not possible for the Christians to break with the world, for the world itself was becoming Christian.[2]

No doubt a more sophisticated view prevailed: do not seek out trouble, but if challenged, then hand over the sacred books to be burned (or better still hand over some heretical books which deserved to be burned) and make the perfunctory sacrifice. The Emperor did not require conversion, only compliance.

> When the Persecution broke out in the spring of 303 a large proportion of clergy and congregations hastened to sacrifice and surrender the Scriptures without evident fear of the consequences hereafter.[3]

The nature of the schism was therefore as much sociological as theological. North Africa, less Romanized, more nationalist, retained the rigorist view concerning the salvation of martyrs and also the rebaptism of the lapsed and *traditores,* those who had handed over the scriptures. Caecilian represented the newer, 'reasonable' attitude of compromise. It is therefore not at all difficult to see why Constantine did not think it necessary to consider the theological issues involved. He sided with the representative of that tradition which had shown itself most willing to work closely with the state. Not that the Emperor was planning to continue the persecution:

that had been ruled out as an ineffective policy. But he recognized in Caecilian and his supporters the forerunners of those church-statesmen who do not allow principles to interfere with conduct and who are not given to tasteless and futile gestures, such as being crucified. The Emperor would not be slow to note the institution-alizing of religion among this party, who considered that it was still in order for a priest to celebrate the eucharist even although he had betrayed his Lord. Harnack makes the point rather abrasively, but then the issue had been one of life and death.

> The Donatist crisis – after the Diocletian persecution – taught the Church to value ordination as imparting an inalienable title *(character indelebilis)* and to form a stringent view of the 'objec-tivity' of the sacraments; or, to use a plainer expression, to regard the Church primarily as an *institution* whose holiness and truth were inalienable, however melancholy the state of its members. *In this thought Catholicism was first complete.*[4]

Nothing could have pleased Constantine more. Without reference to the theological issues involved, he and the Catholic party spoke the same language.

Constantine's intervention began with a letter to Caecilian, in-forming him that 3,000 folles were being transferred to him from imperial funds. This was a very large sum of money indeed, but the Emperor assured the bishop that if this was not enough to guarantee success, more would follow from the royal treasurer. 'I have given him orders in person that if Your Steadfastness should ask him for any sum, he is to arrange for its transfer to you without question.'[5] We have already examined this letter briefly, in Chapter VII, to see if Constantine's letters and edicts contained explicitly Christian references. Now on closer inspection we see that Constantine treats the whole issue as if it were a purely political dispute which could be resolved by spreading money around. But, more ominously, Con-stantine declares his support for what he calls the 'Catholic church', meaning the Caecilian party, and invites the bishop to report to the civil authorities, Anulinus the Proconsul or his Vicar, any activity against Catholics by the opposition, who are referred to as 'certain persons of unstable character'. Religion was too important for Constantine to leave the matter to be resolved at a religious level. He intervened to bring about a political solution which would be acceptable to him. Schism is to be treated as a civil offence.

This was a very important departure in relations between church and state. Constantine then wrote to Anulinus ordering that clergy were to be exempt from municipal duties and obligations. There were great financial implications in this exemption, and there is evidence that rich families of Carthage were quick to see in it a means of tax avoidance. However, the exemption was specifically given to those who supported Caecilian. Once again Constantine offered great fiscal inducements to end the schism. The Donatists were greatly concerned at this new imperial intervention: 'the Devil rewarded the lapsed clergy not only with the restoration of ecclesiastical honours, but also with royal friendship and earthly riches'.[6] Previously all Christians had been subject to persecution by the state. Now the Emperor took it upon himself to intervene in an internal dispute. He would decide who was Catholic and who schismatic; the protection and patronage of the state would be bestowed on those whom he favoured. Those who were schismatic in his eyes would be subject to prosecution under the law.

The circumstances of the Donatist schism and the subsequent history of the Donastist church in North Africa is complex and fascinating, but it falls outwith our particular interest. We are intent on showing that both the motives and the criteria behind Constantine's intervention in the Donatist schism were purely political. They provide no grounds whatsoever for claiming that he acted as a Christian. Indeed, when examined in some detail, his intervention was anything but Christian.

The Donatists saw clearly the implications of Constantine's intervention and appealed to him to send judges from Gaul to hear the dispute between them and Caecilian. As W. H. C. Frend notes, 'This is one of the decisive moments in the history of the early Church.'[7] The Emperor was asked to intervene in a matter which previously would have been settled within the church. It is interesting to note that the Donatists did not appeal to Constantine as a Christian, but as a good and pious ruler. Constantine arranged for a hearing to take place in the Lateran Palace in Rome, but the bishop of Rome, Miltiades, added to the tribunal several Italian bishops. This meant in effect that Constantine had not authorized merely a civil hearing, but an ecclesiastical council. Thereafter no one objected to the Emperor summoning a council of the church when he wished a dispute settled. We should not assume that when the Emperor summoned a Council he was acting as a Christian who had the well-being of the church at heart. He called such councils whenever religion threatened to become a divisive force within his Empire.

The hearing took place in 313 and found against Donatus, but since Miltiades was not regarded as neutral and had himself been a *traditor*, this decision did nothing to end the dispute. The following year Constantine summoned the Council of Arles, at which attended representatives of all his provinces. After condemning the practices of the Donatists, the Council went on to discuss other matters, but 'The Emperor wearied of the whole affair *(taedians)* and sent them home.'[8] In other words, Constantine's interest was not theological but political. He had not summoned a council for the well-being of the church, but for the welfare of the Empire. When the dispute still continued, Constantine in some exasperation decided to go to Carthage to hear the dispute himself.

> What more can be done by me, more in accord with my constant practice, and with the very office of a prince, than after expelling error and destroying rash opinions, to cause all men to agree together to follow true religion and simplicity of life, and to render to Almighty God the worship which is his due?[9]

Of some interest here is the fact that Constantine simply disregards the canons passed at Arles and the findings of the council in Rome. In other words, he used these councils as devices to serve his political policy. He set no store by their theological conclusions. In this he was quite pragmatic: they had not done the one thing required of them, to end the schism, and therefore they were worthless. It is left now to the Emperor to intervene when the church cannot put its own house in order. As Frend says: 'Constantine is in fact acting as though he were on a higher plane than the religious powers on earth, rather as God's own Vicar than an ordinary mortal.'[10] But then that is exactly the conclusion to which we came in Chapter III, 'Constantine as Messiah'.

In passing we might mention a letter attributed to Constantine which represents him not only as a Christian, but as holding a very much higher view of episcopal pronouncements. About the year 375, Optatus, Bishop of Milevis, published his treatise 'On the Schism of the Donatists'. To this work were appended several documents collected at an earlier period, including six letters attributed to Constantine.[11] In five of these letters the material is already familiar. Reference is made to 'Almighty God', 'Supreme God'; there is no mention of Christ and no association of the Emperor with believers. His concern is for the continued prosperity of the empire, to which schism is a threat. Only in Appendix V do we find a Christian letter, addressed 'To the Catholic Bishops'. After sifting through the works of Eusebius and considering the religious policy of Constantine, we have a fairly precise understanding of the beliefs, concerns and attitudes of the Emperor. We must simply say that on such critical grounds this letter is incompatible with what we know of Constantine.

The letter includes several specifically Christian phrases, such as 'Christ the Saviour' and 'the mercy of Christ'.[12] Beyond this the writer associates himself with those whom he addresses through the greeting, 'Constantine Augustus, to his dearest brothers, the Catholic Bishops . . .', and in the appeal, 'O most holy Bishops of Christ the Saviour, my dearest brothers . . .'. But most striking is the writer's pained reaction to the appeal made to him by the Donatists. 'They ask judgment from me, who am myself waiting for the judgment of Christ.'

I cannot be accused of hitherto simply setting aside evidence which was not congenial to my emerging view of Constantine's religion, but if we are to maintain a critical approach to the material we must conclude that this letter does not come to us directly from Constantine. Indeed even Vassal-Phillips in his introduction to this letter is forced to admit as much.

> Moreover, this letter may perhaps have been touched up by an ecclesiastical secretary, of whom Constantine had several in his household. One of them, Hosius, the celebrated Bishop of Cordova, was certainly closely involved in these African controversies.[13]

This would suggest that we might adopt the same approach as in my treatment of the oration 'To the Assembly of the Saints', i.e., to view this as an original letter from Constantine which may have been christianized by the addition of a pious introduction from the hand of a later polemicist. When we look more closely, we see that the last main paragraph deals with practical arrangements which Constantine has made for dealing with the Donatists. The tone is quite familiar to us, and the religious references to 'our God', 'Heavenly Providence', 'Almighty God' and 'Saviour' are those already dealt with in previous chapters in which I concluded that Constantine was not a Christian. This letter, which appears to be composite, does not require me to change my position. Historically it misrepresents Constantine's view of the bishops at Arles. He did not stand by them, but decided to go over their heads to settle the schism.

Constantine did not in fact go to Carthage nor did he resolve the dispute, even although in 317 he passed oppressive legislation, confiscating Donatist property and exiling their leaders. Not for the first time was it demonstrated that persecution strengthened the church, and in 321 Constantine was forced to admit defeat and grant toleration. His original intervention had not been on religious grounds, and so his withdrawal from the dispute is unproblematic. It, too, was a calculation. At that time another controversy threatened the unity of the church, this time in Egypt. The Donatist church was the church of North Africa and did not threaten the unity of the church elsewhere. But this new dispute stemming from Alexandria threatened to divide the Empire.

2   The Arian Heresy

The Arian controversy concerned disagreement on the eternal relationship of the Father and the Son. Later in the century it was to lead to the trinitarian controversy. If that thought produces a certain heaviness of heart, we can be encouraged by the fact that our immediate interest in the controversy does not require that we enter this metaphysical minefield. Indeed our interest is not so much in the theological content of the Arian debate as in the part which the Emperor played in attempting to resolve it. However, we must give some indication of the rise of the controversy and why it came to the attention of Constantine.

The dispute first arose in Alexandria, one of the great centres of Christian scholarship in the early church. One of its most brilliant sons was Origen, who was head of the famous catechetical school, and who eventually suffered as a martyr at the beginning of the Decian persecution. Unlike the West, the East had a tradition of speculative philosophy and a tendency to enquire into the subtle depths of the divine mysteries. Origen bequeathed to his school doctrines which were not unambiguous, and the Arian controversy was, in the first instance, the result of emphasizing one side of his teaching on christology. Arius was a presbyter, in charge of a church in the Baucalis district of Alexandria. He was not a young man when about the year 320 he began to publish his views. The actual occasion of the dispute is not known for certain, but it may have been at a meeting of clergy in Alexandria addressed by Bishop Alexander.

> He, in the fearless exercise of his functions for the instruction and government of the Church, attempted one day, in the presence of the presbytery and the rest of the clergy, to explain, with perhaps too philosophical minuteness, that great theological mystery – the unity of the Holy Trinity.[14]

Arius, who is described as 'possessed of no inconsiderable logical acumen', considered the bishop's position to be heretical and offered his own views on the matter.

> If the Father begat the Son, he that was begotten had a beginning

of existence: and from this it is evident, that there was a time
when the Son was not in being. It therefore necessarily follows,
that he had his existence from nothing.[15]

The Son is not of the same substance of the Father. To the less
sophisticated this seemed quite reasonable and the view of Arius
spread rapidly in North Africa. Alexander called a synod in Alexandria and Arius was condemned. In a letter following the meeting
the bishop associated the views of Arius with the anti-Christ, but
noted that Arius had the patronage of the powerful bishop Eusebius
of Nicomedia. Nicomedia was the capital of the Eastern Empire,
and on the eve of the final struggle between Licinius and Constantine,
to end with Constantine's total victory in 324, the metaphysical
dispute of Alexandria threatened the unity of the church in the East.
One of Constantine's first acts when he gained control of the East
was to send his court-bishop Hosius of Cordova to Alexandria with
a letter calling on Alexander and Arius to resolve their differences.
Harnack described this letter as 'one of the most important monu-
ments of his religious policy'.[16]

The letter is preserved by Eusebius of Caesarea in *The Life of
Constantine*.[17] It is described by the biographer 'as exhibiting a
specimen of his watchful care over God's people' and we might
assume that Constantine would reveal himself as a Christian. This
could come about in several ways, but on closer examination of the
letter we see that Constantine does not write as a Christian. This
would seem once again to be an anomaly, yet an anomaly only for
those who assume the Emperor was a Christian. It is sometimes said
by those who assume that he was converted to Christianity, that
because most of his subjects were pagan, Constantine could not
openly present himself as a Christian. As we have seen, the more
obvious explanation is that he was not a Christian in the first place.
However, if he had any hesitation about declaring himself in his
general edicts, surely he would have spoken openly in writing to
Alexandria. The basis of this dispute was on the nature of Christ and
the eternal generation of the Son. Would he not have begun his
letter calling for reconciliation by at least some reference to the
common faith – his and theirs? But no: 'I call that God to witness, as
well I may, who is the helper of my endeavours, and the Preserver
of all men . . .' Once again, montheism, but not Christianity. Or
again, since he is calling for unity, would he not have sought to move
them by reference to their unity in Christ? But no, he tells them that
the dispute bears on his twofold endeavours. First, he desires 'to
bring the diverse judgments formed by all nations respecting the

Deity to a condition, as it were, of settled uniformity'. Can this be a Christian Emperor addressing fellow Christians? His religious policy is to promote monotheism: beyond that he has no concern for religion. But secondly, he endeavours 'to restore to health the system of the world, then suffering under the malignant power of a grievous distemper'. His political objective, achieved by military means, was to unify the Empire. He is writing to Alexandria therefore, not for the sake of unity in Christ, but because having after almost twenty years achieved the objective of uniting the Empire, at that precise moment he finds this political unity threatened by division within the church. Clearly he is not writing as a Christian, nor has he any concern for the basis of the dispute. His only concern is for his own political aims, and the danger to these aims posed by any ecclesiastical division. He does not address Alexander and Arius as fellow believers; indeed, speaking of Hosius his emissary, he refers to his intervention as 'sending some of yourselves'. He is here standing outside the church observing this irritating squabble.

The central doctrines of the Christian faith came to final formulation through controversies which required further detailed and more subtle definitions. In this sense the Arian controversy was one of the most important stages in the development of Christian orthodoxy. It consumed the energies of a theological generation and has been a central issue in the history of doctrine ever since. How, then, did Constantine view the controversy? There are several phrases in the letter which indicate his judgment on the matter: 'truly insignificant', 'an unprofitable question', it is the result of 'misused leisure', 'insignificant questions', 'trifling and foolish verbal difference', 'points so trivial and altogether unessential', a 'truly idle question'. Not surprisingly, Constantine's letter failed to resolve the issue: he denied that there was an issue. His attitude has puzzled those who assume that he was a Christian. 'The well-meant, but bungling effort was in vain.'[18] But Constantine was not a simple-minded layman who could not see the importance of the distinctions made. He was not a Christian, and his only interest was in securing religious unity. His appeal was to a lowest common denominator of monotheism. Compared with his vocation to unify the Empire such questions were not only ineffectual but evil.

The same pattern was emerging as in the case of the Donatist controversy, in which the Emperor's initial intervention had failed to resolve the matter. He therefore determined to follow the procedure which he had developed and called a council of the church. The Donatist controversy had been a matter of concern to him in the West: the Arian controversy was of the East. It is said that the Council of Nicaea, 325 was the first 'ecumenical' council, being drawn from the whole of the now unified Empire. However, the issue was of no particular interest to the West, and while over three hundred bishops attended from the East, only a handful came from the West. The Emperor's experience with the Council of Arles was that, left to themselves, the bishops would go on endlessly on matters which he regarded as unimportant. He therefore attended the council, having paid for the transport of the bishops. He had not spent such a sum of money in order to allow theologians to play games. This was an investment in order to further his religious policy and he went prepared to press through a formula to unify the church.

At the outset the Arian position was rejected and Eusebius of Caesarea introduced the creed of his own church. This was amended significantly to include the assertions, 'begotten, not made', and 'of one substance *(homoousion)* with the Father'. Thus Arius' views were specifically excluded. In fact it is only in this negative respect that the Nicene formula is specific. The terms remained ambiguous, but if new doors to heresy were opened, the Emperor seemed to be content at least to close this one.

> While different groups might read their own theologies into the creed and its key-word, Constantine himself was willing to tolerate them all on condition that they acquiesced in his creed and tolerated each other.[19]

Ecclesiastical unity was his objective, not the semantic refinement of metaphysical speculation.

> The Emperor asked only that the bishops should accept the creed: he declined to allow any official interpretation of its meaning: it was to be an eirenicon and not a source of further disagreements.[20]

Eusebius described the appearance of the Emperor at the Council: it would have been a brave man who would have objected to his presence or disagreed with his creed. Constantine may well have feared extensive and tedious discussions on other matters, but since most of the canons agreed on concerned discipline and authority within the church his purpose was also well served. Nicaea marked a further stage in the centralization of power, in parallel to the administration of the Empire itself. Alföldi is quite justified in drawing attention to the fact that Christianity was much more institutionally organized than the pagan cults.[21] This may have been a factor in Constantine's original choice of the God of the Christians, but it was certainly a potential which he was to encourage and exploit.

The Nicene controversy was to continue long after the death of Constantine, but in all the intrigue and complexities we see the same attitude maintained: the Emperor was not guided by considerations of theological truth or orthodoxy, but of reaching a formula which would provide a basis for unity and of then attempting by political means to enforce that unity. The attack on the Nicene position was led by Eusebius of Nicomedia, and one by one the supporters of the creed were disposed of. The impression is that Constantine would happily have settled for a rejection of the creed if *this* would have secured unity. Indeed he accepted a new creed presented to him by Arius, when the latter returned from banishment.

There is a letter from Constantine to the church in Nicomedia, warning against supporting their bishop, Eusebius. The letter begins with a theological defence of Nicaea and this of course raises the question of its authenticity.[22] From what we know of Constantine it is most unlikely that he would present such arguments for the resolution of the controversy. The author appeals to his audience, 'we are Christians', but he presents a very careful statement of the faith in accordance with the Nicene position, claiming that the 'Lord God' and 'Christ the Saviour' are Father and Son, that the Son is of the same 'substance' as the Father. These two features of the letter conflict with the extensive evidence we have concerning Constantine's religion and religious policy, i.e. the openly Christian position of the writer and also the attempt to promote unity through theological argument. Does this mean that the letter has been forged? There is another, less abrasive, conclusion to which we might come. Although the text of the letter as it stands is found only in Galesius of Cyzicus and also in Athanasius, a shorter version is found in Theodoret.[23] It has been assumed that the latter version preserves only part of the original letter from Constantine. But on closer inspection we see that the letter in Theodoret is entirely in keeping with both Constantine's religion and his religious policy. As in the case of the oration 'To the Assembly of the Saints', and also the letter to the bishops of the Council of Arles, we may draw the conclusion that the longer version is composed of an original letter from Constantine, to which has been added an introduction by a Christian theologian. The writer's interest was in defending Nicaea: Constantine's interest was in achieving unity in the church, whether through Nicaea or in spite of Nicaea.

The one man who comes out of the whole controversy with credit is Athanasius, bishop of Alexandria, successor to Alexander in 328.

Of Athanasius it might truly be said he feared God more than man and set theological truth above the imperial religious policy. In other words, he was a very dangerous man as far as the Emperor was concerned, and it is hardly surprising that he was banished five times. Though orthodox, Athanasius was not even-tempered and dealt violently with schismatics in Egypt. Eusebius of Nicomedia used this as the basis for having Athanasius condemned at the Council of Tyre in 335. Athanasius petitioned the Emperor.

> But Eusebius of Nicomedia clinched the issue by producing testimony that in a rash moment Athanasius had threatened to call a dock strike at Alexandria, stopping the vital corn supply to Constantinople, if the Emperor failed to support him.[24]

Constantine, who was uninterested in Athanasius' theology, at once banished him to Gaul. And with the mention of corn supply we have a certain feeling of *déjà vu*, for it is with this that I began my account of Constantine's intervention on the Donatist schism. We must not forget that Constantine was running an Empire and that for him bread was more important than theology. Religion had its place, but only as it served that greater purpose of unifying the Empire. Any threat to the religious unity of the Empire was treason, not simply schism or heresy. Virtue lay in the re-establishment of unity, without regard to metaphysical niceties. Constantine's religious policy is all of a piece, consistent and single-minded. It provides no evidence for asserting that he was a Christian, but much evidence for judging that he was not.

PART THREE

THE IDEOLOGY OF CONSTANTINE

In Part One of this study we examined the religion of Constantine. Although it has been assumed that Constantine was a Christian, we saw that on closer inspection there is very little evidence to support this view. To the contrary, there are good grounds for asserting that he was not a Christian. Once this view is accepted, the old anomalies and inconsistencies disappear. Constantine was a religious man with very precise beliefs, attitudes and values. But these were certainly not Christian.

In Part Two we considered his attitude towards religion. It played an important part in his ambition to conquer and unify the Empire. His religious policy flowed from his own personal religion. Religion played a part in his imperial policies. This guided not only his beneficence towards the church but also his intervention in the internal affairs of the church. Religion was too important to his strategy to leave in the hands of the ecclesiastics.

Now in Part Three we turn to a more fundamental question, the effect which Constantine had on the church, and through that on the development of Western culture. It may seem surprising to claim that, by comparison, the question of whether Constantine called himself a Christian or not is relatively unimportant, but a moment's reflection makes it clear that the two are separate issues. From our examination of the sources it seems impossible to conclude that Constantine was a Christian, but we need not delay our enquiry into the more fundamental question until final agreement has been reached on this point. Because of his relationship to the church, Constantine was able to influence it and Christianity at a profound level. We must now consider how Constantine's values infiltrated the church: not how he was converted to Christianity, but how through his religious policy he succeeded in converting Christianity to his position.

IX

CONSTANTINE'S COVENANT RELIGION

1 Pre-Christian

In Chapters II and III we discussed Eusebius' presentation of the religion of Constantine, in the oration 'In Praise of Constantine'. We were forced to the conclusion that Christ is omitted from that religion, indeed that Christ is set aside as if he had never existed. More than that, Constantine replaces Christ as the manifestation of the purpose of God and the instrument of God's salvation of mankind. Since no one has seriously questioned the authorship of this oration or the fact that it was given in the presence of its subject, it is surprising that this view of Constantine's religion should have attracted so little attention. It is extraordinary that Constantine's religion should be thus described by a Christian bishop. We have concluded from this that Eusebius must have described it accurately and faithfully.

We might therefore expect that the oration 'In Praise of Constantine' would read as a pagan narrative. If Christ is omitted, set aside and even replaced it should read as if it belonged to some other religious tradition. Yet the oration has a strange quality about it; it is not so much non-Christian as actually pre-Christian. It is for this reason that its true significance has never been spelt out. It is about the God of the Christians, delivered by a Christian bishop, and it makes frequent use of biblical language and images. To the casual reader, or one who assumes that Constantine was a Christian, it appears to be a Christian work, notwithstanding the fact that Christ is not mentioned but replaced. Its subject is the Sovereign and the sovereign, God and the king, but God here is the God of the Christians – before the doctrine of God was influenced by the revelation in Christ. That is to say, in the religion of Constantine we are not taken outwith the Christian tradition so much as transported back to an earlier stage in its development. The religion of Constantine takes us back to the context of the Old Testament. It is as if the religion of Abraham, Isaac and Jacob, the religion of Moses and Joshua, of David and Elijah, of Zechariah and Daniel, is at last fulfilled not in Jesus but in Constantine.

Nor does this only come about at the end of his reign: it is the conclusion to which we might have come in the opening chapter, in discussing the receiving of the *labarum. Remoto christo*, there is no mediator through whom Constantine might receive either vocation or guidance. We are at once transported back in history to the religious time of the patriarchs. The scene is one of theophany. There is the covenant between God and Noah:

> And God said, 'This is the sign of the covenant which I make between me and you and every living creature that is with you, for all future generations: I set my bow in the cloud, and it shall be a sign of the covenant between me and the earth.'[1]

For Moses there is the burning bush and later the cloud and fire.

> And the Lord went before them by day in a pillar of cloud to lead them along the way, and by night in a pillar of fire to give them light . . .[2]

And so it continues, a sign given to one man of a covenant through which the people will be saved. But the covenant is made through the one, and if he were to fail to respond then salvation must be postponed. It is the recurring theme of the one man who has faith, who risks that the covenant is to be trusted. And above all in the ethos of patriarchal religion, it is covenant and not merely command: there is a gain, a reward. Not some possible life after death, not some spiritual blessing that warms the heart and leaves the belly empty. No, a covenantal religion which rewards faith with security, with land, with long life, with wives, children, cattle, water and, in a hot land, cool shade. The religion of the labarum, this saving sign in the sky, is the religion of covenant. But a covenant which rewards faith not with sanctity only, but with booty. And if this covenantal religion is continuous with the old, then no man was ever promised more nor had more bestowed upon him: the Roman Empire. The religion of Constantine, which begins with the labarum, is in this respect the climax of covenantal religion and as such it is pre-Christian, as if Christ had never been. As we shall see, it is also and profoundly anti-Christian. But this is where it begins, at the conversion of Constantine, and it is in complete continuity with the religion which Eusebius so faithfully describes in the oration.

If Constantine stood squarely within the Christian tradition, then

Eusebius would have spoken of his faithfulness to Christ, his *imitatio Christi*. But apparently Eusebius cannot do this, for the simple reason that Constantine was not a follower of Christ. Yet since Constantine was a devotee of the God of the Christians, Eusebius has the Old Covenant at his disposal. In language and images from the Old Testament he can describe Constantine's unmediated relationship to God, without Christ. We have already noted that it is Constantine who brings the fulfilment of promises made in the book of Daniel. It is Constantine who 'fulfils the predictions of the divine prophets, which ages and ages ago proclaimed that "the saints of the Most High shall take up the kingdom." '[3] In this way Constantine fulfils the religion of the Old Testament, without Christ.

Such is his boundless admiration for the Emperor that, in the *Life of Constantine*, Eusebius compares the experience, vocation and achievement of Constantine with that of Moses![4] He too lived in the court of the oppressor as a youth, 'in this respect again keeping up his resemblance to the great prophet Moses'.[5] Indeed the drowning of Maxentius in the Tiber is compared to the destruction of the chariots of Pharaoh in the Red Sea.[6] The labarum is given in a theophany comparable to those of the Old Testament: its use in battle is the primitive testing of God through combat. It might seem that these are simply images used by Eusebius, not by Constantine. Yet there is at least one intriguing parallel which comes from the Emperor himself.

In the wilderness, where there could be no permanent buildings for a people on the move, Moses made a special portable tabernacle in which he could pray to God for guidance.

> Now Moses used to take the tent and pitch it outside the camp, far off from the camp; and he called it the tent of meeting.[7]

In the *Life*, Eusebius tells us that Constantine made such a tabernacle.

> He pitched the tabernacle of the cross outside and at a distance from his camp, and there passed his time in a pure and holy manner, offering up prayers to God; following thus the example of his ancient prophet . . .[8]

In passing, we might note that the Greek text described this portable tent which Constantine used on the field of battle as a 'tabernacle' (ἡ σκηνή), and not a 'tabernacle of the cross'.[9] This is another example in which the English translation christianizes the original. In this case Eusebius is suggesting that Constantine consciously followed the example of Moses. It is certainly in the Old Testament

rather than the New Testament that Constantine finds models for
his vocation and activity.

According to Eusebius the covenantal religion has a strong
materialist base: 'This One, the Supreme Sovereign, our triumphant
sovereign himself praises to us, having fully perceived in Him the
cause of his empire.'[10] Neither marriage into the house of Hercules
nor birth into the royal house of the Sun gave Constantine any
prospect of capturing the Empire. It was delivered to him by the
God of his personal covenant. But what was Constantine's role in
this success story? Certainly not that of a humble man who rejected
the aid of legions of angels. No, but still, the role is strangely
familiar. Constantine in his day was the fulfilment of the promise of
God to send a king like David to save his people. It is this model, so
powerful and so pre-Christian, that best describes Constantine's
role. The Logos conducts a battle with spiritual powers, while 'His
friend, armed against his enemies with standards from Him above,
subdues and chastizes the visible opponents of truth by the law of
combat' (II.86). Religion of covenant: religion of crusade. The king
like David came to mean the Messiah, and as we have seen, this is
the role of Constantine in the perspective of his new religion.
Happily for him his enemies are God's enemies, and their defeat is
not simply good business but righteousness.

As in patriarchal times, the reward is longevity; God 'bestows on
him additional long periods of rule' (III.86). The language is almost
that of an insurance policy: 'increasing the benefits in return for the
rites paid Him' (III.86). By the time of his Jubilee the Emperor is
not quite so active, but there is the patriarchal reward of his sons,
who now take over the daily chores. But still, the Empire is ruled by
one monarch and not by four. In this respect also, Constantine
marks a return to earlier times, the theocratic state which Israel saw
dramatically justified in the time of David. Nor will it do to say that
the ancient world knew no other model. In the time of the Republic
Rome deliberately closed the door to monarchy because of the evils
which seemed inevitably to attend it. And Constantine himself had
grown up in the Empire under the tetrarchy. No, it is appropriate
that Constantine, a king like David, should restore not only monarchy but theocracy: the King in heaven and the king on earth.

Of course Constantine as Messiah goes far beyond David as
Messiah. This is true at a material and military level. But David was
a flawed hero, not least in the matter of morals. By contrast
Constantine displays divine virtues.

Above care for money, stronger than the passion for women,

victor of physical pleasures and demands, the conqueror, not the captive, of ill-temper and wrath, this man truly is the Autokrator, bearing the title that conforms to his moral conduct (V.89).

Bring back David, one might say, but if Constantine seems too good to be true, then that also serves Eusebius' presentation of the sovereign as more than mortal man. His reward is not simply longevity, for God lengthens his reign, 'and extends it even into far distant eternity' (VI.91). Once again, this is the culmination of covenantal religion.

Constantine is therefore a messianic figure, but the hopes for the Messiah reflected the changing circumstances of the Jews. By the time of the writing of the book of Daniel in the second century BC it was clear that no earthly warrior, even one like David, could overcome the power of evil which was represented by the Seleucid empire under Antiochus IV. The Messiah would have to overcome evil in both it spiritual and material forms. This is illustrated in the apocalyptic works of the inter-testamental period.

> And as for the lion whom you saw rousing up out of the forest and roaring and speaking to the eagle and reproving him for his unrighteousness, and as for all his words that you have heard, this is the Messiah whom the Most High has kept until the end of days, who will arise from the posterity of David, and will come and speak to them; he will denounce them for their ungodliness and for their wickedness, and will cast up before them their contemptuous dealings.[11]

It is this combination of Davidic and Levitical Messiah which Eusebius uses in describing the person and work of Constantine, who leads the people into righteousness by his own example, 'calling in a great voice that all can hear and proclaiming for everyone on earth the laws of genuine piety' (II.86). As the power of evil increased in the world, sectarian Judaism anticipated the final confrontation with the Messiah. Eusebius applies their eschatological account of their times to the circumstances which faced Constantine at the beginning of his rule. It is a situation in which mankind is becoming insane in its madness for strange gods, gods that reduce life to sensuousness, even gods of death. Like an apocalyptic writer he paints a picture of a world which is on a downward spiral to destruction. 'In such a situation, what had the Sovereign of the oppressed to do?' (VII.96). In such desperate straits the apocalyptic faith called on God to send forth his Messiah. Like some pro-

grammed war-machine the Messiah would be unleashed upon the
unsuspecting world.

> And then, stretching out His right hand for requital of His
> enemies, He eliminated them with a single nod, avenging Himself
> with heaven-sent blows and forcing them, even against their wills,
> to recite their crimes with their own lips (VII.96f.).

Four centuries later than expected, yet God at last sent forth his
agent to defeat his enemies and those that persecuted his faithful
few. But the conflict was now at a level inconceivable to David, and
the Messiah was hardly a mortal man, the 'invincible warrior'. Yet
the Levitical note is also struck, for in defeating the enemies of God,
this victor overcomes evil not by destruction of the evil doer but
with salvation: he 'even saved the godless, to teach them to live
piously' (VII.97). The 'prefect of the Supreme Sovereign' (VII.97)
overturned their gods and led the people to the truth. For the sake
of righteousness, not to mention his treasury, Constantine, like a
latter-day Moses, melted down their gods. Like a latter-day Elijah,
the sovereign is a religious empiricist. He, too, can demonstrate the
power of his God in defeating his enemies. And as David settled in
Jerusalem and made it a capital worthy of his new Empire, so did
Constantine choose the unlikely backwater of Byzantium to transform it into the wonder of the age. But David at least carried, in
good time, the ark of the Lord God to grace his capital: here was
guaranteed the presence of God. Well, Constantine was not short of
such a religious symbol when he entered Rome:

> he proclaimed to all men the Victory-Bringing Sign and erected
> in the midst of the ruling city this great trophy against all enemies,
> this explicit and indestructible salutary Sign of the Roman Empire
> and safeguard of the Universal Kingdom (IX.99).

Of course we are not suggesting that there is any conscious effort to
present Constantine in an Old Testament guise, yet there are many
features about his religion and his own role which take us back to
another age, before Christ. But this is no regression to another time;
rather, it is the fulfilment of covenantal religion and above all the
outworking, after four centuries of waiting, of the prophecies
concerning the coming of the Messiah. They longed for the kingdom.
Now dawns the age of lasting peace after decades of strife. Now
breaks forth, on a world of darkness and despair, the light of truth
and the hope of those who waited upon the Lord. The religion of
Constantine is as pre-Christian as it is anti-Christian.

2   Anti-Christian

It might be thought that if Constantine is seen fulfilling the expectations of the Jews in the inter-testamental period, then in some sense he also bears witness to the coming of Christ. This would certainly be a very convoluted process. In the Gospels, John the Baptist is presented as such a witness and forerunner, but he at least was born before Jesus. It would be a very odd witness who was born almost three centuries later. But perhaps it could at least be argued that Constantine would belong within the same tradition, fulfilling at a later date some further expectations not fulfilled in Jesus. But this is to assume that Jesus fulfils and does not contradict such expectations. Historically Christianity emerged from Judaism and claimed to be the fulfilment of many of the expectations of the Jews. But the fact that it emerged indicates also that some aspects of Christianity marked a radical departure from Judaism. What we are examining now is the possibility that Constantine is continuous with precisely those elements in Judaism which Christianity rejected. This should come as no surprise, since in Chapter III we saw that Constantine was represented as a Messianic figure and that in the process Christ was set aside. To be more precise, we might say that Constantine more obviously fulfilled the messianic expectations, at least of the sectarian Jews, than did Jesus. There is a marked contrast between the picture of Constantine, the king like David, and the figure of Jesus, whom the church believed to be the Messiah.

In fact the comparison between the two figures seems to favour Constantine in every respect. Eusebius stands in the presence of the emperor, to praise him as the one chosen by God to save his people. Jesus has no place on this occasion. If we insist that the comparison takes place, then he stands in the court in such a way as to recall the trial before Pilate or the appearance before Herod. This is surely not the Messiah upon whom the hopes of the Jews depended. The contrast is more striking since the king is in fact the successor of the very Caesar who appointed Pilate. Eusebius holds that monarchy derives from God and subjects should therefore recognize in the monarch the will of God (III.87). Those who offend the law of Caesar would, on this view, deserve their fate. The perspective of Eusebius is that of the king and not that of the accused.

God's saving purpose is fulfilled through the sovereign, who exercises kingly power. This is his 'divine calling'. This contrasts in every respect with the calling of Jesus, which leads him away from the little that he had in Nazareth. And if some of his followers thought that his vocation was to be the Messiah in the traditional sense, the sense now protrayed so gloriously in Constantine, then John's Gospel disabuses us of such a view. 'Perceiving then that they were about to come and take him by force to make him king, Jesus withdrew again to the hills by himself.'[12]

And if truth be told, which one looks more like a Messiah? Is it Constantine, born to the purple, who wears his rich robes easily as one who has never doubted his right to them? Or is it the son of the carpenter who, while being tortured and used for sport by the soldiers after his arrest, was made to wear a royal robe because it was so incongruous? Who looks more the part of the king who fulfils the longing for a successor to David? Surely it is the emperor in his court, surrounded by the evidences of wealth, rather than one who can only say, 'Foxes have holes, and birds of the air have nests; but the son of man has nowhere to lay his head'?[13]

There is also the question of those who attend the king. On the one hand there is the sovereign, lord of the Empire, commander of the army, surrounded by 'his entourage of attendants, the myriads of his armies, the subservient and obedient multitudes of heavy-armed men both on foot and on horse alike . . .' (V.90). On the other hand there is Jesus, with his little band of disciples drawn from diverse backgrounds, but with this in common: that none comes from the military or the ruling class. On this comparison Constantine seems more in keeping with the picture of a king like David. But the situation is, if anything, worse. It is not that Jesus is the ruler of a little insignificant band, at least a large fish in a small pond. Apparently his relationship to his small band is quite the opposite to Constantine's relationship to his subjects. Jesus instructed his disciples in quite a different order. 'The kings of the Gentiles exercise lordship over them; and those in authority over them are called benefactors. But not so with you; rather let the greatest among you become as the youngest, and the leader as one who serves.'[14]

Jesus will not even act as a king towards his own followers. 'If any one would be first, he must be last of all and servant of all.'[15] Fine words: very unlike the words of a Messiah, but fine and noble sentiments none the less. Worse is to follow: Jesus then acts out the words, when 'he rose from supper, laid aside his garments, and girded himself with a towel. Then he poured water into a basin, and began to wash the disciples' feet, and to wipe them with the towel with which he was girded.'[16] The contrast here is not between two kingly figures distinguished only by the numbers of their followers, the wealth of their possessions or the extent of their power. If Constantine is anti-Christian, it is because he is the kind of Messiah who was steadfastly rejected by Jesus and the early church.

But there is no doubt that the most marked contrast between Constantine and Jesus concerns combat. We have already noted that Constantine seems to fulfil the expectations of that covenantal religion which looked for a military leader like David. When times were bad, the Jews looked for a king like David to deliver them. When times were much worse, they knew that even such a king was of no avail: it must be a larger-than-life king, the chosen agent of God. This apocalyptic longing is fulfilled in the coming of Constantine, who 'subdues and chastises the visible opponents of truth by the law of combat' (II.86). This is what they looked for as the world became more deeply under the influence of evil, as the faithful were persecuted even to death. Then God sent his Messiah. But which Messiah? 'These things the Supreme Sovereign enacted from heaven when He put forth an invincible warrior as His attendant . . .' (VIII.97). They cried to God for such a Messiah and he was sent, if three centuries later. And according to such covenantal religion, the Messiah gains his reward: more than any mortal could have dreamed of, reaching into eternity itself. Indeed, so well does Constantine fulfil the expectations and fit the picture of the Messiah, it is almost embarrassing to turn to Jesus as the Messiah. He has no sword in his hand, nor army at his disposal. His coming could hardly be described as God 'stretching out His right hand for requital of His enemies . . .' (VII.96). In their suffering they cried for a deliverer: Jesus came and suffered even more than most. Constantine's life is a success story: by comparison the life of Jesus must be counted defeat. The symbol of Constantine's life is the labarum, through which he brought terror to his enemies and freedom to his subjects. The symbol of Jesus, however, is a cross. Not a highly polished and beautifully worked masterpiece of a silversmith, grand enough to grace the neck of a prince of the church attending a royal banquet. No, a device which brought to the victim degradation, humiliation and such agony hour after hour that death must have seemed a welcome door to a better place. A device which brought terror to those who might have sympathized with him for a time, lest they share his fate.

But we must not see these two pictures of the Messiah as complementary in any sense. They are in stark contrast. Constantine is the culmination of that covenantal religion which hoped for a king like David, a warrior whose power, even ferocity, would increase in direct proportion to the grip of evil around the necks of the righteous. We have been declaring Constantine anti-Christian in that he fulfils a vision which Christians rejected. The Messiah, according to the church, does not succeed as did Constantine: he is defeated, in

Constantine's terms. And if to the eyes of faith he has the victory in the end, then it is by a route and to a goal which is completely and irrevocably alien to everything that is represented in the Constantinian Messiah.

Military might separates the two models of Messiah, but once again we must see that it is not the distinction between the king of a great army and the king of a small band. The distinction goes deeper until the two are incompatible. Historically the contrast is dramatically exemplified in the torture and execution of Jesus. Was he treated thus because he lacked a few bodyguards? The attempt by a friend at Gethsemane was insufficient to prevent his arrest. However, more fundamental is the rejection by Jesus of such a course of action.

> Then Jesus said to him, 'Put your sword back into its place; for all who take the sword will perish by the sword. Do you think that I cannot appeal to my Father, and he will at once send me more than twelve legions of angels?'[17]

Indeed the contrast between the two images of Messiah is further sharpened when the early church used the military metaphor to describe their faith.

> Finally, be strong in the Lord and in the strength of his might. Put on the whole armour of God, that you may be able to stand against the wiles of the devil.[18]

The military image is the more intriguing to the writer precisely because the military option itself is not open.

> Therefore take the whole armour of God, that you may be able to withstand in the evil day, and having done all, to stand. Stand therefore, having girded your loins with truth, and having put on the breastplate of righteousness and having shod your feet with the equipment of the gospel of peace; above all taking the shield of faith, with which you can quench all the flaming darts of the evil one. And take the helmet of salvation, and the sword of the Spirit, which is the word of God.[19]

Eusebius recalls this metaphor of the *milites christi* when he remembers those who were persecuted for righteousness sake, before the coming of Constantine: 'as soldiers of God, they fortified their hearts with virtue, and held laughable every manner of death . . .' (VII.96). They refuse to kill other people: does that make them cowards? They refuse to betray their Lord: does that make them guilty of treason? In face of such accusations the church calls them 'soldiers of Christ', the force of the metaphor being in the refusal to be like a soldier of Caesar. They have their orders and their equipment, 'the breastplate of faith and love, and for a helmet the hope of salvation.'[20]

It is therefore not surprising, but quite inappropriate, when Eusebius applies the metaphor to his sovereign.

> But he, fortified with the armour of piety, arrayed against the multitude of his foes the Saving and Life-Giving Sign like some safeguard and shield against evils, and gained a victory over his enemies and the spirits alike (IX.99).

The striking, dramatic image of the church is that those who wear no helmet risk all for their Lord. Those who have no sword or shield to protect them go forth to meet death as those invulnerable to blows. It is totally inappropriate to use the image of one who goes out to kill and maim, wearing the best armour of the age. Paul speaks to Christians as he goes in chains, not chain-mail. Once again we note that the contrast locates Constantine in a position not only anti-Christian, but pre-Christian. He is the instrument of God: it is not his faith which wins him the victory. The victory is won by sword and sinew. Here is the faith not of the church but of the Psalmist: 'O sing to the Lord a new song, for he has done marvellous things! His right hand and his holy arm have gotten him victory.'[21] As we shall see, Constantine's victory was over the church and its Christ.

X

THE GREAT REVERSAL

From our discussion we have concluded that Constantine was not a Christian, indeed that his religion was actually anti-Christian. If we adopt the view of the editors of the Theodosian Code and take religion to be a rather peripheral issue for the Emperor, then this conclusion might seem to have little significance. However, religion was not simply a personal or private matter for Constantine. It is at this point that we must examine in more detail the function of religion not only with regard to motivating and legitimizing Constantine, but also in the social and cultural unification of the Empire. In other words, we must examine the ways in which religion performed an ideological function for Constantine. If the religion of Constantine is profoundly anti-Christian, it is not simply at a dogmatic level, but rather because at an ideological level it expresses values which are anti-Christian. In this chapter we shall consider the mechanism by which religion comes to perform its ideological function within Constantine's imperial strategy. In the next we shall look more closely at the values which make it incompatible with Christianity. And finally, we shall look at the most ominous question of all, the extent to which the Christian church was influenced by Constantine and came to substitute his values for its own. Christ omitted: Christ denied.

1   Reflection or Projection

In 1933 Norman Baynes declared that scholars had not paid to the oration 'In Praise of Constantine' the attention which it properly deserved.[1] Right though Baynes was, it is clear that even he failed to take seriously enough the extraordinary claims made for Constantine in the text. His attention was focused upon that constant feature of the ancient world, the intertwining of the religious and the political. He claimed that the oration was the first clear statement of the political philosophy of the new Christian Empire.

> The basis of that political philosophy is to be found in the conception of the imperial government as a terrestrial copy of the rule of God in Heaven; there is one God and one divine law, therefore there must be on earth but one ruler and a single law. That ruler, the Roman emperor, is the Viceregent of the Christian God.[2]

We have dealt with this already in Chapter II, in the section 'Model Sovereign', where we learned of 'the all-pervasive Logos of God, from whom and through whom bearing the image of the higher kingdom, the sovereign dear to God, in imitation of the Higher Power, directs the helm and sets straight all things on earth'.[3] The reflection is unflawed, and 'outfitted in the likeness of the kingdom of heaven he pilots affairs below with an upward gaze, to steer by the archetypal form' (III.87). God has 'modelled the kingdom on earth into a likeness of the one in heaven . . .' (IV.88). Baynes sees, of course, that this presentation does not come from biblical or Christian thought, and he suggests that Eusebius has here borrowed from the Hellenistic philosophy of kingship. There were different strands, but they find echoes in the oration. Plutarch says that God has set a fair image of himself in the heavens, the sun, and also on earth a similar *mimema*, namely the king, in so far as the king seeks to be guided by the Logos. The wise king models himself upon the heavenly Logos. Ecphantus held that the Logos was incarnate in the true king, giving him power to help and to save his people. The king is the shepherd of his subjects. His virtuous activity is a *mimesis* of divine virtue.

According to Baynes, the oration shows us how Eusebius has christianized this line of thought, adapting to his purpose. Diotogenes saw the king as a god among men. Eusebius sees this particular king as the viceregent of God. Diotogenes held that the state is a *mimesis* of the cosmos. Eusebius converts this sentiment to imitation of the kingdom of heaven. For Diotogenes the Logos supports and empowers the king. For Eusebius the Christian king is inspired by Christ the Logos. 'Was it indeed thus that the scholarship of Eusebius was employed to fashion the political philosophy of the Byzantine world?[4] Well, Yes and No. To the question of political legitimation we shall return in a moment. But first let us look more closely at the model of *mimesis* or imitation. We have seen in Chapter II how Eusebius repeated the model of imitation, and to this extent Baynes was correct. But in Chapter III we saw that Eusebius was certainly not concerned to christianize the model. It would be truer to say that Eusebius simply took over the Hellenistic philosophy of kingship: he did not present the Logos as Christ. Indeed Christ is not only set aside for the moment, but permanently excluded. And this brings us to the consequences of the imitation – whether we attribute the model to Eusebius or to Constantine himself.

In order to see the consequences it is instructive to turn to a relatively modern parallel. The Hellenistic philosophy referred to goes back to Plato and his theory of Forms, or Ideas.

> The Platonic Idea is the pure, archetypal essence, in which those things which are subsumed under the same concept, participate. Aesthetically and ethically, it is the perfect in its kind, to which the given reality remains perpetually inferior. Logically and ontologically considered, it is the object of the concept.[5]

Well, that seems clear enough. Thus all instances of justice may be more or less just as they participate in the Idea or Form of Justice, and imitate it. Plato actually uses the term *mimesis*. Thus the never quite perfect kingdom on earth reflects the True Kingdom in heaven; the mortal king, if guided by the wisdom of the Logos, reflects the perfect King in Heaven. Logically as well as ontologically: we understand kingship because of the Idea of Kingship, not because of the rather flawed examples of it here on earth. This is the powerful tradition of Idealism, and it has been suggested (with the brash confidence of an examination question which invites a critique) that Western philosophy is simply a series of footnotes on Plato. On this view Hegel's system of Absolute Idealism must be counted a rather extensive note. But in this sytem we find the same pattern of thought. Hegel was concerned with the developing consciousness of Spirit, 'a process in which an object yields up a universal meaning or unifying pattern of which it is an instance.'[6]

> For there to be consciousness of something, that thing must to some extent depart from the mutual externality of existence in time and space, and from the hard definiteness of sense. It must declare itself as a case of some general kind, of which no case is perhaps an adequate embodiment: it must align itself with other objects in a connected picture governed by some unifying rule.[7]

What Plato and Hegel have in common here is the assumption that the phenomenal world is not self-explanatory: the mundane is to be understood when it is seen as an example, imperfect example (imitation/*mimesis*), of that which can be conceived of, but never fully encountered. That is the essence of Idealism, and it is not difficult to understand its powerful, even hypnotic attraction for the human mind, in the midst of a world of flux, chance and change. And it has been of fundamental importance in European history that this idealist assumption corresponds to the religious premise that the world is understood only *sub specie aeternitatis,* from the perspective of heaven. 'Hegel developed his ideas, not so much in reaction to the opinion of philosophers, as in deep ponderings on the meaning of the Christian religion . . .'[8] It is for this reason that critical social theory in the nineteenth century confronted Idealism indirectly, through its critique of religion.

The attack was first mounted in 1830 in an essay by Ludwig Feuerbach, entitled 'Thoughts on Death and Immortality'. Almost inevitably the most perceptive criticism of Hegel came from a one-time disciple. The intention of the essay was 'To cancel above all the old cleavage between this side and the beyond in order that humanity might concentrate on itself, its world and its present with all its heart and soul'.[9] In this and his magnum opus *The Essence of Christianity,* Feuerbach seemed to substitute a materialist anthropology for a religious idealism. This is not the place to give an account of Feuerbach's overlapping theories of religion, but we must pay particular attention to his projection theory.

> Man – this is the mystery of religion – projects his being into objectivity, and then again makes himself an object of this projected image of himself, thus converted into a subject.[10]

We might refer to this as the Great Reversal. It is Feuerbach's critique of religion: man creates God in his own image. Or rather, man selects those aspects of the life of mankind (the species as it was then called) which he most admires and values, and projects them away from himself. Thus objectified and alienated they stand over against man. Their creator then 'forgets' that he made them. They appear more real and enduring than the experience of any individual. The critique of religion is also his critique of Hegel, and of course it was Feuerbach who taught Marx how to stand Hegel on his head. The whole system of Absolute Idealism, which had seemed itself so objective and enduring, was shown in an instant to be a socially constructed reality. Feuerbach had demonstrated that what had been taken to be revelation from above, was in fact projection from below. Religion tells us nothing about another world, but tells us indirectly about man and his self-consciousness. 'By his God thou knowest the man, and by the man his God . . .'[11] It was left to Marx to extend the critique of religion into a broad critique of Hegel's philosophy and on to an analysis of politics and economics. Critical philosophy began with religion because the same pattern of reversal found in religion pervaded the whole of society. 'This state, this society, produce religion, an *inverted world consciousness,* because they are an *inverted world*'.[12] The point is not whether Feuerbach and Marx are to be followed in their conclusions, but rather that in this theoretical analysis they do uncover an unconscious movement in the social construction of reality.[13] For example, it is not necessary to assume the truth of atheism in order to recognize that the understanding (or doctrine) of God in any society at a given time is influenced or determined by the view of man in that stage of cultural development.

And this brings us back to Norman Baynes and Eusebius' oration. Baynes claims that Eusebius has made use of, and adapted, the Hellenistic model of *mimesis*: the king is an imitation, a reflection of the King in heaven. But *mimesis* here is actually based on Platonic idealism. In the light of our discussion of Feuerbach we must enquire whether the Great Reversal applies to Plato as to Hegel. Are we dealing with revelation or projection? If indeed we are confronted by an imitation, who is imitating whom? In the oration, are we dealing with a reflection in which all is 'on earth as it is in heaven'? Or to the contrary, and probably unconsciously, are we presented with the precise reversal of this model, in which all is 'in heaven as it is on earth'? In other words, does the use of the model of *mimesis* simply have the effect of legitimizing the actions of the sovereign and deifying his values?

2   In Heaven as on Earth

As we have already noted, the subject of the oration is the relationship of the Sovereign and the sovereign. It is as well before Eusebius is launched into full flight to make the prosaic point that the audience for the oration is the sovereign, surrounded by his court: that side of the equation is objectively there. But Eusebius is soon to speak of 'the Highest Sovereign and the holy escort'.[14] Clearly this way of speaking about God and the heavenly hosts is inspired by the company gathered for the festival. Idealism speaks as if in this equation the Sovereign was known, and the oration is to bring out the true but as yet unknown nature of the sovereign. But in the face of the Great Reversal it would be more realistic to say that the sovereign is well enough known, too well to some. It is the Sovereign who is unknown. The question, which has as much ideological as theological significance, is whether the equation works in the other direction. Is the true nature of the Sovereign clarified by looking at the sovereign? We shall see that the unknown Sovereign is gradually coloured in the hues of the earthly sovereign.

The oration gets under way with praise first of all to God, 'whose kingdom's throne is the vault of the heavens above, while the earth is footstool for His feet' (I.84). He is encircled by 'celestial armies', secure 'within the royal halls'. The sun and moon stand 'like torchbearers at the palace doors' (I.84). This is not imitation but projection. And so it continues: 'armies of angels', 'petitions', 'first rank' and even the term 'kingdom' (I.85), all combine to re-enforce that heaven, which no man has seen, is very much like earth, provided the appropriate spot on earth is chosen, i.e. the imperial court in the presence of the Emperor. When we hear that he imitates the 'Governor of the entire cosmos' (I.85), what we gather from this is that the unknown Logos is a higher version of the sovereign. When we are invited to consider the crusading victories of the Emperor, this image is then magnified to help us understand the counterpart of this crusade above the earth. The models of earth are used to illuminate the heavens: the 'Ruler of All' designates the sovereign 'Victor'. The Logos is 'Supreme Commander' and 'heavenly armies encircle Him, an infinite number of supernatural troops' (III.87).

And now Eusebius lays on his audience a significant problem.

> But how came it to man to perceive these things? Who brought them to human hearing? How can matters that are not of flesh and the body be elucidated by a tongue of flesh? Who has seen the invisible Sovereign and beheld these powers in Him?' (IV.88).

But there is no mystery. The answer is quite simple: projection. Eusebius has not had these things supernaturally revealed to him, nor has he as in a theophany beheld the Sovereign who is invisible. No, he has looked upon the known and the visible and projected them into objectivity. It is not that by a cosmic alchemy the sovereign takes the form of the Sovereign. Rather, by simple projection, the Sovereign takes on the form of the sovereign, though of course much enlarged. We are not here discussing the existence of God, but how God is conceived of, the actions attributed to him and the values which are to be regarded as divine.

This, then, is the model for the oration. In keeping with the Jubilee celebrations, the subject is of the relationship of the Sovereign and the sovereign. The title, 'In Praise of Constantine', would suggest that the panegyrist is congratulating the Emperor on being conformed to the model of divine Sovereign. But in the light of the Great Reversal we must look more closely to determine the grounds of congratulation. As we have already seen in Chapters II and III, Constantine is to be congratulated in that through his relationship to God he has personally gained great rewards, may expect even greater in the life to come, has brought unity and harmony to the Empire and, without immodesty, may be said to have saved the world. But on the specific point of *mimesis*, what is added to this accolade? The answer has already been hinted at when we noted that the Sovereign/sovereign equation is as much ideological and theological. To give an example, leaving Constantine aside for the moment, if a king should come to power by force of arms, by plotting the death of his rivals, executing them and their families and taking it upon himself to reorganize the lives of the people of his new lands, then in imitation (*mimesis*) of this a new pretender might at any time attempt to wrest from him the throne with all its power and privilege. What is there to silence the voice of any rebellion or stay the sword of ambition? Well, of course, there is the king's army and his system of informers. But these provide no guarantees and are rather expensive to run. A much more effective and cheaper form of protection is provided by religious legitimation. The young pretender does no more than imitate the king when he hacks his way towards the throne. But what if the king is the imitation of God? In more religious times than ours this doctrine of *mimesis* had the power to turn back the sword and even subdue the murmur of conspiracy. In the course of praising Constantine for his imitation of the divine Sovereign, Eusebius uses his position as bishop and ecclesiastical scholar to bestow religious legitimation not only upon the Emperor, but on the manner of his rule.

The first task which Eusebius sets himself in this respect is to challenge the apparently arbitrary nature of monarchy, the relativity of this form of government. He first of all links the sovereign to the natural order. To do this he propounds a natural theology:

> the entire species of mankind in general, people of every race, shape and tongue, all in common alike and individually, though divided in their opinion on other matters, agree on this alone, calling on the One and Only God with an inbred logic, a self-taught and self-learned knowledge (IV.88).

The natural world also bears witness to its maker, displaying that inherent rationality and order that comes from the Logos,

> from whom and through whom, bearing the image of the higher kingdom, the sovereign dear to God, in imitation of the Higher Power, directs the helm and sets straight all things on earth (I.85).

The *mimesis* is here the bridge by which the sovereign becomes part of the eternal and natural order of things. But more than that, the salvation of the world is part of that divine scheme of things. The work of the Logos is not simply to make men rational, but to make them capable of responding to God's redeeming call. In imitation, the sovereign,

> like some interpreter of the Logos of God, summons the whole human race to knowledge of the Higher Power, calling in a great voice that all can hear and proclaiming for everyone on earth the laws of genuine piety (II.86).

The Emperor is part of the natural order and part of the scheme of salvation for the world. In this he passes from the realm of the contingent to the necessary. But Eusebius also hints at a point to which he will return: the laws of the Emperor are part of that necessary scheme of salvation.

Lest we lose sight of the wood for the trees, let us be reminded of what is happening. It is apparently imitation, by which what goes on on earth reflects what is the case in heaven. This is the first stage. The second stage in our analysis is to point out that through the Great Reversal we are seeing not reflection, but projection. By this objectification, what is the case in heaven is actually an idealized version of what is going on on earth. But in religious legitimation we see the third and final stage. Now what goes on on earth is proclaimed as necessary, rational and just because it is patterned on heaven. Yet as we have just seen, what is the case in heaven is actually patterned on earth. So that the effect of religious legitimation here is, under guise of pointing a reverent finger upwards, to advocate unquestioned acceptance of whatever the Emperor is and does. Since 'God's laws' in this case are simply projections of the king's laws, it is merely a disguised tautology to claim that the king's laws should be accepted because they are modelled on God's laws.

Eusebius in the Oration rings the changes on these two themes, the legitimation of monarchy, in particular *this* monarch, and the legitimation of the rule of law, in particular *these* laws of Constantine. A minor variation is when he legitimizes the house of Constantine, as a dynasty. Naturally the Emperor declined to return to the old tetrarchy, from which he himself had emerged, and which could only be a training ground for rebellion. He appointed his own sons as the Caesars. Well, not quite, since this would mean they were simply appointed by a man, albeit the saviour of the universe. God himself has blessed the Emperor with assistants, having readied some one of his sons for partnership in the royal throne at each tenth anniversary, as if to prolong the bloom of a flourishing plant (III.87).

And now Eusebius addresses himself directly to the question of the legitimation of monarchy as such. The tetrarchy has been set aside, not simply for tactical reasons, but for theological reasons.

He grows strong in his model of monarchic rule, which the Ruler of All has given to the race of man alone of those on earth (III.87).

Is this argument incredibly dated, especially to those who are fortunate enough to enjoy an alternative system of government which unfailingly produces quite outstanding leaders every four years? It was not incredible to the Anglican theologian F. D. Maurice writing of such matters in the mid-nineteenth century. Let us digress for a moment to consider Torben Christensen's summary of Maurice's position.

Monarchy and aristocracy thus belonged to the Divine Order. To abolish them and introduce Democracy, which Maurice always understood as the government of self-will, was consequently tantamount to denying God and His constituted universe and robbing men of the witness of the unchangeable laws in God's dealing with mankind.[15]

No one was attempting to abolish monarchy in the time of Eusebius, but he was intent on establishing absolute monarchy. However, Christensen's account of Maurice brings out clearly the basic argument and what is held to be at stake. It will be of no surprise to readers to learn that Maurice was a Platonist. Eusebius underlines his point.

Monarchy excels all other kinds of constitution and government. For rather do anarchy and civil war result from the alternative, a polyarchy based on equality. For which reason there is One God, not two or three or even more (III.87).

This line of argument, while important, cannot be pursued here.[16]

Eusebius turns now to his other theme: one God and therefore one law. 'There is one Sovereign, and His Logos and royal law is one . . .'(II.87). There is a happy ambiguity here by which those who heard the oration would make the identification of God's laws not written on tablets of stone, and the imperial laws which imitate them. The section ends with a similar association of ideas. The Logos 'has provided a model of the royal power' (III.88) to man.

He alone is strong in real strength, and the Parent of Justice itself, the Father of Reason and Wisdom, the Source of light and life, the Holder of Truth and Virtue, and so the Leader of the Empire itself, and of every form of rule and power (III.88).

The tetrarchy has gone because there is but one God. Monarchy exists in imitation of the rule of heaven. Every form of rule and power on earth reflects the reason, wisdom, truth and virtue of the rule of heaven. But as we have seen via the Great Reversal and religious legitimation, this argument tells us nothing about heaven. It simply gives *carte blanche* to the Emperor to rule as he rules and to call it just.

So we come from a slightly different direction to Eusebius' treatment of a mystery. 'But how came it to man to perceive these things?' Eusebius is arguing for the acceptance of monarchy, absolute monarchy, and the justice of imperial laws. But his argument is not on practical grounds or in terms of efficiency. Man accepts these things (or so the orator would like to believe) as natural, as part of the eternal order of things, not simply as expedients or contingent arrangements. Now, says Eusebius, this surely is a mystery.

'So how did the concepts of legitimate authority and royal power ever penetrate men's minds? How does the principle of autocracy occur to solid flesh and blood? Who made known to those on earth Ideas, which are invisible and formless, or Essence, incorporeal and shapeless?' (IV.88).

This is the thoroughly Platonic theory of Forms and Ideas. Men accept these things because they are imitations of their eternal counterparts in heaven. The mystery is solved: the Logos has revealed them on earth. And for those who trust less in concepts and theories, the Logos has of course provided a material expression, namely the sovereign and his just laws. That is what Eusebius would like to think, but we have seen that the Great Reversal suggests that if in the fourth century men accepted these things – and if they did, why was Eusebius arguing at such length to justify them? – it was through projection, not revelation; through religious legitimation, not actual imitation. To conclude the argument, Eusebius slips in a rather neat point at the end. Man has been made *logikos* and recognizes the legitimacy of monarchy and imperial laws, but the mark of those instructed by the Logos is to know 'how to rule and be ruled' (IV.88). Previously the oration has been about the sovereign, the tendency to alienate him from other men, but now the rest of the audience is brought into the scheme. What have they been inspired to do? To know how to be ruled! Is this through fear of loss or greed for gain? No, they play their part in the eternal order by being loyal subjects of the sovereign.

The question of loyalty of course is intensified in this context. Heinrich Heine went so far as to suggest that Kant's linking of ethics and a rational faith in God was inspired by the attitude of the Prussian police towards freethinkers, that is 'whoever tears himself away from his God will sooner or later break with his earthly superiors too'.[17] But in our context, the reverse is Eusebius' point: to break with Constantine is to break with God. And as for a pretender, no one would merit the title 'true sovereign' who did not have the virtues of Constantine. But from the Great Reversal we can see the circularity of that argument. No one must dare to replace Constantine since this would be to break with God. Why, because by projection and religious legitimation only one who acts as Constantine does displays the divine virtues: only 'this man truly is Autokrator'. So Eusebius weaves the argument: Monarchy, this monarch, loyalty to this monarchy, no alternative to him. 'He alone deserves to wear the royal purple which so becomes him' (V.89).

Does this virtuous sovereign have armies to protect him, servants to wait upon him at all times? Are his clothes of finest materials, heavy with the crustations of precious metals? Yes, but all these things are quite distinct from his life, like a modern pious prelate who owns absolutely nothing, not even his chauffeur driven car, and certainly not the jet plane which takes him wherever he wishes to go.

One final point might be added, because not all who live within the Empire have the capacity to understand the philosophy of Eusebius, or the patience to attend to his convoluted oration. For them there is something which gathers up theory and gives it objective, visible expression, namely the labarum. No mass movement can succeed without such a tangible symbol. Did Constantine rebel against his legally constituted rulers, did he reach the throne by hacking, maiming and killing those who stood in his way? It remains only for Eusebius to offer a religious legitimation of Constantine's path to the monarchy. It was not the war of an adventurer, but the crusade of a saint. Did he act simply from uncontrollable ambition? No, 'these things the Supreme Sovereign enacted from heaven when He put forth an invincible warrior as His attendant' (VII.97). It was a crusade because it was conducted behind the labarum. And what of this strange device, neither cavalry standard nor religious artefact? Was it conceived of by chance one hot afternoon as Constantine lay in his tent doodling on a piece of

papyrus? Or was it the brilliant compromise which one of his astute
political advisers dreamed up as a public relations exercise? Perish
such unworthy thoughts! It was not devised by men, but written on
the clouds of heaven.

> Setting this victorious trophy, apotropaic of demons, against the
> idols of error, he has won victories over all his godless foes and
> barbarians (IX.99).

In this holy crusade the barbarians are simply identified, not as the
enemies of Rome, but the enemies of heaven. With a nudge and a
wink, did the tough centurions welcome the battles which brought
them land and booty? Not so Constantine.

> But he, fortified with the armor of piety, arrayed against the
> multitude of his foes the Saving and Life-giving Sign like some
> safeguard and shield against evils, and gained a victory over his
> enemies and the spirits alike (IX.99).

The oration 'In Praise of Constantine' might at first seem the sickly
sweet offering of a fawning panegyrist. If only it were as harmless as
that! As to religion, far from being Christian, it is incompatible with
Christianity. But its real purpose emerges as ideological rather than
theological. Eusebius through the model of imitation (*mimesis*)
praises Constantine as one who has put himself completely at God's
disposal and become in all things conformed to the will of God.
However, by the Great Reversal it is clear that something much
more subtle and insidious is going on in the text. It is not Constantine
who has been conformed to God, but rather what is attributed to
God is first found in Constantine. Long before Constantine's 'conversion', he had determined by any means possible to become sole
ruler of the Empire. Did that change when he associated himself
with the God of the Christians? No, the same project was now given
divine blessing. Long before his 'conversion' he had decided that
persecution was counter-productive. Did his conversion mean that
he was at the disposal of the church? Far from it; the church was
incorporated into his grand plan and became an instrument in his
unification of the Empire. But above all, what of his values? Was he
so changed at his 'conversion' that he now conducted himself
according to the will of God, as revealed in Jesus of Nazareth?
Under no circumstances. We have noted that in the oration Christ
is set aside and finally contradicted. With this we move to the most
important issue of all. If Constantine had been a Christian, even if
he had called himself a Christian, then we might have expected his
life and actions to have been conformed to the values of Jesus Christ.

Yet the evidence is that in this also Christ is set aside. At first sight this might seem a purely theological issue, and it will be discussed in the next chapter. But something more important is at stake. Through Eusebius' oration the values of Constantine are represented as being Christian. But in fact it is clear that Constantine's values did not change. Through the Great Reversal these values, which stand in contradiction to those of Christ in matters of wealth, power, ambition, personal relations, social organization and religion, are now assumed to be Christian values. It is in this way that European history is determined by the values of Constantine, as if they were the values of Christ. But this is the essence of ideology, that the underlying reality is the inversion of what appears to be the case.

XI

THE LABARUM OR THE CROSS

In the previous chapter we noted that the oration 'In Praise of Constantine', written to serve various purposes, is of more lasting significance for its ideology than its theology. While overtly dealing with religious matters, Eusebius legitimizes not only monarchy but the political values of Constantine. The hearer (now reader) is led unsuspectingly to identify the values of the sovereign with those of the Sovereign. Although the oration is not explicitly Christian, the effect on the church was to identify the values of Constantine with those of Christ, to assume that Christian values were manifest in the life and actions of the Emperor. We are not arguing that the values of Constantine should be rejected simply because they are not Christian; rather, it is important to distinguish his values from those of Christ. It would be one thing for European history to be guided by the values of Constantine rather than those of Christ. It would be quite another for it to be guided by those of Constantine, while mistakenly supposing that the two were the same. And most tragic of all would be if the church itself, following the argument of Eusebius, should take over the values of Constantine and thereby deny the values of Christ. Inconceivable though this might seem, it is in fact what has happened since the fourth century. We shall illustrate this in the next chapter, but in the present chapter we shall take time to contrast the values of Constantine and Christ, since whatever his religion, Constantine stood in contradiction to the fundamental teachings of Jesus of Nazareth.

1 Locus of Revelation

Everyone's experience is different, and in consequence it may well be that no two people believe the same things about something as complex as a developed religion. When experts gather to debate there are normally more positions than participants: why should we be surprised if Eusebius heralds for Constantine a religious position which is not orthodox? Should we be taken aback if the Emperor's religion focusses more on crusade than contemplation? But we are not dealing with minor eccentricities, nor is it the private affair of a humble citizen. It is the Emperor, and he is not being accused of wearing no religious clothes, but of wearing the uniform of the opposition.

Are we claiming more than this, that the religion of the soldier is less subtle than that of the theologian? In this case, however, the point is that the religion of Constantine was actually anti-Christian. It is not merely a less subtle religion than that of the Christian theologian; it is a religion which is squarely based on assumptions and values which were rejected by Christ. Constantine fulfilled that covenantal religion which was not only pre-Christian, but which formed the substance of the temptations overcome by Christ. From our previous study of the sources it would appear that we are actually dealing with two religions, or at least with two different revelations of God. Constantine is presented as the manifestation of God on earth. But this manifestation is not only different from Christ, but incompatible. Indeed, it yields a picture of God which is specifically denied by Christ's life and teaching. We must now spell out what is involved in these two revelations. Although it is in the first instance theology, through the Great Reversal the theology of Constantine provides an absolute legitimation for his own values. The tragedy would be if the Christian church were to take over the revelation of God which is claimed to have taken place in Constantine, and allow it to exclude the revelation in Christ.

What, then, is the picture of God revealed in the religion of Constantine, as enunciated by Eusebius? Eusebius describes the sufferings of the faithful who were brutally tortured and treated in bestial ways. 'In such a situation, what had the Sovereign of the oppressed to do? (VII,96). In covenant religion God has always sent a deliverer: Moses to the Hebrews, David to Israel, Cyrus to the Jews in exile, while to those suffering under the Seleucids he sent Judas Maccabaeus. And now in that great line comes Constantine.

> And then, stretching out His right hand for requital of His enemies, He eliminated them with a single nod, avenging Himself with heaven-sent blows and forcing them, even against their wills, to recite their crimes with their own lips (VII,96f.).

Indeed, one might wonder what justice there is when Hollywood has as yet failed to take up this truly epic narrative. As the screams of the persecuted ring out, so comes Constantine like the cavalry over the hill, to cut and thrust, to sever limbs and decapitate the unrighteous. The film would almost direct itself, so familiar are we with the general scenario. But one claim Eusebius makes for Constantine, not made for Moses, David, Cyrus, Judas Maccabaeus – or Charlton Heston for that matter – is that not only was Constantine God's instrument, but in the actions of Constantine, God is revealed. He is not simply the instrument, but the model. How does God act towards his enemies? He sends 'an invincible warrior' against them, to kill them.

That view has a long history in religion, though on inspection there are precious few examples of such interventions, given the almost constant oppression suffered by the righteous in any genera-tion. It may or may not be a credible religious faith, but at least one thing is certain, it has nothing to do with *Christian* faith. In the time of Jesus the faithful were also persecuted and the religion of the Jews was subject to constraints. 'In such a situation, what had the Sovereign of the oppressed· to do?' The Christian answer was, to send Jesus of Nazareth. To send 'Christ', we might say, as long as we remember that the content of the title 'Christ' was thereby com-pletely changed. Indeed, that change neatly summarizes the incom-patibility between the revelation in Constantine and the revelation in Jesus. What was God to do? Many people took Jesus for their enemy. Indeed those who were enemies seemed to be prepared to unite at least in their attempts to be rid of him.[1] But the Gospels do not suggest that Jesus saw anyone as an enemy. When Judas led the Temple guard to arrest Jesus in Gethsemane, Jesus addressed him not as one who was to bring him torture, humiliation and a terrible death, but with the title 'friend'.[2] According to Christ, although some people take God as their enemy, no one is an enemy of God. To believe this and act upon it is of course a matter of faith, but at least it is a genuine revelation. It is something new and not just a repetition of relationships on earth.

Two revelations: Constantine and Christ. In the case of Constan-tine, God is like the Emperor, only more so. Does the Emperor wage war on his enemies to destroy them? Then so does God. Does the Emperor carefully plan the downfall of his rivals and kill with them their families and followers? Then so does God. Revelation? But who needs such a revelation? It tells us nothing new about the world: it only confirms our worst fears that this is how things have always been and are likely to continue to be so. Is the Emperor jealous of his honour so that he will avenge himself at the first opportunity? Then so acts God, according to this revelation. But it is no real revelation at all. By the Great Reversal it is simply a way of legitimizing what Constantine does in any case. Of course the Christians who had recently suffered persecution might welcome such deliverance, rejoicing in the downfall of their persecutors. But is this action the intervention of God? Does God eliminate the opposition, or does he not forgive them, seventy-times-seven times?[3] There are certainly two incompatible positions here, but does Constantine really tell us anything that deserves the name revelation? Do his actions not simply confirm the observable law of every age and culture? Does it need to be called an epiphany of the invisible God before we recognize that the world is ruled by force and that the will of the powerful becomes the law of the land? Is this what the prophets risked all to proclaim? Is it for this truth that holy men and women allowed themselves to be parted from their families and to be killed in agony? Surely a 'revelation' should be declaring something more than an *apologia* for the grasping and exercising of power? If the king has power to rule, to pronounce judgment, to go to war and defeat his challengers, then apparently the King of kings has such power but infinitely so. And if this is 'revelation', that there is a God in heaven who is like the kings of the earth, but more so, then should this bring comfort and joy to shepherds in the fields, to the widow, the orphan and the immigrant? If Constantine, sword in hand, surrounded by men who have proved that they can kill and take without remorse, should proclaim that heaven is like this but more so, should his audience rejoice or should they weep for despair of it?

Of course if Jesus had proclaimed such a 'revelation' he would never have been crucified. He would have been cultivated by the authorities, religious and political, perhaps sent on speaking tours of trouble spots throughout the country. That 'revelation' is not theology, but ideology. It is the guise in which Constantine required the loyalty and support of his subjects. Naturally those who had been persecuted would welcome such a protector, but at a more fundamental level there is no good news in the announcement that as on earth, so in heaven, arbitrary power rules. It is the revelation in Christ that God does not act as do the kings of the earth. It may seem in turn utopian or naive to many, but it is not an ideological duplication or imitation of the world as we know it. It is the claim that at a profound level reality is completely different from the common view of it.

From the foregoing it will be clear that we are not dealing with marginal or peripheral differences. Here are two completely contrasting religious world-views. The one seems very straightforward and recognizable, now manifest in Constantine. Indeed, as we shall discuss later, nothing is more ominous than the fact that it does seem natural and straightforward. In stark contrast is another view which seems to be contradicted by reality at every stage, except by those who have attempted to live out such a faith. The two views could hardly be more contrasted and yet it is the non-Christian one which seems most natural, even to Christians.

Perhaps we might allow ourselves a slight digression, to illustrate the incompatibility of the two. The situation is not without parallel. In the middle of the nineteenth century Soren Kierkegaard considered that throughout Denmark true Christianity had been entirely submerged by something which was not the Christian religion, but a religious form of Hegel's philosophy. So strongly did he feel about the contrast that in *Philosophical Fragments* he undertook 'a project of thought'[4], an intellectual exercise, in which he would draw up two lists. One would represent Christianity as then understood, the other would be the complete opposite of that position. Then to everyone's amazement, he would show that this 'opposite' religion was true Christianity. If we allowed ourselves a brief Kierkegaardian digression we might describe the locus of revelation in two ways. First of all there is Constantine, and I need spend little time describing him since he has been the subject of our study. Born to the purple, he knows how to gain absolute power, and equally, how to exercise it. In battle he has no equal. His wealth is beyond the imagination of his subjects. His court is splendid, his appearance awesome. It is his will which guides the nations and peoples within his Empire. Who would dare deny him the title, 'the Great'. To call him the model of the King of heaven, the reflection of the eternal Ruler of the universe, seems natural and fitting. For this reason he is hailed as the manifestation of God on earth. Do you wish to know of God? Then look first to the Emperor.

If it does not seem too contrived, not to mention absurd, let us picture therefore a figure who in every possible respect stands in contrast to the Emperor. If Kierkegaard were to assist us, then he would no doubt begin the search not in a palace but in a humble cottage, or if that be not contrast enough, then let us begin in a stable! 'If the God had permitted himself to be born in an inn, wrapped in swaddling-clothes and laid in a manger, could the contradiction have been greater . . .?[5] For the *mimesis* of God on earth, let us look not to the son of Emperor Constantius, but to the son of an artisan. Let the child be illegitimate, or at least let his birth be surrounded by rumours. Already the contrast will appear unfruitful, but if Constantine was raised in the imperial court of Diocletian, then let us picture one who lived in the most obscure and least fashionable corner of the Empire, not a citizen but a subject. And if Constantine was trained from earliest times to rule the Empire, let us picture one who learned the trade of a carpenter.

Certainly in their origins and in their early lives there could hardly be a greater contrast between two men. We need hardly ask the question, in which life is the manifestation of God on earth? In which is the Sovereign to be reflected? Yet it might be said that many a king came from an unpromising background, including Constantius. Might it not be that the man from the obscure village could find himself suddenly presented with the opportunity to achieve greatness, an unexpected invitation to receive great power and wealth. How then would he respond?

> Again, the devil took him to a very high mountain and showed him all the kingdoms of the world and the glory of them; and he said to him, 'All these I will give you, if you will fall down and worship me'.[6]

Matthew makes this the last, presumably the greatest, of the temptations. Is it simply that Jesus began life further back than Constantine, but essentially on the same road? No, when presented with the goal of Constantine, he turns away. Why, because of the 'condition' attached by the devil? How naive we should be to read it thus. This is not the condition attached. The evil is not in an extra act, but in the thing itself, in the striving to possess and control the kingdoms of the world and the people therein. What Jesus is rejecting is the very thing that Constantine calls his 'religious vocation', his driving ambition to rule the world.

At a crucial point in the life of each man a choice has to be made, the acceptance of a vocation. The way forward for Jesus is to reject the way of Constantine. In whom now is God to be manifest? In other words, here is a new teaching about God, that God does not call men to world power, that God is not manifest in such a man. Up to that point Jesus lived the life of the middle class in his village. He was not one of the poor and he had financial security and social status. But from the time that he accepted his vocation he rejected wealth, status and security – precisely those things which were to concern Constantine continuously till the time of his death. The imperial court is replete with the symbolism and the reality of wealth, status and security. The God of Constantine can be represented as a heavenly Sovereign simply by expanding each of these. But the God revealed in Christ is apparently to be found by those who have none of these things. 'Blessed are you poor, for yours is the kingdom of God.'[7] When we say that Constantine was not a

Christian, it is not simply because he does not speak of Christ, but because he represents in every aspect of his being precisely what Christ rejects, point for point. The God revealed in Christ cannot be manifest in Constantine, and if this point needs any further confirmation, it is in considering the circumstances of the death of Christ, on the authority of Caesar.

2 Kenosis

In Parts One or Two we might have taken the trouble to point out that Constantine does not mention the efficacy of the death of Christ, which has been so central to Christianity not only in the doctrine of the atonement but in the mystery of the eucharist. But by this stage we are beyond merely noting such omissions. Our interest is in the incompatibility of the religion of Constantine and the faith of the early church. We have pointed out the divergence of the careers of Constantine and of Christ. As Constantine goes on for three decades to greater and greater triumphs, Christ survives his perhaps not even three years and meets humiliation and a cruel death. In which is God manifest? It might seem surprising but it is at this point that the church has been in great danger of borrowing assumptions from the other model.

We know little about the life and ministry of Jesus. Were it not for the events surrounding his death, then of course we should know nothing at all. But the events of the life of Jesus were of surprisingly little interest to the early church and can even be described in a remarkably bland manner: 'he went about doing good and healing all that were oppressed by the devil, for God was with him.'[8] As already noted, he turned away from a movement to make him king, that is, to proclaim him Messiah. Indeed it is not easy to see why he was killed. There was, of course, a long and distinguished tradition of martyrdom in Israel.[9] Prophets were persecuted and even killed because of their radical reinterpretation of the faith. Small comfort to them that if their words were subsequently confirmed by events they were rehabilitated posthumously as true prophets. Not surprisingly, therefore, Jesus anticipated his own death. He was accused of encouraging the breaking of the sabbath and reinterpreting the Law. The three predictions of his death have been filled out with hindsight to include the intervention by the Romans, but since he had no overt quarrel with them, it is more likely that he foresaw a final confrontation in Jerusalem and that he would meet a prophet's death at the hands of his own people, not by crucifixion but stoning.

O Jerusalem, Jerusalem, killing the prophets and stoning those
who are sent to you. How often would I have gathered your
children together as a hen gathers her brood under her wings, and
you would not.[10]

The initiative for the arrest, trial and condemnation of Jesus came
from the Jewish leaders. For reasons which are now obscure, they
succeeded in involving the Roman procurator whose brief was to
maintain the *pax romana*. Although for theological reasons Christians have represented Pilate as vacillating, as weak rather than evil,
in reality he was a ruthless petty tyrant, described by Agrippa I in a
letter to Caligula as 'inflexible, merciless, and obstinate' with a
record of terrible crimes and excesses.[11] His first consideration was
not the justice of a case, but preserving at least a veneer of peace. To
such a man nothing could be more dangerous than a religious leader
who sets limits on what could be required by Caesar.

Up to that point little is said by the early church to suggest that in
the life of Jesus God is manifest in a unique way. Everything hinges
on his death. Fortunately we need not here discuss the meaning and
nature of the resurrection: was it an objective event which might
have been observed by non-Christians, or was it the name of a
spiritual experience to those who became Christian? The important
point is that the resurrection transformed the followers of Jesus,
both in their religious beliefs and in their behaviour. It marks the
beginning of specifically Christian faith, and it includes the assertion
that it is in the life and death of Jesus that God is uniquely manifest.
This takes us a very long way from the manifestation of God in the
triumphs of Constantine, but unless a fine distinction is made, then
there is a real danger that the church will fall back to the model of
Constantine. To illustrate this, let us indulge once more in a
Kierkegaardian digression. In what sense might it be said that God
is manifest in such an unlikely figure, one so humble who goes about
doing good until he is tortured to death? Let us consider the case of
a king incognito.

Once upon a time there was a young king, who announced to his
equerry that he intended to dress like a commoner, go into the
market place and countryside and there come into direct contact
with his people. The equerry protests and advises him of the danger
and impropriety. (Actually the equerry is much more worldly than
the king and knows perfectly well that the plan cannot work. He
also suspects that the king could not face the reality of the situation
if it did work.) But the king, out of compassion, or perhaps boredom,
insists – as we all hoped he would – and determines that the very

next day he and the foot-dragging equerry will set out, thus disguised, to enter the world of his subjects.

We might speculate that the next day is rather chilly and so the encounter with the real world is postponed. Then, after a hearty four-course breakfast, the king dons the ragged cloak of the country folk and goes walk-about to meet the people, incognito. Tempting though it might be, we cannot take time to follow his exploits, with which he regales his yawning courtiers for months afterwards. Everything went splendidly. He was warmly received wherever he went and the conversations that he heard in the local inn all seemed to be of how fine was the life of the people under such a noble king. In other words, the equerry had left nothing to chance and had laid out a great deal of money to make sure that when this 'stranger' appeared he would not be beaten up or told what a disaster the king was. And to round off a perfect day the king cut across the royal park on his way back to the castle. Unfortunately this was a capital offence for common people, and he was arrested by a party of soldiers patrolling the grounds. Near tragedy. They already had a rope over the branch of a tree, ready to carry out summary justice, when the 'stranger' threw open his ragged cloak to display his credentials. They gasped and sprang back in amazement: it was indeed the royal personage. Just time for three relieved cheers before the experiment came to an end and the king was safely back in the security of his castle. What a day it had been! He had been a commoner for a day and experienced life as it really is for the ordinary folk. He had set aside his kingly power and status and had shared their lot.

At least it pleased the king to think so, but we know that nothing could have been further from the truth. He neither became a commoner nor did he share their lives. A king he was before, after and even during his little sojourn. If he had not been still a king, then he would have been executed.

A pleasant little interlude, but the intention of painting such a picture is to use it in dealing with our question about the locus of revelation. There is a picture similar in some respects in Paul's letter to the Philippians.

Have this mind among yourselves, which you have in Christ Jesus, who, though he was in the form of God, did not count equality with God a thing to be grasped, but emptied himself, taking the form of a servant, being born in the likeness of men. And being found in human form he humbled himself and became obedient unto death, even death on a cross. Therefore God has highly exalted him and bestowed on him the name which is above every name, that at the name of Jesus every knee should bow, in heaven and on earth and under the earth, and every tongue confess that Jesus Christ is Lord, to the glory of God the Father.[12]

This is a very familiar passage to Christians, but its interpretation is important for our discussion and it may be that the familar understanding is misleading. The picture comes from an early stage in the life of the church and already implies the pre-existence of Christ. According to Paul the Son of God sojourns on earth for a time and then returns to heaven. But he does not appear on earth as the Son of God. Rather, he 'empties' himself of his majesty and appears as a man. For this reason, the episode is usually called *kenosis*. Perhaps the relevance of our Kierkegaardian digression will now be clear. Did the Son of God come to his own people in the manner of our romantic king, so that the suspecting eye might have been able to see through the disguise and detect nevertheless the presence of God? This might seem an absurd question, but of course in the gospels we are told that at least the demons and evil spirits recognized him. 'And whenever the unclean spirits beheld him, they fell down before him and cried out, "You are the Son of God". And he strictly ordered them not to make him known.'[13] As the king throws around him the ragged cloak of the people, does the Son of God put on the Galilean robe? Is this the Son of God incognito, not a king to the casual observer but underneath every inch a king? He emptied himself, but of what? Obviously of divine omnipresence: he was located in time and space. And omniscience: he was a Jew of his time and place. But even that had been contradicted in Christian history, since many have believed that his knowledge was not so restricted. And omnipotence: he did not exercise the power of God. Here again, the miracles are taken to be indications of such power. But we should look also to the tradition of the resurrection. Our romantic king was almost killed before his real identity prevented the tragedy. But Jesus was killed. Yet the belief that he rose from the dead would seem to assert that being the Son of God he could not be killed, not as others are killed. So that the parallel with our romantic king is not quite so absurd as it first appeared. In Christian piety the *kenosis* was a good deal less complete than is at first sight implied by Paul.

It is not difficult to see why the first major heresy in the church was Docetism, that form of Christian faith which believed that Jesus was not really human at all, that he did not really participate in human experience and of course that he did not die a human death.[14]

And although Docetism is vehemently rejected in theory, its continuing influence is considerable. Indeed, when Christians begin from a certain premise, Docetism is inevitable, no matter how it is rejected in theory. The premise is that Jesus was a pre-existent figure, either the Messiah or the Son of God. Starting with this assumption, then, we are always confronted with the king who is never really other than a king, in spite of his lack of power, in spite of his vulnerablility, in spite of his humiliation and unjust execution. And it is from this premise that it is assumed that God is manifest in a king, precisely when most a king. If this were the case, then of course Constantine would be a much better candidate than Jesus. Once this approach is adopted, then Christianity loses its dramatic and revolutionary originality and falls back into the religion of Constantine, the repetition of the tired platitude that God is manifest in kingly power, wealth, status and security.

To sharpen the issue again, the question of the locus of revelation is this: was God revealed in this earthly sojourn, in spite of the weakness, the humiliation and the defenceless death, or does the uniqueness of Christian faith lie rather in this, that it is precisely in the weakness, humiliation and defenceless death that God is revealed? Here lies the contrast between the religion of Constantine and the faith of the early church. As Paul Althaus puts it:

> The full and undiminished deity of God is to be found in the complete helplessness, in the final agony of the crucified Jesus, at the point where no 'divine nature' is to be seen.[15]

Jurgen Moltmann makes the same point.

> God is not greater than he is in this humiliation. God is not more glorious than he is in this self-surrender. God is not more powerful than he is in this helplessness. God is not more divine than he is in this humanity.[16]

It is for this reason that Christianity turned away from the king like David, from the long-expected Messiah and from the invincible victor whom Eusebius recognized in his Emperor. And the reason is this, that the God of the Christians cannot be revealed in such a figure. There is after all a Christian *mimesis,* but it is not the glorious autocrat who defends his honour by killing his enemies. The *mimesis* of God, for Christians, is the one who sets aside his garments and washes the feet of his disciples, who touches the leper and will harm no man, not even his persecutors and not even to save his own life. The labarum is not the cross. They symbolize two quite incompatible approaches to life and two quite contradictory revelations of God.

152 The Ideology of Constantine

The most dramatic evidence of this is that the victorious trophy of Constantine is covered in blood, but the blood of other people.

XII

THE NEW IMPERIAL CULT

In the previous chapter I spelt out in some detail the difference, indeed incompatibility, between a religion which takes Constantine to be the locus of the revelation of God and a religion in which God is manifest in Christ. The two are not different phases of the same religion: they represent diametrically opposed alternatives. If that were the end of the matter it would be remarkable enough. But there is one further stage, and a most unfortunate development at that. In Chapter III we discussed the process by which Eusebius presents Constantine as the new Messiah, a process in which Constantine actually replaces Christ. Now of course this did not develop into a new religion in which Constantine was hailed as a saviour. If it had, then at least the choice would have been clear. Instead, a much more subtle and insidious development took place. The values of Constantine replaced the values of Christ *within* Christianity.

In Chapter X we analysed the Great Reversal. If a religion had centred upon Constantine, then, by this reversal, what is said about God and the Logos would actually have derived from Constantine. It would be his life-style, motives, values and attitudes which would have been attributed to God and the Logos. Although in the oration 'In Praise of Constantine' Eusebius did not attempt to Christianize this religion, it was inevitable that Christians would begin to adapt it to their religion. In other words, by the Great Reversal, what is said of Constantine now informs what is said of Christ. Christ remains at the centre of Christianity, but the values of the historical Jesus are now replaced by the values of Constantine. This is seen nowhere more dramatically than in Byzantine art, in which Christ is represented as seated in a heaven which looks suspiciously like Constantine's court in Byzantium. In this chapter we must therefore examine the process by which Constantine transformed Christianity into his own imperial cult.

1   In This Sign Conquer

At the beginning of this book we reviewed those dramatic and romantic words addressed to the young Constantine as his struggle, existential, political and strategic, was resolved at his conversion: 'In this sign conquer.' Who could then have foreseen how complete would have been his conquest? There was Maxentius at Milvian Bridge, the Western Empire, and eventually Licinius and the whole of the Empire, East and West. And if that were not enough, he also conquered the barbarian tribes which pressed again and again at his borders. Who could have predicted such complete conquest at that stage? And yet, as in the case of other Emperors and Empires, we might wonder what was achieved in the long term. The Roman Empire has long since gone, and the Byzantine as well. Before the century had ended, the Goths could no longer be contained and had the Empire at their mercy. But there is one conquest made by Constantine, the effect of which still continues to the present day, his most surprising yet least acknowledged. At his conversion Constantine embraced his new personal covenantal religion, symbolized by his own labarum. 'In this sign conquer': and he did. He conquered the Christian church. The conquest was complete, extending over doctrine, liturgy, art and architecture, comity, ethos and ethics. And this is the greatest irony, that Constantine achieved by kindness what his predecessors had not been able to achieve by force. Without a threat or a blow, and all unsuspecting, the Christians were led into captivity and their religion transformed into a new imperial cult. All who heard of the promise thought that Constantine had conquered his enemies: no one seemed to notice that he had conquered his new friends. But this achievement, unheralded then, unrecognized now, represents Constantine's greatest conquest, the one which has persisted largely unchallenged through the centuries in Europe and wherever European Christianity has spread.

Eusebius presents Constantine as the saviour of the world and certainly the saviour of the church. This is quite misleading, even dangerously misleading. Only a sadist would wish that persecution continue in the church, only a masochist welcome it, and yet suffering seemed an inescapable experience for early Christians. They were persecuted by the Jews in Acts and in Paul's letters were subject to persecution by the Jews of the dispersion and at times also by Gentiles. But this was no mystery or paradox, since Jesus himself had been persecuted and cruelly put to death. And this not by chance, but inevitably. Indeed Mark's Gospel seems to be written to demonstrate to persecuted Christians that they only followed in the steps of one whose witness caused even enemies to unite against him and conspire to bring about his death. As we have seen, the history of the church till the fourth century was of random and often intensive persecution. Whenever the Emperor or the traditions of the Empire seemed threatened, it was open season on persecuting Christians. And yet this tiny minority, insignificant, weak and defenceless, not only survived but grew. Tertullian's aphorism is as frightening as it is memorable. 'We multiply whenever we are mown down by you; the blood of Christians is seed.'[1]

In the last chapter it was argued that the new revelation in Christianity is that God is revealed in weakness and in suffering which does not betray love, but is willing to go down to death rather than seek victory through evil. The continuity between the witness of the historical Jesus and the faith of the early church is clear to see. Paul describes both the weak and humiliated, and also the new revelation which is made manifest in and through them too.

> For consider your call, brethren; not many of you were wise according to worldly standards, not many were powerful, not many were of noble birth; but God chose what is foolish in the world to shame the wise, God chose what is weak in the world to shame the strong, God chose what is low and despised in the world, even things that are not, to bring to nothing things that are.[2]

Their Saviour had himself been weak and humiliated, and they shared in his suffering. This is not the repetition of what everyone knows about the 'real' world. This is the contradiction of everything that we have ever been taught to believe about how things are. It needs no special revelation to tell us how to learn about the ways of the world, to get and exercise power. But as already observed, if there is a new revelation in Christ, it is that God's way with the world contradicts this worldly wisdom and power. 'For the foolishness of God is wiser than men, and the weakness of God is stronger than men.'[3] The early church learned through persecution the truth of this new revelation. To Christians themselves, therefore, it was not at all incredible that persecution could actually strengthen the church: it brought precisely the experience in which God was made known to them in strength.

Nor should it have been so surprising to the church that this new strength should prove too much for their enemies. Diocletian lost heart in persecution; Galerius died of it. With the Edict of Toleration the church was vindicated, and with it in a real sense the faith that God is manifest in weakness and suffering love. And it is therefore all the more tragic that Christians should, in this moment of victory, forsake the revelation in Jesus, for its opposite in Constantine. The church did not need the protection of Constantine; it had already taken on the Empire, century after century, and had in the end been victorious. But the victory was not gained through the way of the labarum, but through accepting the cross. And this is the tragedy: having been sustained through all their sufferings and troubles, Christians were just about to be seduced away not only from that but from the profoundly revolutionary faith revealed in Christ. Eusebius invited them now to put their faith in a new saviour, one who had no intention of being weak or of suffering, one who was dedicated, through an apparently divine vocation, to being strong and exercising his power on those who opposed him.

Through that divine foolishness and weakness the church had been able to continue under persecution, demonstrating that it was possessed by that true knowledge and inner strength which the world could neither understand nor defeat. If Constantine had in turn persecuted the church, he too would have failed to conquer it. How was it then that he was able to succeed where his predecessors had failed? How was it that by a little kindness, a word of praise here, a grant to build a new church there, he was able to induce the church to forsake what they could not be made to forsake under threat of torture or death? The Emperor offered so much, beyond the dreams of Christians recently under constant threat. He offered in effect at least a share in the kingdoms of the world. When Satan is seen to offer such rewards, the temptation is rejected. When one comes professing to be a follower of the One God, then his offer is accepted. Or were they in fact one and the same? What a small price to pay! In this sign conquer. What a stroke of genius! To lead them in such thankful festival, like a pied piper whose gifts turned their gaze from the Christ and caused them, like Peter, to sink! The policy of successive pagan emperors had failed. They had tried to dam the river and it had engulfed them. What genius to reverse the policy and, purporting to assist the river in its course, actually to divert it along a newly prepared route! And so the Emperor had his way by insisting that they had their way. Where now the steadfastness, if necessary unto death? They could trust him, could they not, this 'friend of God'? And once again the Son of Man was betrayed with a kiss.

Not that the betrayal took place in a moment. It was a gradual process. Gradually the church came to have faith in the Emperor, to trust him and to see in him and in his ways the hand of God. Not in a moment and yet, in historical perspective, the transition was accomplished in an alarmingly short space of time. Three centuries they had held out and kept faith with the Crucified One. Now within a generation, if Eusebius is to be believed, the transformation was complete. The church was completely loyal to the Emperor, the new saviour who had succeeded in displacing the historical Jesus. They no longer had to renew their faith in the Crucified One by withstanding persecution. Their needs now were met by Constantine, who asked only that they should follow wherever he led. The 'foolishness of God': that was no longer necessary. Christian leaders were now drawn into the imperial court as 'advisers'. Christians, it would seem, were no longer foolish but wise in the ways of the world. The 'weakness of God': nor was that necessary. Christians were given status and power in the Empire, so that they might also in turn enjoy a little persecution of pagans.

Constantine, one of the most shrewd and able emperors in the history of the world, is often represented as if in things religious he was rather naive. How unlikely! Whether unconsciously, whether intuitively, yet effectively nevertheless, Constantine pursued a policy which achieved the conquest of the church, and this was the greatest prize of all, the prize which able predecessors had not been capable of gaining. But if Constantine had become a humble member of the church, then it could hardly be a conquest. In that case he would have been overcome. What made it victory was not the fact that he gained the support of the church, but that in the process he completely altered the nature and the basis of the Christian faith. That was his real achievement, and yet it has gone unnoticed. It is assumed that the church remained constant in its faith, but was able to support Constantine because he had forsaken the imperial designs on the church. Forsake nothing: Constantine achieved far more than the transfer of loyalty. He managed to eliminate from Christianity precisely that which prevented Christians previously from being totally loyal to the Emperor. Since then it has been assumed that the church remained constant and the Emperor became a Christian. Thus was the church able to support him. Quite the contrary is the case. Constantine did not become a Christian, but he was able to tempt the church to forsake its faith in the Crucified One. He showed them that the time for that kind of faith was over. God had sent them one in whom they could trust, one who was neither foolish nor weak. They were surrounded by enemies, and there came to them one who had been instructed to make a sign that approximated to the cross. He had been ordered to conquer in that sign. But when we look at the situation more closely, there is something not quite right about it. After the Edict of Toleration it could be argued that the church had no enemies. In the Cross of Christ, it had already conquered. The enemies surrounding them were not actually their enemies at all, but Constantine's. Since his goal was the unification of the Empire under his absolute control, the most obvious and proven enemy that he faced was the Christian church itself. 'In this sign conquer': and he did. The most formidable enemy to his aspirations was the church, and he was able to convert it to absolute loyalty to him within a few short years.

In this conversion, Constantine achieved that which had eluded his illustrious predecessors, and for that alone he might be judged an extraordinary ruler. He had managed to neutralize the enemy which had always threatened the unity of the Empire. But if one thing emerges from this study, it is that Constantine the Great deserved that title more than we at first imagine. He not only neutralized the threat to the unity of the Empire; he went far beyond this, using Christianity as the new basis for unity. At least that is what has been mistakenly said. But as we have seen, it is true only in a very qualified sense. The faith of the church after the new Judas kiss was not the same as the faith that had withstood the imperial cult throughout the centuries. It was no longer the faith in the Crucified One, no longer the faith in *Christos Kurios* who was irreconcilable with the claims of *Caesar Kurios*. No, after the Judas kiss Caesar was none other than the 'friend of God', and could no longer be thought of as an enemy. It is not true that Constantine gave up all idea of an imperial cult in favour of Christianity. Rather, a transformed Christianity became the imperial cult by any other name. We have already seen how this could happen; let us simply draw attention to the process by which in fact it took place.

From Alexander the Great onwards there was a tradition of the imperial cult in which the Emperor was divine. Few of the Emperors were concerned about being divine. The issue was whether their policies could be given divine status, that is, could claim absolute force. This is the underlying purpose of the imperial cult, not the absurdity of thinking a man divine, but the obscuring of the equal absurdity of accepting a man's policies as divine and therefore meriting absolute acceptance. Constantine would have liked his policies to have been so accepted. The obstacle to this was a Catch 22 situation. He could not unify the Empire unless he could gain the support of the Christian church. But he could not be given divine status within Christianity. And yet, as we have seen, Constantine was able to achieve his objective nonetheless. By the Great Reversal, his policies were considered to be the will of the Logos. Incredible though it now seems, apparently no one noticed that these policies were incompatible with the historical Jesus, the revelation of God seen in him and confirmed in the experience of the church throughout the centuries of persecution. Constantine thus not only defeated the church, which his predecessors had failed to do, but enlisted the aid of the church in unifying the Empire. And to add insult to injury, when Constantine reconstructed the imperial cult by which the wisdom of the world and the ambition of one man were given the absolute status of divine law, the church actually pronounced this cult to be Christianity!

2   The State Religion

The Empire strikes back. The church was not dealing with a Diocletian or a Galerius, but with someone more dangerous than these two combined. And most dangerous of all because he seemed to be both friend of God and benefactor of the church. He gained more by this convoluted route than he could ever have achieved by confrontation. He was content to give up personal deification for that greater goal, the deification of all that he stood for. And all this without the need of persecution. Far from it, the church, notably in the person of Eusebius, could not wait to legitimize this achievement and commend the wisdom and power of this world as if they were the foolishness and weakness of God himself. Who conquered whom? Did the Empire become a Christian state? No: Christianity sold its birthright for a pension and became the state religion. Effectively this marks the beginning of the history of Christianity as we know it. It lays down the new norms by which Christianity is to be understood. More ominously, it provides the perspective by which the earlier form of Christianity is now interpreted.

Wealth and property provide good examples of the change in perspective which is associated with the establishment of Christianity as a state religion. The early Christian view of wealth and possessions is very strict. Little though we know of the life of Jesus until his conversion by John the Baptist, it is probable that he lived quite comfortably in Nazareth. If he was the son of a craftsman he would by the standards of the time be middle-class, certainly not one of the 'poor of the earth'. This would be true also for most of his disciples, self-employed fishermen or civil servants. But Jesus gave up this security in order to proclaim the kingdom of God. He required this also of his disciples and in a famous saying he required it also of a rich young man. 'You lack one thing; go, sell what you have, and give to the poor, and you will have treasure in heaven; and come, follow me.'[4] These words are recorded, of course, not for historical interest, but as a dominical saying, a requirement which the Lord of the church lays upon his followers. This requirement has been diluted over the years; it has been reinterpreted and 'spiritualized'. We shall take this point up in a moment, but much more important than any particular reinterpretation is the fact that Christians felt free to interpret, to dilute the requirement. We are suggesting that this change in attitude can be associated with the new norms of Christianity when it becomes a state religion. But the gospel passage seems to close the door already to such a dilution. Jesus continues, 'Truly, I say to you, it will be hard for a rich man to enter the kingdom of heaven. And again I tell you, it is easier for a camel to go through the eye of a needle than for a rich man to enter the kingdom of God.'[5] These words are hard to bear, and over the centuries some clever minds have been given the task of explaining that they do not mean what they say. But our interest here is in the obvious change of norms which underlies such a reinterpretation. Previously we saw that the historical Jesus was set aside in favour of Constantine. Here the values of Jesus are set aside in favour of those of the Emperor. It is the task of a dutiful state religion, therefore, to bring its own traditions into line with the imperial policy and values.

It is of some significance that the sharpest critics of Christianity have distinguished between the life and values of later Christianity and the life and values of Jesus and his early followers. Lenin drew a parallel between the way in which words of Marx had been conveniently forgotten, 'as if it were a piece of old-fashioned "naivete", just as Christians, after their religion had been given the status of a state religion, "forgot" the "naivete" of primitive Christianity with its democratic revolutionary spirit'.[6] Lenin is here referring to the Jerusalem community. We might be forgiven for thinking that the first actions of the early community after the death and resurrection of Jesus would be of quite fundamental importance for the later church. They had lived communally with Jesus, and their first actions, when they had to take some initiative, involved setting up what Troeltsch called the 'Primitive Christian communism of the Book of Acts'.[7] Once again we see that a norm from the early church has ceased to be a norm for the later church. Of course there was disagreement in the early church on the correct attitude towards wealth and possessions. Towards the end of the second century Clement of Alexandria, in a work entitled *Can a Rich Man be Saved?*, was diluting the requirement of the Gospels, while Tertullian was taking a hard line, insisting that the example of Jesus was normative. 'He always defended the poor and condemned the rich.'[8] But the important point for our discussion is that when Christianity became a state religion, the norms for discussing the issue changed. Up till then Christians might have failed to keep the norms of Jesus and the early church. But with the revaluation of all values, there was no longer any need for guilt about the matter. The older requirements did not obtain.

Thus the church welcomed into its midst the rich and property-owning members of society. We can imagine how delighted were the Christians who could remember only a few years previously how such people had been on the side of the persecutors. Surely there would be no recriminations on that score? And surely no one would be so tasteless as to suggest that according to Jesus of Nazareth such people could not enter the kingdom of God? No doubt some bright young theologian would find a way of spiritualizing these hard words: everyone is welcome, if their 'hearts' are right with God.

At every point we see the revaluation of values, the conforming of Christian values and attitudes to those of the Emperor, the 'friend of God'. In the oration, 'In Praise of Constantine', Eusebius seems quite oblivious to the hard words of Jesus as he describes the great wealth and property of the Emperor. It is apparently enough for the bishop to claim that the sovereign is 'high-minded' and not seduced by such trinkets. This is a very specific illustration of the issue. It is assumed that the Emperor is a Christian. But the Emperor is wealthy. Therefore since he is the imitation of the Logos (Christ) in heaven, this must mean that the Christ approves of wealth – properly used, of course. How churlish it would be to recall the hard words of Jesus! If the Christ in heaven is represented by the Emperor, then the sovereign's conduct must be a better guide to conduct in these new circumstances. So runs the *apologia*. The result is that the historical Jesus is no longer the norm of conduct or values for the church. His words and witness are now interpreted in the light of the Christ in heaven (whom *we* of course know to be simply a projection of Constantine the Great). The more wealth he bestows upon the grateful church, the more they interpret these blessings as from God. But the more they accept from the Emperor, the more committed are they to his values. Every benefaction accepted binds them more closely to the state. The wealth and property are significant, but they are in fact the objectifications of the church's new allegiance, and like any other objectifications they become ties that bind. It is easy to talk about changing values, but once values are given form in stone and precious metals it is easier to believe that these values must be right. The process gains momentum. With each new building, with each new costly project, it is more and more difficult to raise the question whether all this is a betrayal of the One who 'always defended the poor and condemned the rich'.

Precisely at the time when the church was being drawn into a new relationship with the state, exchanging one set of values for another, Pachomius was setting up the first Christian monastery, in southern Egypt. The absorption into the state was not to go without protest or, at times, sharp criticism. Even so, the important change was the state religion, against which monasticism protested. The monastic ideal, which seemed closer to the example of Jesus, was not the norm for the church at large. It was hardly surprising, therefore, that the monastic orders as they developed came to possess great wealth and properties. In these circumstances poverty became an ideal. Monasticism was originally a middle-class movement; to choose poverty had a certain attraction, if the poverty was practised within the security of a wealthy community. But in the church at large, disparity of wealth and poverty was not seen as disgraceful or blasphemous. After all, without the poor, how could the rich practise charity? In the earlier period Jesus had declared, 'Blessed are you poor, for yours is the kingdom of God'.[9] But under the new order, blessed were those who *gave* to the poor.

We have spent some time on this example of the revaluation of Christian values, the consequences of Christianity becoming the new imperial cult, the state religion of the Emperor who excluded the historical Jesus. But of course there are many other examples. If Christianity is now the state religion, then it must become a department within the civil service: after all, the purpose of an imperial cult is to work for the benefit of the state. Thus the leaders of the church become confidants and advisers to the Emperor. What did they advise him to do? Sell all he had and give it to the poor? Beat his swords into ploughshares? Anyone familiar with administration will know that such fundamental matters of principle do not appear on the daily agenda for running a busy empire. All too soon the bishops would be entirely taken up with the implementation of policies and the solving of local problems. The echoes are clearly audible today. 'Someone has to do it.' 'Better to work from within the system in the hope of changing it.' 'If we work with the Emperor on one issue he will listen to us on other issues.' 'Tell them to leave the petition here, I must attend a dinner for the opening of the new chamber of commerce.' Yes, the bishop who only a few years ago was a front-line target for persecution is now a civil servant, and his loyalties are now to the sovereign who pays his salary and repairs the roof on the church.

But there is even more to it than that, because the functionaries of the state religion must be a credit to the state. If the state religion is to legitimize the state itself, then it must institutionalize the values and imitate the structure of the state. In those far-off days when Jesus walked the dusty roads of Palestine, the leader could be recognized as the one who washed the feet of his followers. The first was last and servant of all. But now under the new régime the leader was recognized by no such paradoxical reversal. It would not have been fitting for a servant of Constantine to have acted in such a humble manner: it would have reflected on the dignity of the Emperor himself. In former days Jesus spoke to the people of John the Baptist, that Elijah *redivivus*, whose rough robe symbolized the single minded commitment which his faith required. 'Why then did you go out? To see a man clothed in soft raiment? Behold, those who wear soft raiment are in kings' houses.'[10] But now that the bishop of Rome had been given the use of the old Lateran Palace, even Christians might be seen wearing rich apparel and living in 'kings' houses'.

Once again we must make it clear that the things themselves are not the issue, but what they symbolize. The examples taken together show Christianity reflecting the structure and the values of the empire. An example of this concerns authority. It is said repeatedly in the Gospels that Jesus spoke 'with authority'. Indeed this was one of the major sources of conflict with the 'authorities', the religious leaders. They ask him, 'By what authority are you doing these things, or who gave you this authority to do them?'[11] The leaders stand in a chain of command. They have been given authority, and in turn they can confer authority. Clearly Jesus did not stand within this chain. 'I will ask you a question; answer me, and I will tell you by what authority I do these things. Was the baptism of John from heaven or from men?'[12] Jesus claims that his authority comes from God, as did that of John, this man who did not belong in kings' houses and who indeed was beheaded for outspoken 'authoritative' criticisms of Herod. John seemed to be autocratic, in that his authority was not bestowed upon him by a chain of command. But of course Eusebius described Constantine as an autocrat, claiming in effect that his authority was derived directly from God. And so it might be intriguing to ask the inhabitant of the Lateran Palace by what authority he does these things? Does he act as one who stands in the chain of command from the Emperor, or the chain of command of the one who had no earthly authority (and, for that matter, nowhere to lay his head)? Perhaps the question would be shrugged off. But once again the issue concerns what is being symbolized. The authority of Jesus led him to act as a servant. Inevitably those who live in palaces exercise authority over those under them. The distinction was anticipated in the gospels. 'The kings of the Gentiles exercise lordship over them; and those in authority over them are called benefactors. But not so with you . . .'[13] Sooner or later those who live in palaces come to be called 'princes of the church', and people do homage to them in the manner of the 'kings of the Gentiles'. Why? Because the model is not a Christian model but an imperial model. When we recall the humiliation of Jesus by the soldiers of the authorities, it is beyond comprehension that his followers should wear symbolic crowns and adorn themselves in the royal colour. Beyond comprehension if it were not that the church, as the religious arm of the state, should now replicate the symbols of authority of the state itself.

'In this sign conquer.' Was there any aspect of Christianity that Constantine did not overcome? The progression was logical and inevitable. The church began to imitate the state. The imperial model of authority was accepted, so that the princes of the church lived in palaces and exercised dominion over an administrative district, parallel to the civil administration of the Empire. They accepted stipends from the state and adopted the life-style appropriate to the servants of Constantine. Once this transvaluation of values was complete, everything followed: Christians owning slaves and raising their own armies, and finally the emergence of the papal states.

But again we must insist that this is no carping criticism, as if in some sadistic way we wished that persecution might have continued. The point is that these developments were made possible and then inevitable because the basis of Christianity had been changed. From the beginning of the fourth century there was a dramatic change in the church. It might be said that this was because of changed circumstances. To be sure, the circumstances were greatly changed, and must have been like the answer to the church's prayers. But the point is not that the new developments were unforeseen, unpredictable or unprecedented. It is that the new developments were incompatible with the old faith. They were the contradiction of the faith that had overcome evil with good, that had been strengthened in adversity. 'Beloved, do not be surprised at the fiery ordeal which comes upon you to prove you, as though something strange were happening to you.'[14] But in the new state religion, such testing would have been not simply strange but unthinkable and unnecessary. Those who trusted in the wisdom and power of Constantine no longer tested out the weakness and foolishness of God. 'But rejoice in so far as you share Christ's sufferings, that you may also rejoice and be glad when his glory is revealed.'[15] But the church now turned from sharing the sufferings of Christ, and set its eyes on the glory already revealed in Constantine.

XIII

CONSTANTINE AND POLITICAL THEOLOGY

1 Challenging the Tradition

In Part Three we have been examining the way in which Constantine's imperial ideology infiltrated Christianity, to displace Jesus of Nazareth and transform the values of the early church. Although this represents a specific interaction of politics and religion, it would not be correct to describe it as a political theology. The phrase 'political theology' is widely used now in Christian circles, to characterize developments which have taken place mainly since the late 1950s.[1] What these developments have in common is a dialectical relationship in which Christianity has become politically conscious – usually through Marxist analysis – but has then gone on to criticize ideologies, including Marxism, from *religious* principles. The importance of an injection of political theory is not simply to make Christians 'wise as serpents', but rather to make them aware of the extent to which Christianity has been unconsciously under the influence of values which are fundamentally alien to it.

The task of political theology has been, therefore, in the first instance to unmask the fact that Christianity has been assimilated to ideologies which are quite incompatible with it. By definition this is no easy task. To anyone under the sway of an ideology, everything seems quite 'natural' and straightforward. The injection of political theory is to raise to consciousness the fact that what seems natural is socially constructed, what seems necessary is not only contingent but indeed arbitrary. This is the first problem. The second is to discover what are the genuinely Christian values which have been overlaid or displaced. This is especially difficult since the displacement took place many centuries ago. That is to say, the 'tradition' does not provide an objective norm by which to re-establish the original values. The tradition of 1600 years is itself part of the problem.

It may now be clear why this study of Constantine is intended to assist the development of political theology, and more generally is intended as a contribution to the renewal of Christianity in the modern world. If alien values are to be unmasked and replaced, then it is necessary to understand how they entered Christianity in the first place. It has been our contention that they entered when Constantine's imperial ideology infiltrated the Christian church at the beginning of the fourth century. From that time the original values have been displaced, so that they themselves now seem remote from Christianity. Since then a long tradition has built up incorporating the alien values. It is for this reason that it is difficult for political theology to proceed. In the first place it is difficult to argue convincingly that certain institutions should not exist within the church. For example, we have seen that the nature of authority changed with the influence of the Empire. The church came to be organized by a hierarchical system of government which paralleled the administration of the state. But this system of government was developed over a period of centuries to carry out the objectives of the Empire, that is, to gain power and wealth for the ruling class at the expense of the defeated subjects. It would seem, *prima facie,* most unlikely that an authority based on such values and objectives would be able to serve and edify the Christian church, which was originally based on values in direct opposition to those of the state. Yet it is difficult today to argue against such hierarchical organization simply because it itself, over the centuries, has become part of the tradition. The period before the infiltration by imperial ideology is now proportionately very short, and is that period of the life of the church of which historically we know least.

A second reason why it is difficult for political theology to proceed is that Jesus of Nazareth, his life and teaching, were also displaced by the influence of Constantine. It may come as a shock to young Christians to discover that their Founder gave specific teaching, such as, 'it is easier for a camel to go through the eye of a needle than for a rich man to enter the kingdom of God'[2], or 'call no man your father on earth'.[3] But it may be even more shocking for them to discover that pointing to these words does not bring about any change in the values or the practice of the church. The tradition has now taken over, the tradition that comes from Constantine's imperial values, and Jesus of Nazareth is simply displaced. Of course, if Jesus should have said something which for quite other reasons coincides with imperial values, *then* his words are reverently quoted and used to provide religious legitimation. An example of this would be the hard words on marriage and divorce: 'What therefore God has joined together, let not man put asunder.'[4] Since this serves the purpose of social cohesion and simplifies questions of ownership of property, this saying has been given prominent status. Needless to say, the saying 'if any one would be first, he must be last of all and servant of all',[5] has been set aside since it conflicts with the imperial view of hierarchical authority, even though it is much more fundamentally Christian than the teaching on divorce.

In the introduction I made the point that the reign of Constantine is a fundamental turning-point in the history of Europe, and not only Europe. From that time the imperial ideology, with all its implications for the accumulation of wealth and the exercise of power over the weak, was given religious legitimation by the church. As we have seen, this is a quite extraordinary step, and in itself was a far greater accomplishment by Constantine than the frightening off of a few hairy barbarians in the north. In order to legitimize imperial values, it was necessary for Christianity to be completely transformed from within. But the process does not simply run forward from the beginning of the fourth century. In other words, in order to legitimate the Empire under which it had originally suffered, it was necessary to re-write or at least re-interpret the history of Christianity. And it is for this reason that it is almost impossible to challenge the church as it is by reference to the gospels or the practice of the early church. It is a matter of hermeneutics, of the perspective from which interpretation takes place. It is not that the perspective of the early church provides the norm for critically assessing the life of the church today. To the contrary, after Constantine, it is the church under the sway of imperial values which now provides the perspective for reading the Bible.

If things are so cut and dried, we might wonder how it is that the consciousness of this transformation, this betrayal of Christianity has come about. In terms of social theory we might point out that socialization is never complete, the social determination of consciousness is never absolute.[6] In religious terms we might attribute it to the Holy Spirit. However we describe it, and these are not mutually exclusive, the awareness that Christianity was originally something else, and is now under the sway of alien values, has never been entirely lost. This is to be seen in two directions. One is in the development of Marxism. It is not a religion, but as an ideological system it competes with religion in terms of providing a universe of meaning and purpose for those who live within it. We have already noted Lenin's observation that even in his day the words of Marx were no longer decisive for 'Marxists', even as the words of Jesus were no longer decisive for Christians. It is a curious parallel.

Miranda has recently examined the extent to which present-day Marxists are willing to misrepresent Marx on the subject of religion.[7] Without falling into cultural imperialism and pronouncing Marxism a Christian heresy, we can clearly see a close relationship between the two, even if 'Original Marxism – Estranged Offspring'[8] sounds rather patronizing. It was the intention of the young Marx to unmask false consciousness over the whole range of social life and relationships. In Chapter XI analysed the 'Great Reversal' of consciousness which is at the heart of Constantine's ideological infiltration of Christianity. Original Marxism is not the enemy of Christianity. Indeed, it is alienated not from early Christianity, but from that form of Christianity which serves Constantine rather than Christ. Original Marxism is the enemy of the ruling class, but if Christianity since Constantine identifies itself with this class and its values, then it is hardly surprising that the church has often seen Marxism as its own enemy. How convoluted and even tragic if it should be left to Marxism to maintain that critical distance from the modern capitalist state which characterized the attitude of the early church towards Caesar. We cannot pursue this point further, but it is not surprising that some Marxists have responded warmly to that thin line of protest within the church against Constantinian Christianity. The East German Marxist philosopher Ernst Bloch has a way with aphorisms: 'The best thing about religion is that it makes for heretics.'[9] To be declared heretical by the norms of orthodox Constantinian Christianity may be a source of relief and encouragement to those who seek to follow Christ. The protest does not come from outwith, but from within the church. 'The Bible has always been the church's bad conscience.'[10] It preserves the witness to Jesus and the early church, even when this witness is ignored or only selectively observed.

The protest against Constantine Christianity has been preserved, therefore, in movements such as Marxism, which have had to develop outside religion, though they have been indebted to early Christianity. But as already noted, there has been a thin line of protest even within the church. I drew attention to the fact that precisely at the same time when Christianity was succumbing to the imperial embrace, Pachomius was withdrawing from that assimilation and, like a new Elijah, seeking the self-determination of the desert. How has the Empire dealt with this protest? It has not been able to declare it an enemy of Christ in the way that Marxism has been condemned. But the ruling class knows above all how to rule. Each protest movement has, in turn, been incorporated into mainline Christianity. The reason is not difficult to find. Harnack gives the clue in speaking of the institutionalizing of religion. Protest movements themselves eventually become institutionalized and they follow the example of the imperial model. The monastic movement began with withdrawal from involvement in the culture and economy of the Empire. 'Blessed are the poor, for yours is the kingdom of God.' But of course to choose to live the life of the poor is a decision that can only be taken by the rich. And to *organize* a community around a vow of poverty soon requires both money and property. The imperial model has the victory in the end. At the other end of the time-scale, in our own day those who lead the protest, especially in poor Third World countries, are not normally silenced. Constantine demonstrated that this was counter-productive. No, they are uprooted from that environment which first made them conscious of the betrayal of Christ, and placed upon a conveyor-belt which transports them to one world conference after another, assisting them to gain a 'wider' perspective on things, a more 'realistic' appreciation of the problems involved. The Catholic church is still organized on the model of Constantine sitting above the council of bishops: the World Council of Churches is modelled on the United Nations Organization. Both models have served the ruling class well, but neither springs from Christian values.

2   Established Religion

In the previous chapter I discussed the transformation which came about within Christianity as it became Constantine's imperial cult. Although the transformation was without precedent, it bears an interesting relationship to certain historical examples from still earlier times. In his book *The Gnostic Religion* Hans Jonas makes an important point about state religions which become disestablished.[11] He provides three examples, the first being the case of the Jews exiled to Babylon in the sixth century BC. This traumatic experience forced them – or made it possible for them, depending on one's point of view – to transcend the narrow boundaries of country, nation and race.

> We find the position fully realized in Second Isaiah, who enunciated the pure principle of monotheism as a world cause, freed from the specifically Palestinian limitations of the cult of Jahweh. Thus the very uprooting brought to fulfilment a process which had started, it is true, with the older prophets.

The second example comes from the overthrow of Babylon by the

Persians, through which the Babylonian religion ceased to be a state cult.

As one of the institutions of the monarchy it had enjoyed a defined official status, and this connection with a local system of secular power had supported and at the same time limited its role. Both support and restriction fell away with the loss of statehood.

If this seems a rather negative and unfortunate development, it had unforseen consequences.

The fate of subjection and political impotence in the Persian Empire forced the Babylonian religion to stand henceforth on its spiritual content alone.

It was now one religion among others and had to compete with them at a spiritual and theological level.

Political uprooting thus led to a liberation of spiritual substance.

The third example is of the old Persian religion of Mazdaism, which travelled from Iran with each conquest. But with the collapse of the Persian Empire it too became one of the many competing cults, and if it had lost status, it had also lost the negative associations of its imperial past. Both abroad and within Persia itself intellectual development took place, resulting in 'the transformation of traditional religion into a theological system whose characteristics approach those of a rational system'.

Having given those examples, Jonas admits that there is a temptation to raise their common characteristics to the level of a historical law, as if disestablishment automatically or inevitably led to a creative flowering of spiritual or truly religious potential. Naturally our interest is directed towards the corollary of such a historical pattern. In effect Constantine's religious policy was to make Christianity an 'established' religion. If disestablishment tends to lead to creative development at a truly religious level, does establishment have the opposite effect?

Jonas notes that during the exile prophetic religion in Israel reached its fulfilment, notably in its conception of God as God of mankind and not of one nation. But it could be argued that it also reached a spiritual depth in the prophetic songs concerning the Suffering Servant. In the early church the figure described in Isaiah 53 is identified with Jesus at the Passion; indeed, it may be that the experience of the Suffering Servant is taken as a model by the gospel writers to fill out their limited knowledge of the actual events of the treatment of Jesus at his trial and conviction.[12] But certainly there is a continuity of revelation here: God is manifest in one who suffers even to death, not in the kings of the earth who exercise power.

If we are to follow the pattern uncovered by Jonas, then we see that with the restoration of the Jews, their religion – Judaism – reverts to characteristic concerns of country and nation (it would be ironic indeed to call it 'blood and soil'). With the establishment of Judaism as a national cult again, the prophetic creativity is lost and its energies are channelled into organization (law) and building. Christianity emerged from the later apocalyptic tradition which had close ties with the prophetic. 'There are differences between Jewish and Christian apocalyptic, and yet they are essentially one . . .'[13] But this in itself did not lead Christianity out of the milieu of a state cult. The original disciples were rather limited men. The gospel writers frequently represent them as incredibly unimaginative. 'Jesus said to them, "Take heed and beware of the leaven of the Pharisees and Sadducees". And they discussed it among themselves, saying, "We bought no bread" '.[14] They are frequently said to misunderstand or not to understand Jesus. Few were active in the church after the death of Jesus; indeed, the gospel writers are not even sure of their names. We might even say that to claim to stand in such an apostolic succession is an admission of considerable humility. It was when Christianity was carried beyond Palestine, into the Hellenistic culture at large that it developed in a creative and deeply religious way: 'the making of the Christian synthesis was hardly a corruption, a dilution, but rather an enriching.'[15] It was the disestablishment of Christianity from the state cult of Judaism that enabled it to become a world religion.

Our present study, however, has been of a time when Christianity, having passed through a most creative period of spiritual development, became the established religion of the Roman Empire. We should not be surprised if that new position had two main consequences: first, the rapid institutionalization of Christianity in matters of order and organization; second, a corresponding lack of creativity in the spiritual and truly religious. Enough has been said in previous chapters to indicate that these are the directions in which Constantine encouraged the church to move. On the first consequence, the established religion adopted the ethos of the state in matters of order and organization. On the second, its responsibility was now to seek the welfare of the Emperor and the state. This of course inhibited the voice of prophetic criticism and led to the identification of the enemies of the state as the enemies of the church. But there is one further development which might seem to contradict this tendency of established religions to be less creative in spiritual things. The establishment of Christianity was to lead to a flowering of Byzantine art and architecture.

In the original plan of this book there was to be a section of at least two chapters on Byzantine art and architecture. Sadly the book has reached such proportions that it is not practicable to introduce this vast subject at this stage. This is unfortunate for several reasons. The most important is that nothing illustrates the thesis of this book better than the representation of Christ sitting in the heavenly court, surrounded by the trappings of power, wealth and privilege which characterized the imperial court of Constantine. Nothing better confirms the argument that, through the Great Reversal, it is the character and values of Constantine which now in-form the picture of Christ. And at the same time we see why the *kenosis* is circumvented, why it is believed the God is not revealed in Jesus while he is a suffering servant, but when he is restored again as a king.

The second reason why it is unfortunate that art and architecture cannot now be included is because its omission leaves us in the realm of words and concepts, while the vast majority of Christians in the ancient world (possibly in the modern world), being illiterate, are more influenced by the objectifications of oil and stone than the finer points of rational argument. Even those who could not hear or understand the Platonic exposition of the oration 'In Praise of Constantine' would understand in the new Byzantine churches that Constantine was the very model of Christ in glory.

The third reason why it would have been more satisfactory to deal with art and architecture – with coins and statues also – is that it is possible to make claims in these media which could be too blatant if spelt out in words. We have not discussed the rather delicate subject of whether Constantine saw himself replacing Christ, in the arrangements which he made for his burial.[16] We might recall an exchange recorded by Eusebius in the *Life of Constantine*, when a priest,

> presumed so far as in his own presence to pronounce him blessed, as having been counted worthy to hold absolute and universal empire in this life, and as being destined to share the empire of the Son of God in the world to come. These words, however, Constantine heard with indignation, and forbade the speaker to hold such language . . .[17]

It may be that the indignation was not that the priest should express thoughts quite foreign to him, but rather that he should accurately and publicly spell out what was symbolized, even unconsciously, in the architecture of the Church of the Apostles.

A final reason for regret, however, is that the development of art and architecture should not be viewed independently of the new status of Christianity as an established religion. Although in one sense they indicate a spiritual development, they developed as a compensation for the loss of the prophetic dimension. The channelling of religious energies into art and architecture represents a development of the aesthetic approach to religion which in practice means the de-politicizing of religion. With the establishment of Christianity the prophetic, critical dimension loses its central place, the place which it had in the teaching of Jesus. It would be a false dichotomy to say that it represents a concern for beauty rather than truth, yet we cannot escape the conclusion that if the time, energy and wealth which have gone into the aesthetic expression of religion had been channelled into the establishment of justice and peace, the history of Europe would have been dramatically different. But with the establishment of Christianity as the state religion, the responsibility for justice and peace passed from the church to the state. What was left but to represent the imperial court in the most beautiful colours imaginable on the ceilings of the churches? When the voice of prophecy was silenced, what was left but the singing of beautiful psalms? The development of the aesthetic is the consequence of the de-politicizing of religion. Who can speak against beauty, but when its pursuit represents a flight from prophetic social criticism, the beautiful in religion becomes ugly and evil.

It would be quite false to think of Constantine as a deeply religious man. His religion was neither profound nor particularly edifying. So far as his convictions were concerned, he was fanatically committed to his religion: without it he would not have achieved his life's ambition of absolute power. Whether historically this was the case does not alter the fact that Constantine believed it to be so. At an empirical level, the more success he achieved, the more deeply held were his religious convictions. But intensity at such a pragmatic level does not guarantee profundity at a spiritual level: perhaps it precludes it. Constantine integrated politics and religion in his own life, but his religion was not Christianity. Christianity was enlisted in his own personal crusade to gain control of the Empire and in the process Christianity was transformed.

'Render therefore to Caesar the things that are Caesar's, and to God the things that are God's.'[18] So commanded Jesus, at a time when Caesar claimed to be God. For almost three hundred years the church withstood the absolute claims of the Emperor. With what relief did they now attend Constantine, the 'friend of God', to grant him his heart's desire. He did not claim to be God. All he asked was that the church should legitimize everything he stood for and call it the will of God. In this guise the imperial ideology conquered the church. It is for political theology to expose this ideology and the betrayal of Christ.

NOTES

I The Gods at War

1. Lactantius, *De Mortibus Persecutorum* XXX; ET *The Works of Lactantius*, T. & T. Clark 1871, Vol. 2, p. 192.
2. R.A.B. Mynors, *XII Panegyrici Latini*, Clarendon Press 1964.
3. Tertullian, *Apology*, The Loeb Classical Library, Heinemann 1931, XL.2.
4. Lactantius, *De Mortibus* XII.
5. 'Look up to heaven the Christians . . . we are for ever making intercession for all the Emperors', Tertullian, *Apology* XXX.4.
6. This is an estimate made by Norman Baynes in *Constantine the Great and the Christian Church*, Oxford University Press 1931, p. 4. It is based on material in Adolf Harnack, *The Mission and Expansion of Christianity*.
7. Karl Marx, 'A Contribution to the Critique of Hegel's Philosophy of Law: Introduction', *Collected Works*, Lawrence & Wishart 1975, Vol. 3, p. 175.
8. Ludwig Wittgenstein, *Philosophical Investigations*, Blackwell 1963, p. 47.
9. The phrase is used to describe Schutz's position by Helmut Wagner, 'Introduction', *Alfred Schutz on Phenomenology and Social Relations*, University of Chicago Press 1970, p. 16.
10. Jacob Burckhardt, *The Age of Constantine the Great*, Routledge & Kegan Paul 1949, p. 292.
11. Paul Keresztes, *Constantine: A Great Christian Monarch and Apostle*, J.C. Gieben, Amsterdam 1981, p. 8.
12. It is as Elijah *redivivus* that John the Baptist appears, and it is Elijah who represents the prophets, as Moses represents the Law, at the Transfiguration.
13. I Kings 18. All biblical quotations in English are from the Revised Standard Version of the Bible.
14. Augustine, *Confessions*, Book VIII, ch.8, Sheed & Ward, New York 1943.
15. This is tacitly recognized even in a work which confidently affirms Constantine's conversion: Hubert Jedin and John Dolan (eds.), *History of the Church*, Vol. 1, *From the Apostolic Community to Constantine*, by Karl Baus, Burns & Oates 1980, p. 416.
16. Eusebius, *De Vita Constantini* I.27; ET 'The Life of Constantine', in Henry Wace and Philip Schaff (eds.), *Nicene and Post-Nicene Fathers* (New Series), Vol. 1, *Eusebius*, Oxford 1840.

17. *Vita Constantini* I.28.
18. Baynes, *Constantine the Great*, pp. 60–5.
19. F.L. Cross (ed.), *The Oxford Dictionary of the Christian Church*, Oxford University Press 1957.
20. Lactantius, *De Mortibus* XLIV.
21. Eusebius, *Vita Constantini* I.29.
22. *Vita Constantini* I.31.
23. Baynes, *Constantine the Great*, pp. 97ff.
24. Gaston H. Halsberghe, *The Cult of Sol Invictus*, E.J. Brill, Leiden 1972, p. 167.
25. Eusebius, *Vita Constantini* I.41.
26. *Vita Constantini* I.40.
27. *Corpus Inscriptionum Latinarum* VI.1139; ET in J. Stevenson (ed.), *A New Eusebius*, SPCK 1957, p. 302.
28. Ibid.

II   Constantine the Friend of God

1. Baynes, *Constantine the Great*, p. 56.
2. Ivar Heikel, *Eusebius Werke*, Vol. 1, J. C. Hinrichs'sche Buchhandlung, Leipzig 1902. ET published by Samuel Bagster & Sons, London 1845, and revised by E. C. Richardson for *Nicene and Port-Nicene Fathers* (New Series), Vol. 1, *Eusebius*. The most recent ET is provided by H. A. Drake, *In Praise of Constantine: A Historical Study and New Translation of Eusebius' Tricennial Orations*, University of California Press, Los Angeles 1975.
3. *Vita Constantini* I.45–46.
4. Drake, op. cit., ch. 3.
5. Quotations are taken from Drake's translation and will be identified by the Oration chapter, followed by the page number in Drake, e.g. I.85.
6. W. Wrede, *Das Messiasgeheimnis in den Evangelien* (1901); ET *The Messianic Secret*, James Clarke 1971.
7. Mark 1.34; 3.11f.; 8.29f.; 9.9.

III   Constantine as Messiah

1. *Cur Deus Homo?*, ET by S. N. Deane, *Saint Anselm: Basic Writings*, Open Court Publishing Co, La Salle, Illinois 1962, p. 177.
2. John 1.11.
3. The significance of this doctrine of *mimesis* will be discussed more fully in Ch. IX.
4. Daniel 7.18.
5. I Corinthians 2.9; cf. Isaiah 64.4.
6. John 6.15.
7. Richard Krautheimer, *Early Christian and Byzantine Architecture*, quoted by Drake, *In Praise of Constantine*, p. 170.
8. This will be discussed in more detail in Ch. IV.

IV   The Life of Constantine

1. Quotations are from *Nicene and Post-Nicene Fathers* (New Series), Vol. 1, *Eusebius*. References are to Book and Chapter, e.g. I.23.
2. Theodoret, *A History of the Church: From AD 322 to the Death of Theodore of Mopsuestia, AD 427*, Henry G. Bohn, London 1854, I.18.
3. Isaiah 53.3.

4. I Corinthians 10.4; cf. Exodus 17.6.
5. Cf. Theodoret's interpretation of angels as the activity of the Son: G. W. Ashby, *Theodoret of Cyrrhus as Exegete of the Old Testament*, Rhodes University, Grahamstown, South Africa 1972, pp. 61f.
6. I Corinthians 12.12.
7. I Corinthians 12.13.
8. John 13. 34f.
9. John 15.1,4.
10. I. A. Heikel (ed.), *Eusebius Werke*; also F. Winkelmann (ed.), *Eusebius Werke* I, Akademie-Verlag, Berlin 1975.

V Against Pagan Despisers

1. Drake, *In Praise of Constantine*, p. 31.
2. *Vita Constantini* IV.33.
3. Drake, op. cit. Although Drake separates the oration 'On Christ's Sepulchre' from 'In Praise of Constantine', he continues to follow the traditional chapter numbering. Thus 'On Christ's Sepulchre' begins at Ch. XI. As in the previous chapters of the present book, references combine the chapter of the oration and the page number in Drake, in this case XI.103.
4. *Vita Constantini* III.60.

VI The Assembly of Saints

1. Eusebius, *Vita Constantini* IV.32.
2. Daniel de Decker, 'Le "Discours à l'Assemblée des Saints" Attribué à Constantin et l'Oeuvre de Lactance', in J. Fontaine and M. Perrin (eds.), *Lactance et Son Temps*, Editions Beauchesne, Paris 1978, pp. 75ff.
3. Baynes, *Constantine the Great*, p. 56.
4. Quotations are from *Nicence and Post-Nicene Fathers* (New Series), Vol. 1, *Eusebius*, Assembly I.
5. Ibid., II.
6. *Vita Constantini* IV.22.
7. Heikel, *Eusebius Werke* I, p. CII.

VII Legislation on Religion

1. Penguin Books 1965.
2. Lactantius, *De Mortibus*, Ch.XXII, p. 184.
3. Ibid., Ch.XXXVIII, p. 199.
4. Isaiah 44.28.
5. 'Constantine', *Cambridge Ancient History* XII, Ch.20, p. 706.
6. Lactantius, *De Mortibus* XLVIII.
7. 'Constantine', p. 686.
8. Eusebius, *The History of the Church*, X.5 (subsequent references are cited in the text).
9. *Cambridge Ancient History* X, Ch. 15, p. 465.
10. Eusebius, *Vita Constantini* II.24.
11. Luke 13.1–5.
12. *Vita Constantini* II.25.
13. Clyde Pharr, *The Theodosian Code and Novels and the Sirmondian Constitutions*, Princeton University Press 1952, Book 2, Title 8, Section 1. References will be given in the form 2.8.1.
14. Matthew 3.9.

15. Rosemary Radford Ruether, *Faith and Fratricide: The Theological Roots of Anti-Semitism*, Search Press 1975, p. 104.
16. Ibid., p. 116.
17. *Vita Constantini* III.18.
18. *The Theodosian Code* 16.8.1; cf. 8.5.
19. Ibid., Constitution 4.
20. Ibid., 16.9.1; cf. Constitution 4.

VIII   The Unity of the Church

1. The Donatists sent a letter to Constantine by Anulinus which they described as 'a document of the Catholic Church containing charges against Caecilianus, and furnished by the party of Majorinus': Marcus Dods (ed.), *The Works of Aurelius Augustinus*, Vol. VI, *The Letters of St Augustine*, Vol. 1, Letter No. 88, T. & T. Clark 1872.
2. W.H.C. Frend, *The Donatist Church*, Clarendon Press 1952, p. 141.
3. Ibid., p. 142.
4. Adolf Von Harnack, *History of Dogma*, Dover Publications, New York 1961, Vol. V, pp. 41f.
5. Eusebius, *The History of the Church*, X.6.
6. Quoted by Frend, *The Donatist Church*, p. 146.
7. Ibid., p. 147.
8. Ibid., p. 152.
9. Ibid., p. 158.
10. Ibid.
11. *S. Optat: Milevitani Libri VII: Corpus Scriptorum Ecclesiasticorum Latinorum* XXVI, edited by Karl Ziwsa, F. Tempsky, Vienna 1893.
12. O. R. Vassall-Phillips, *The Work of St Optatus*, Longmans Green 1917, pp. 395–8.
13. Ibid., p. 394.
14. Socrates, *History of the Church*, Henry G. Bohn, London 1853, Book 1, Ch. 5.
15. Ibid.
16. Harnack, *History of Dogma*, Vol. IV, p. 11.
17. Eusebius, *Vita Constantini* II.64–72.
18. Williston Walker, *A History of the Christian Church*, Scribner, New York 1959, p. 108.
19. J. N. D. Kelly, *Early Christian Doctrines*, A. & C. Black 1958, p. 237.
20. Norman H. Baynes, 'Constantine', *Cambridge Ancient History* XII, Ch. 20, p. 697.
21. Andrew Alföldi, *The Conversion of Constantine and Pagan Rome*, Clarendon Press 1948, p. 14.
22. Gerhard Loeschcke and Margaret Heinemann (eds.), *Gelasius Kirchengeschichte*, J. C. Hinrichs'sche Buchhanddlung, Leipzig 1918, pp. 192–9.
23. Theodoret, *A History of the Church*, I.20.
24. Henry Chadwick, *The Early Church*, Penguin Books 1967, p. 135.

IX   Constantine's Covenant Religion

1. Genesis 9.12f.
2. Exodus 13.21.
3. Drake, *In Praise of Constantine*, III.87; Daniel 7.18.
4. *In Praise of Constantine* I.12.

5. *Vita Constantini* I.20.
6. *Vita Constantini* I.38.
7. Exodus 33.7.
8. *Vita Constantini* II.12; cf. Socrates, *History of the Church* I.18; Sozomen, *History of the Church*, Samuel Bagster and Sons, London 1846, I.8.
9. So Heikel, *Eusebius Werke*, and Winkelmann, *Eusebius Werke*.
10. Drake, *In Praise of Constantine*, I.84. Further references are cited in the text.
11. II Esdras 12.31f.; cf; Bruce M. Metzger (ed.), *The Apocrypha*, Oxford University Press 1965.
12. John 6.15.
13. Matthew 8.20.
14. Luke 22.25f.
15. Mark 9.35.
16. John 13.4f.
17. Matthew 26.52f.
18. Ephesians 6.10f.
19. Ephesians 6.13–17.
20. I Thessalonians 5.8.
21. Psalm 98.1.

X   The Great Reversal

1. Norman H. Baynes, 'Eusebius and the Christian Empire' (1933), reprinted in *Byzantine Studies and Other Essays*, The Athlone Press 1955, pp. 168–72.
2. Ibid., p. 168.
3. Drake, *In Praise of Constantine* I.85.
4. Baynes, op. cit., p. 172.
5. Friedrich Ueberweg, *History of Philosophy*, Scribner, Armstrong & Co, New York 1876, Vol. I, p. 115.
6. J. N. Findlay, *Hegel: A Re-examination*, Allen & Unwin 1958, p. 41.
7. Ibid.
8. Ibid., p. 30.
9. Quoted by Frederick Gregory, *Scientific Materialism in Nineteenth-Century Germany*, D. Reidel Publishing Co, Dordrecht, Holland/Boston 1977, p. 16.
10. Ludwig Feuerbach, *The Essence of Christianity*, reprinted Harper & Row, New York 1957, pp. 29f.
11. Ibid., p. 13.
12. Karl Marx, 'A Contribution to the Critique of Hegel's Philosophy of Law' (see Ch. I n. 7), p. 175.
13. Peter L. Berger and Thomas Luckmann, *The Social Construction of Reality*, Penguin Books 1967.
14. Drake, *In Praise of Constantine*, Prologue.
15. Torben Christensen, *Origin and History of Christian Socialism*, Universitetsforlaget I, Aarhus 1962, p. 295.
16. Cf. Jürgen Moltmann, *The Crucified God*, SCM Press 1974, p. 325.
17. Quoted by S. Körner, *Kant*, Penguin Books 1955, p. 128.

XI   The Labarum or the Cross

1. Mark 3.6.
2. Matthew 26.50.

3. Matthew 18.22.
4. Soren Kierkegaard, *Philosophical Fragments*, Princeton University Press ²1962, Ch. 1.
5. Ibid., p. 71.
6. Matthew 4.8f.
7. Luke 6.20.
8. Acts 10.38.
9. Ethelbert Stauffer, 'The Principal Elements of the Old Biblical Theology of Martyrdom', *New Testament Theology*, SCM Press 1955, pp. 331–4.
10. Matthew 23.37.
11. Philo, *De Legatione ad Gaium*, quoted by Vincent Taylor, *The Gospel According to St Mark*, Macmillan 1957, p. 578.
12. Philippians 2.5–11.
13. Mark 3.11f.
14. J. N. D. Kelly, *Early Christian Doctrines*, pp. 141ff.
15. Paul Althaus, 'Kenosis', *Die Religion in Geschichte und Gegenwart* III³, 1243; quoted in Jürgen Moltmann, *The Crucified God*, p. 206.
16. Moltmann, *The Crucified God*, p. 205.

XII   The New Imperial Cult

1. Tertullian, *Apology*, L.14.
2. I Corinthians 1.26–28.
3. I Corinthians 1.25.
4. Mark 10.21.
5. Matthew 19.23f.
6. V. I. Lenin, *The State and Revolution*, Progress Publishers, Moscow 1969, p. 41.
7. Ernst Troeltsch, *The Social Teaching of the Christian Churches*, Harper & Brothers, New York 1960, Vol. I, p. 63.
8. Quoted by Julio de Santa Ana, *Good News to the Poor*, World Council of Churches, Geneva 1977, p. 59.
9. Luke 5.20.
10. Matthew 11.9.
11. Mark 11.28.
12. Mark 11.29f.
13. Luke 22.25f.
14. I Peter 4.12.
15. I Peter 4.13.

XIII   Constantine and Political Theology

1. Alistair Kee (ed.), *A Reader in Political Theology*, SCM Press 1974; id., *The Scope of Political Theology*, SCM Press 1978.
2. Luke 18.25.
3. Matthew 23.9.
4. Mark 10.9.
5. Mark 9.35.
6. Alfred Schutz, *The Phenomenology of the Social World*, Northwestern University Press 1967, pp. 3f.
7. Jose P. Miranda, *Marx against the Marxists: The Christian Humanism of Karl Marx*, SCM Press 1980.
8. Robert Brank Fulton, *Original Marxism – Estranged Offspring*, The Christopher Publishing House, Boston 1960.

9. Ernst Bloch, *Atheism in Christianity: The Religion of the Exodus and the Kingdom*, Herder & Herder 1972, p. 9.

10. Ibid., p. 21.

11. Hans Jonas, *The Gnostic Religion*, Beacon Press, Boston 1958, pp. 15–17.

12. Cf. D.E. Nineham, *The Gospel of St Mark*, Penguin Books 1963, p. 418.

13. D.S. Russell, *The Method and Message of Jewish Apocalyptic*, SCM Press 1964, p. 35.

14. Matthew 16.6f.

15. John Herman Randall, *Hellenistic Ways of Deliverance and the Making of the Christian Synthesis*, Columbia University Press, New York 1970, p. 138.

16. Agathe Kaniuth, *Die Beisetzung Konstantins des Grossen*, Scientia Verlag, Aalen 1974, p. 17.

17. Eusebius, *Vita Constantini* IV.48.

18. Matthew 22.21.

GENERAL INDEX

Aberdeen, 9
Agrippa I, 148
Alföldi, A., 112
Althaus, P., 151
Anselm, 35, 36
Antiochus IV, 121
Anulinus, 91, 105, 179
Apollo, 9, 12, 13, 16, 40
Arianism, 63, 64, 109–114
Ashby G. W., 62
Athanasius, 74, 113, 114
Augustine, 13
Aurelius, Marcus, 10
Ayres, Pam, 86

Baptism, 18, 57, 59
Baus, K., 176
Baynes, N., 11, 17, 20, 25, 79, 80, 85, 89, 90, 128, 129, 132
Berger, P. and Luckmann, T., 132
Bloch, E., 169
Britain, 8, 9, 93
Burckhardt, J., 12, 16, 17

Caecilian, 91, 103, 104, 105, 106, 179
Celtic Church, 20
Chadwick, H., 114
Christensen, T., 136
Church of the Holy Sepulchre, 45, 46, 47, 54, 56, 59, 60, 61, 62, 70, 71, 72, 73, 74, 76, 77, 78
Claudius, 8
Clement of Alexandria, 160
Constantia, 9
Constantine,
    early years – Ch. I
    conversion – see Conversion
    religion – Part One
    religious policy – Part Two
    life – Ch. IV
    and Church – Chs. VII and VIII
    influence on Christianity – Chs. XI–XIII
    baptism – see Baptism
Constantius, 8, 15, 33
Conversion, 11, 12, 13, 16, 18, 20, 23, 25, 28, 29, 34, 37, 43, 57, 59, 104, 116, 118, 139, 154, 158, 176
Council of Arles, 106, 107, 108, 112, 113
Council of Tyre, 114
Covenantal Religion, 30, 45, 62, 100, Ch. IX, 142, 154

Decius, 10, 84, 104, 109
Decker, D. de, 178
Dies Solis, 57, 96
Diocletian, 7, 8, 10, 11, 84, 104, 105, 145, 155, 159
Diotogenes, 129
Divine Patronage, 11, 12, 13, 14, 15, 16, 17, 18, 23, 39, 88
Docetism, 150, 151
Donatism, 91, 103–109
Drake, H. A., 27, 30, 70, 71

Ecphantus, 129
Edict of Milan, 90
Empiricism, 9, 11, 13, 22, 42, 76, 84, 122, 174
Eusebius of Nicomedia, 110, 113, 114
Eusebius Pamphili
    The Life of Constantine – Ch. IV
    In Praise of Constantine – Chs. II, III, IX, X
    On Christ's Sepulchre – Ch. V
    Church History – 88–94
    The Assembly of Saints – Ch. VI

Fausta, 7, 8
Feuerbach, L., 131, 132
Findlay, J. N., 130
Frend, W. H. C., 104, 106, 107
Fulton, R. B., 169

Galerius, 7, 8, 11, 17, 88, 155, 159
Galesius of Cyzicus, 113
Gaul, 8, 9, 13, 17, 106, 114
Gordon, Flash, 47
Gregory, F., 131

Halsberghe, G. H., 20
Harnack, A. von, 24, 104, 105, 110,
   169, 176
Hegel, G. W. F., 130, 131
Heikel, I., 87
Heine, H., 138
Helena, 8, 44, 45, 46, 60, 61, 71, 72
Hercules, 7, 8, 9, 11, 12, 13, 120
Heresy, 23
Hosius, 91, 108, 110, 111

Ideology, 2, 4, 69, 116, 128, 132, 134,
   139, 140, 141, 144, 166, 167, 168, 169,
   175
Imitation, see Mimesis

Jonas, H., 170, 171
Jupiter, 7, 11

Kaniuth, A., 173
Kant, I., 138
Kee, A., 166
Kelly, J. N. D., 150
Kenosis, 149–151, 173
Keresztes, P., 12, 16, 17
Kierkegaard, S., 145, 146, 148, 150
Körner, S., 138
Krautheimer, R., 44

Labarum, 17, 19, 20, 21, 22, 25, 28, 30,
   36, 37, 38, 40, 42, 44, 45, 46, 47, 49,
   54, 55, 67, 68, 118, 119, 138, 151,
   154, 156
Lactantius, 7, 10, 18, 19, 24, 26, 88, 90
Legitimation, 7, 8, 9, 12, 134, 135, 137,
   138, 141, 142, 144, 159, 163, 167, 168,
   174
Lenin, V. I., 160, 168
Licinius, 7, 9, 43, 54, 67, 88, 90, 110,
   154

Majorinus, 103, 179
Mamre, 61

Marx, K., 12, 131, 132, 160, 166, 168,
   169
Maurice, F. D., 136
Maxentius, 7, 9, 17, 20, 44, 54, 84, 103,
   119, 154
Maximian, 7, 8, 9, 43
Maximin Daia, 9, 89
Mensurius, 103
Miltiades, 106
Milton, 86
Milvian Bridge, 12, 17, 18, 20, 21, 31,
   37, 42, 84, 154
Mimesis, 29, 30, 38, 43, 67, 68, 73, 78,
   129–140, 145, 151, 161, 164
Miranda, J., 169
Moltmann, J., 136, 151
Mount Carmel, 13

Natural Theology, 29, 74, 75, 134
Nero, 10
Nicaea, 57, 86, 112
Nineham, D. E., 171
Nock, A. D., 92

Optatus, 107
Origin, 109

Pachomius, 162
Panegyrist, 8, 9, 12, 16, 27, 42, 46, 133,
   139
Persecution, 8, 10, 11, 65, 76, 81, 84,
   88, 89, 90, 93, 104, 106, 125, 139,
   143, 144, 151, 154, 156, 157, 162, 164
Plato, 130
Plutarch, 129
Pragmatism, 11, 12, 22, 29, 30, 37, 39,
   45, 107, 174

Randall, J. H., 172
Remoto Christo, 35–36, 118
Richardson, E. C., 66
Rossignol, 87
Ruether, R. R., 99
Russell, D. S., 172

Santa Ana, J. de, 160
Schism, 23
Schutz, A., 12, 168
Severus, 17
Socrates, 109, 119
Sol Invictus, 9, 16, 20, 22, 46, 57, 96,
   120
Sozomen, 119
Stauffer, E., 147
Stevenson, J., 22

Streeter, B. H., 24
Sun God, *see* Sol Invictus
Sun Worship, *see* Sol Invictus

Taylor, V., 148
Terminus, 10
Tertullian, 10, 11, 154, 160
Theodoret, 60, 62, 113
Theodosian Code, 95–101, 128
Toleration, 11, 12, 155, 157
Trajan, 10

Troeltsch, E., 160

Uberweg, F., 130
Unity, 23, Ch. VIII

Valerian, 84
Vassal-Phillips, O. R., 108

Walker, W., 111
Wittgenstein, L., 12
Wrede, W., 32

INDEX OF BIBLICAL REFERENCES

Genesis
9.12f.   118

Exodus
13.21   118
17.6   178
33.7   119

I Kings
18.19ff.   13

Psalms
98.1   127

Isaiah
53.3   61
64.4   177

Daniel
7.18   39, 118

II Esdras
12.31f.   121

Matthew
3.9   99
4.8f.   146
8.20   124
11.9   163
16.6ff.   172
18.22   144
19.23f.   160
23.9   167
23.37   148
26.50   143
26.52f.   126

Mark
1.34   32
3.6   143
3.11f.   32, 150
8.29f.   32
9.9   32

9.35   124, 168
10.9   168
10.21   159
11.28   163
11.29   163

Luke
5.20   162
6.20   146
18.25   167
22.25f.   124, 164

John
1.11   38
6.15   43, 124
13.4f.   124
13.34f.   63
15.1, 4   63

Acts
10.38   147

I Corinthians
1.25   155
1.26–28   155
2.9   41
10.4   61
12.12   63
12.13   63

Ephesians
6.10f.   126
6.13–17   126

Philippians
2.5–11   150

I Thessalonians
5.8   127

I Peter
4.12   164
4.13   165